T0333000

Praise for *History for Tomorrow*

'Brimming with ideas and insights, this is a welcome,
important and clear-eyed view of how understanding
the past can help us better prepare for the future'
– Peter Frankopan, bestselling author of
The Silk Roads and *The Earth Transformed*

'Enlightening and thrilling. *History for Tomorrow*
tells us who we are and who we could be'
– George Monbiot, bestselling author of
Regenesis and *How Did We Get Into This Mess?*

'*History for Tomorrow* simply fizzes with ideas,
revealing with startling clarity what human beings
have done, and can do, when they organise, cooperate
and help each other. Compassionate, insightful and hopeful'
– Michael Wood, historian, broadcaster and Professor of
Public History, University of Manchester

'This joyful and informative book opens our minds
and souls, helping us to see with new eyes and to believe in
ourselves as a species, so we can meet our predicament
with a belief that change really is possible'
– Gail Bradbrook, Co-Founder, Extinction Rebellion

'Essential thinking about the big issues facing the world today'
– Brian Eno

'An amazing feat of synthesis and imagination, weaving
together many different strands of world history to make
a pattern that can guide us in the present toward a vibrant future.
Krznaric's book is immensely suggestive of positive actions that have
track records; they've worked before, and in new formulations
they can work again. Wise and practical inspiration'
– Kim Stanley Robinson, author of
The Ministry for the Future

'A fascinating account of historical moments
that could serve as beacons of hope for our own times'
– Amitav Ghosh, author of *The Nutmeg's Curse*

'Roman Krznaric has achieved a tour de force with a book
that draws unexpected links between a very wide range of historical
events from all over the world. This is a uniquely hopeful book, which
never romanticizes the past but inspires us to imagine alternative
solutions to address the most urgent issues of our time'
– Dr Hélène Neveu Kringelbach, Associate Professor of
African Anthropology, University College London

'Roman Krznaric turns to the past not for its own sake, but for ours.
In his deft hands, case studies suggest how we can do better – learn
and be capable – as we face the largest challenges of the present'
– Dr Sarah Knott, Sally Reahard Professor of History, Indiana
University and author of *Mother: An Unconventional History*

HISTORY
FOR
TOMORROW

INSPIRATION FROM THE
PAST FOR THE FUTURE
OF HUMANITY

ROMAN KRZNARIC

4

WH Allen, an imprint of Ebury Publishing
20 Vauxhall Bridge Road
London SW1V 2SA

WH Allen is part of the Penguin Random House group of companies
whose addresses can be found at global.penguinrandomhouse.com

Penguin
Random House
UK

First published in the United Kingdom by WH Allen in 2024

www.penguin.co.uk

A CIP catalogue record for this book is available from the British Library

Hardback ISBN 9780753559628
Trade Paperback ISBN 9780753559635

Typeset in 11.25/16pt Sabon Next LT Pro by Jouve (UK), Milton Keynes
Printed and bound in Great Britain by Clays Ltd, Elcograf S.p.A.

The authorised representative in the EEA is Penguin Random House Ireland,
Morrison Chambers, 32 Nassau Street, Dublin D02 YH68

Penguin Random House is committed to a sustainable future
for our business, our readers and our planet. This book is made
from Forest Stewardship Council® certified paper.

MIX
Paper | Supporting
responsible forestry
FSC® C018179

The principal and proper work of history being to instruct,
and enable men, by the knowledge of actions past,
to bear themselves prudently in the present and
providently in the future.

– Thomas Hobbes, from the preface to his 1628 translation
of Thucydides' *History of the Peloponnesian War*

Contents

Introduction

Looking Backwards to Find a Way Forwards

The insights of history are a shared treasury for the future of humanity. We live in an era dominated by the present tense, which vastly undervalues the accumulated experience of the past as a guide for where we go next. Faced with the collective challenges of the twenty-first century, from the threat of ecological breakdown and growing wealth inequality to the risks of artificial intelligence and genetic engineering, we are failing to draw on the immense store of wisdom bequeathed by generation upon generation of our forebears. There is an urgent need to look backwards to help chart a way forwards.

The tyranny of the now increasingly governs public life. Most politicians are too busy responding to today's headlines or following the latest policy trends to press pause and spend time learning from the past. Social media traps our attention in the present moment, while the tech gurus assure us that cutting-edge technologies will come to our civilisational rescue: who needs history when you've got carbon capture, synthetic biology and artificial intelligence algorithms?

When it comes to everyday life, however, it is remarkable just how many of us remain captivated by the past. Millions of people watch history documentaries with fascination, listen avidly to history podcasts, read historical biographies, visit ancient sites on holiday and embark on quests to trace their own family ancestries. Just imagine if we could channel some of this passion for the past into helping tackle the multiple dilemmas facing humankind over the decades to come.

There is good reason to do so. A distinguished lineage of historical thinkers going back to Thucydides, Ibn Khaldun and Thomas Hobbes have argued that the study of the past can help us navigate the future – what is sometimes known as 'applied history'.[1] Its purpose is not to enable us to predict the future like Nostradamus but rather to open up our imaginations. History can remind us how we confronted crises in the past, reveal different ways of organising society that may be long forgotten, uncover the roots of current injustices and power relations, and offer clues for surviving and thriving and making change happen. History is a counsellor not a clairvoyant. It encourages us to ask new questions and recognise that other paths might be possible. Goethe understood the nourishment it provides, declaring, 'He who cannot draw on three thousand years is living from hand to mouth.'[2]

Can history really live up to such promise as a guide in a complex world? In October 1962, in the midst of the Cuban Missile Crisis, President John F. Kennedy turned for counsel to a recent work of popular history, Barbara W. Tuchman's *The Guns of August*, which chronicled the series of misperceptions, miscalculations and bungles by political and military leaders that had contributed to the outbreak of the First World War. Kennedy was worried that an aggressive policy response from the US might lead to a similar cascade of decisions that could provoke Soviet premier Nikita Khrushchev to push the nuclear button. 'I am not going to follow a course which will allow anyone to write a comparable book about this time – *The Missiles of October*', the president told his brother, Attorney General Robert Kennedy. 'If anybody is around to write after this, they are going to understand that we made every effort to find peace and every effort to give our adversary room to move.'[3]

Historians still hotly debate the key turning points in the Cuban Missile Crisis. Yet there is widespread agreement that Tuchman's book played a crucial role in Kennedy's decision to resist the hawks in his administration who wanted to invade Cuba and thereby risk thermonuclear conflict, and to instead take a cautious approach and seek a diplomatic solution – which is what led to the successful resolution of the crisis. According to historian Margaret MacMillan, reading the book made Kennedy 'painfully aware of how a series of mistakes and blunders can produce a major catastrophe.'[4] There are books that have helped to start wars, from the Bible to *Mein Kampf*. *The Guns of August* is among the few that may just have stopped one from happening.

This story is a message for our times, revealing the power of learning from history. It shows that history can serve as a valuable warning, an idea captured in George Santayana's famous aphorism, 'Those who cannot remember the past are condemned to repeat it.'[5] While it might be useful to recollect our mistakes and learn from them – as Kennedy did – if we want history to guide us it is just as important to remember our achievements and be inspired by them. So in this book I take a dual approach to the past, searching for insights in positive examples of what went right as well as in cautionary tales of what went wrong.

I equally believe it is important to challenge the old-fashioned idea that history is all about what Thomas Carlyle called 'the biography of great men' – the decisions and actions of powerful politicians, military leaders, business tycoons and other public figures. This elite view of history has been countered over the past half-century by an alternative school of thinking that highlights the importance of 'history from below'. The work of historians such as E.P. Thompson, Christopher Hill, Natalie Zemon Davis, the public and oral history movements, and the French *Annales* tradition have stressed that too much history has been written from the perspective of those in power, at the cost of sidelining the role played by social movements, community organisations and everyday citizens in shaping the landscape of the past. And this has consequences. As Howard Zinn wrote in his pioneering *A People's History of the United States*, 'Most histories understate revolt, overemphasize statesmanship, and thus encourage impotency among citizens.'[6]

Drawing on this 'history from below' tradition, I have written this book to discover what inspiration can be found in our collective past for tackling the most urgent challenges facing humanity today. The global system is already starting to flicker – megadroughts, melting glaciers, far-right extremism, crumbling welfare states, energy shortages, rampant viruses, cyberattacks. We seem to be heading towards an era of permacrisis. History is a compass that can help us steer a way through the turmoil. I do not claim to have uncovered any universal 'laws' of history (such an endeavour is a fantasy given the vast complexities of the past), nor do I advocate a particular theoretical model or thesis about how historical change happens.[7] Rather, in the spirit of Howard Zinn, my main aim is to bring to light stories and insights from history that can empower change-makers in society – not just politicians and policymakers, but community organisers, student activists, social entrepreneurs, street rebels, educators and other committed citizens who want to make a difference in this critical moment of the human story.

Each of the ten chapters addresses a core global challenge such as water scarcity, widening inequality or the risks from genetic engineering. These have been sourced from the expanding scholarship on civilisational collapse and existential risk, which identifies the fundamental ecological, sociopolitical and technological threats to the survival and flourishing of human societies.[8] I then ask what we can learn from the last one thousand years of history, across multiple cultures and continents, to approach these challenges in more innovative and effective ways. Occasionally, for added perspective, the analysis stretches further back to span Goethe's three millennia. To ensure that the history is as applicable as possible to our multifaceted, globalised world, most of the examples are taken from large-scale, complex, urbanised societies.

4

In the following chapters – which can also be read as self-contained essays – I illustrate the importance of *social* innovations in the making of history, as opposed to technological innovations, which tend to get far more attention. By this I mean innovations in collective action, human organisation and shared ideals for the common good, ranging from the disruptive potential of social movements to the radical possibilities of direct democracy and the hidden history of managing the commons. Each of these innovations – which are the social equivalents of the steam engine or the smartphone – has proven itself capable of propelling whole societies over tipping points of change just as much as new technologies. If we hope to tap into the wisdom of the past, it is essential to draw on all we have discovered about the extraordinary human capacity for cooperation, mutual aid and collective agency. It is time for a relational Renaissance.

In the course of my research I came across a wealth of fascinating historical examples, which stimulated often surprising questions. What insights might the slave uprisings of the nineteenth century offer for overcoming our addiction to fossil fuels? How might the history of capitalism help us understand what it takes to limit the dangers of AI? What could we learn from a medieval Islamic kingdom for creating cultural tolerance in an age of growing migration, or from premodern Japan for eroding hyper-consumerism? How might the conflicts unleashed by the printing press, or the coffee-houses of Georgian London, stimulate ideas for reducing the political polarisation created by social media? From pre-colonial India to revolutionary Cuba, from Qing dynasty China to the struggle for women's rights in Finland, history provides unexpected perspectives and possibilities for traversing a tumultuous future.

By academic training I am a political scientist. Looking at the world through the lens of history has been the common denominator of all my research and writing over the past three decades, from a doctoral thesis examining the legacies of Latin American colonialism to books and articles taking a historical perspective on topics such as work, empathy, democracy and long-term thinking.[9] In *History for Tomorrow*, I see myself as an interpreter or ambassador of the past, delving into the work of professional historians and relating it to the crises of the coming century. In doing so, I am indebted to all those historians whose years deep in the archives have produced the intellectual riches without which this book could not have been written.

I am also indebted to my parents, who first instilled in me the idea of learning from history in the conversations we had around the dinner table when I was a teenager. My father was always telling stories about his experiences of living through the traumas of the Second World War in Poland and fleeing Europe to Australia as a refugee. An even greater influence was my stepmother – herself a refugee who had survived the bombing of her home town in Italy during the war – who was a passionate and committed secondary-school history teacher. After a glass or two of wine she would invariably be off talking about the great characters, movements and events of history, from Giuseppe Garibaldi's efforts to forge the Italian republic to the rise of the trade union movement in industrial England, to the neglected women of history like the medieval polymath Hildegard of Bingen. She had a gift for making history feel so alive and so crucial to our understanding of the world. She spoke about how building lasting peace in the Balkans required awareness of regional animosities going back hundreds of years. How we would never be privatising public services such as water, railways or healthcare if we remembered why our forebears had engaged in long struggles to bring them into public ownership in the first place. How the global ecological movement should be learning from the strategies of the suffragettes and the campaign for Indian independence.

All of this comes with a note of caution. Seeking guidance from the past is a potentially dangerous enterprise since history can be so easily used and abused. Joseph Stalin, Mao Zedong and countless other dictators have been experts at airbrushing their atrocities from the history books. In the Balkan wars of the 1990s, Serb leaders manipulated the past, claiming that Croatia and Bosnia were part of the ancient Serbian Empire, and so rightfully theirs, while the Croats created similar mythologies.[10] Today's populist politicians promote imaginary histories of national purity in their attempts to keep immigrants at the gate. Political power is often founded on the manufacture of public memory.

Acknowledging the many challenges of learning from history is essential. A book of this kind might be seen to be cherry-picking examples from the past. Absolutely true, because cherries are for picking. All writing of history is selective – requiring choices about topics, time periods, relevant actors, the importance of race and gender, the role of culture and technology, the use of quantitative data and other methodological issues. What matters is being clear about the approach. From the myriad of historical contexts, I have consciously selected events and stories that offer inspiration for tackling the ten major crises facing humanity in the twenty-first century, and actively focus on the collective struggles and initiatives of everyday people, since this is the realm in which we have the greatest potential agency. Most of us are not powerful figures in politics, media or business – like John F. Kennedy – who can directly influence public agendas. But history reveals that by acting together in solidarity with others, we can begin to shape an uncertain future. I hope that the cherries I have picked provide food for thought and action.

'The past is a foreign country; they do things differently there,' wrote the novelist L.P. Hartley in *The Go-Between* (1953). Can we really hope to learn from past societies that were so seemingly distinct from our own? I believe that we can, as long as we do so with awareness and humility. It is true that our ancestors were not entangled in digital networks or manipulating the human genome. But they were confronting many challenges that, in essence, mirror those of the present, from poverty and pandemics to warfare and water shortages. Analogies can also help us make connections across time: even a technology as apparently modern as artificial intelligence has its parallels in the past. But it is key to highlight differences as much as similarities, and be wary of making simplistic or misplaced comparisons: every dictator is not another Adolf Hitler, every war is not another Vietnam, every economic crisis is not another Wall Street Crash.[11]

One issue requiring awareness concerns identity and social position. The field of applied history remains largely dominated by white men.[12] Recognising the biases and distortions that can emerge from this, I have drawn on a wider range of scholarship, such as the work of Abeba Birhane and Kehinde Andrews, who bring insights from colonial history to their respective research on racial bias in AI and the contemporary legacies of empire.[13] I am also aware of being a writer from the Global North: that is where the 'we' in this book is mainly located. I have therefore tried, as far as possible, to balance this by presenting histories from the Global South and non-Western cultures alongside Europe and North America (a summary table of cases appears in the Conclusion).

Finally, there is the danger of romanticising the past. It is important to acknowledge that human history is strewn with tragedies: wars broke out, people starved, exploitation reigned, societies crumbled. Yet these should not overshadow the accomplishments. Time and again our ancestors rose up to confront injustices, survive crises and build cities and civilisations, often against the odds, providing a source of inspiration as we face the trials of our own era. There are possibilities and pathways scattered across the last millennium that we have scarcely begun to imagine.

Ultimately, this is a book about the power of thinking historically. Doing so offers an antidote to the tyranny of the now and counters common narratives of progress that look to future technologies for salvation. There are chapters of history that speak to us with a message of radical hope: that by acting together, drawing on the extraordinary cooperative capacities of our species, we may find unexpected ways to navigate through the ecological, political and technological turbulence that is whipping up around us.

As we journey towards tomorrow, let us etch into our minds the Māori proverb, *Kia whakatōmuri te haere whakamua* – 'I walk backwards into the future with my eyes fixed on the past.'

1

Breaking the Fossil Fuel Addiction

Rebel Movements and the Power of Disobedience

The West India Interest was one of the most powerful political lobbying groups in British history. Often known simply as 'the Interest', it brought together plantation owners, merchants, financiers, politicians, lawyers, clergymen and journalists who were all intent on a single aim: preserving slavery in British colonies in the Caribbean. Although most active in the early nineteenth century, its story has unexpected resonances with the ecological struggles of our own times.

In 1807 Britain had abolished the slave trade but not slavery itself, leaving more than 700,000 enslaved people working on British-owned sugar plantations in the West Indies. By the 1820s, public pressure for full emancipation was growing, which prompted the Interest to mount a vigorous oppositional campaign. In 1823 its 'Literary Committee' established a £20,000 annual fighting fund (equivalent to £1.8 million today) to distribute pro-slavery pamphlets and secure articles in leading publications in a blatant effort to sway public opinion in favour of enslavement.

The Interest mustered multiple arguments to make its case. Slavery, said one of its most vehement supporters, John Gibson Lockhart (son-in-law of novelist Sir Walter Scott), was raising Africans out of 'barbarism' and if freed they would likely become 'lawless banditti, revelling in blood'. They were also not suffering a 'thousandth part of that misery' that the anti-slavers claimed, he wrote in *Blackwood's Edinburgh Magazine*.[1] Others asserted that plantation owners could be trusted to regulate the system themselves and were already establishing a code of conduct to ban practices such as whipping women.[2] Emancipation would not just bring 'total economic ruin' on the planters and the thousands of people in Britain whose jobs and livelihoods depended on the slave economy, but would hurt consumers too, who would be forced to buy more expensive sugar from India and other countries.[3]

Perhaps the most influential argument made by representatives of the Interest was to admit that slavery was morally questionable, but to reason that emancipation should be a gradual process over several decades to reduce the turmoil that immediate abolition would entail, as the enslaved still lacked the 'education' and 'civilisation' to exercise their freedom with responsibility. As the Black Studies scholar Kehinde Andrews caustically comments, 'The savages obviously could not be expected to understand how to be free.'[4] One article, written in 1824, suggested '1860 as the nearest period at which … we could arrive at [emancipation] without injury to anyone.' At the same time, the article continued, it was vital to protect 'the rights of the planters' who should receive 'a liberal and just compensation' for the loss of their private property.[5]

Two hundred years later, I was sitting in a TED climate change conference in Edinburgh listening to the then CEO of Shell, Ben van Beurden, make almost exactly the same arguments in relation to fossil fuels. In a thinly veiled case for multi-decade gradualism, Van Beurden said that Shell wanted to 'be on the right side of history' by shifting away from its 'legacy business' of oil and gas production. But this transition had to take place at 'a rate of change that is acceptable' and couldn't happen too fast without the danger of its existing business 'imploding'. In fact, Shell needed to keep producing oil and gas in order to finance its shift to renewables such as wind power. 'We need the legacy businesses to fund the strategy for the future,' he said. 'I cannot let them die or wither on the vine tomorrow.'[6] Moreover, he argued, Shell was obliged to continue producing fossil fuels because there was still so much demand for them from consumers. Given these realities, the company was committing to be carbon net zero by 2050. Anything faster was unrealistic.

Van Beurden's well-honed justifications for gradualism did not go unchallenged. He was sharing the stage with a climate justice activist named Lauren MacDonald, who pointed out the hypocrisy of Shell's green agenda: the company had not just spent millions trying to discredit the claims of climate scientists, but was now lobbying the UK government to obtain drilling licences for offshore oil fields in Scotland. Before dramatically walking off the stage in protest at Van Beurden being given a public platform at a conference about tackling the climate crisis, she pointedly asked him why, 'if you are going to sit here and say you care about climate action', Shell was appealing a recent Dutch court ruling to reduce its carbon emissions. His defensive reply was that the ruling was 'totally unreasonable' as it was asking Shell to reduce its CO_2 much faster than other companies. It was clearly unfair and unjust, so he had a 'duty' to his shareholders to appeal the verdict.[7]

History is speaking to us. Although the harm caused by fossil fuel production differs in fundamental ways from the indefensible crime of enslaving human beings, it is striking how both cases illustrate the power of economic elites to stand in the face of change. Like the struggle to abolish slavery, the struggle to abolish carbon emissions has suffered from the intransigence and snail-paced gradualism of vested business interests and of the governments beholden to them.[8]

It is tempting to believe that rapid progress is being made. At the same conference I heard Al Gore give a rousing and optimistic speech that made it sound like a world of 100 per cent clean energy was just around the corner – prices of renewables were plummeting, the electric car revolution was well under way and even the Kentucky Coal Museum now had solar panels on its roof.

But take an honest look at the numbers. How much have annual global carbon emissions fallen since the alarm bells began to ring at the Rio Earth Summit in 1992? They haven't. Instead they've *increased* more than 50 per cent, rising year on year apart from small dips following the 2008 financial crash and the COVID pandemic.[9] Since Rio, humanity has put more CO_2 in the atmosphere than in all prior history. Despite all the technological advances and pledges from companies such as Shell, renewables provide just 11 per cent of global energy, most of which is hydropower, with only 2 per cent from wind and 1 per cent from solar.[10] Nothing but a slither of the total. To stay below 1.5°C of heating, global CO_2 emissions now need to fall 8–10 per cent annually for at least the next decade. To put that in perspective, CO_2 dropped only 6.4 per cent when the world economy went into COVID lockdown in 2020, with businesses closed, aircraft grounded and streets emptied.[11] We need more than that. Every year.

The time for gradualism is long over. The case for rapid and transformative change is all too clear. But how can this be achieved when powerful fossil fuel companies are still fighting to keep the pumps running and most governments are too timid to implement the kinds of radical policies that they are willing to undertake in wartime or when a pandemic hits? What hope is there when renewables have hardly made a dent in the steel and plastics industries and when China will still be getting 40 per cent of its energy from fossil fuels in 2050?[12] Shouldn't we recognise that most energy transitions in the past – such as from wood to coal, or from horse power to mechanical engines – have been painstakingly slow, taking 50 to 100 years?[13] In other words, how can we contend with the glacial pace of change in a rapidly heating world?

To rely on miracle technologies is a dangerous fantasy. Carbon capture and storage (CCS, which injects carbon from the atmosphere deep underground) will likely provide part of any solution but the technology remains at a stage of infancy and there is currently little evidence that it can draw down CO_2 at anything like the speed and scale required to avoid severe climate breakdown.[14] Other tech innovations, such as geoengineering, are not just risky but almost wholly untested. There is, however, another way: to put our hope not simply in technological innovations but in the innovative strategies of rebel movements to create disruptive change. Where better to look for insights than to return to the struggle to abolish slavery?

A Tale of Two Rebellions

The pro-slavery lobby in Britain managed to keep emancipation at bay throughout the 1820s. They were helped in no small part by the abolitionist movement itself, which in 1823 had united in the London Society for Mitigating and Gradually Abolishing the State of Slavery Throughout the British Dominions. The name said it all. Its leading figures, such as William Wilberforce and Thomas Fowell Buxton, were fundamentally conservative and readily bought into the paternalistic pro-slavery argument that enslaved Africans were not yet ready for freedom, so emancipation had to take place at a measured pace.[15]

By 1830, however, there was a growing frustration with this gradualist strategy. Radical women activists, such as Elizabeth Heyrick, were calling for immediate emancipation. A new Whig government was also now in power, deposing the pro-slavery prime minister and hero of Waterloo, the Duke of Wellington, and bringing more abolitionists into government. But even still this was not enough to tip the balance.

The turning point came the following year in an act of disruption and defiance that created shockwaves in Britain: the Jamaica slave revolt of 1831. One of a series of rebellions that had erupted in the Caribbean over the previous two decades – including in Barbados and Demerara – the Jamaica uprising was the greatest revolt against enslavement in British history and a crucial event in its demise. According to historian David Olusoga, it was 'the final factor that tipped the scales in favour of abolition'.[16]

It was led by an enslaved worker and Baptist deacon named Samuel Sharpe. Thirty-one-year-old Sharpe had originally planned a peaceful sit-down strike to demand wages just after Christmas, when the sugar harvest usually began. At the same time, he began to see the need for more militant action, holding secret meetings after church services to galvanise his supporters and organising them into militia groups with 'colonels' and 'captains'. On 27 December the rebellion began with an attack on the Kensington plantation, which stood on a high ridge. The rebels set it alight, with the flames visible for miles around sending a signal for attacks on surrounding plantations.[17]

Burning of the Roehampton Estate, Jamaica Rebellion, January 1832.

The revolt was incendiary in every sense, spreading rapidly across the island. Soon over 20,000 enslaved people had joined the rebellion, setting fire to more than 200 plantations and seizing control of a wide swathe of northwest Jamaica. Although completely outgunned by government forces, it took until the end of January 1832 finally to subdue them. As government soldiers were closing in on one plantation, a woman put down her washing and ran to set fire to the sugar works, shouting out before being shot, 'I know I shall die for it, but my children will be free.'[18] By the end of the insurrection, over 200 rebels had been killed in the fighting compared to 14 whites.

And then came the official reprisals. Some 626 rebels were tried for treason and 312 sentenced to death. White colonisers crowded around the gallows to watch the executions, especially of the now-notorious leader Samuel Sharpe, who mounted the steps to his death quoting verses from the Bible. His owners were paid 16 pounds, 10 shillings in compensation for the loss of their property. It was a reminder, as British Jamaican author Andrea Levy observed, that to the colonisers 'slaves were more like cattle than people.'[19] Almost 150 years later, in 1975, Sharpe was declared a National Hero of Jamaica.

The Jamaica Rebellion had an electrifying impact in Britain. On the one hand, it spurred the abolitionist movement to push for immediate emancipation, with members of the public horrified not just by the violence meted out against the rebels but by the white mobs who were now terrorising missionaries who had supported them. On the other hand, it spread the fear of further insurrection among the establishment, who were afraid of losing total control of the island, just as the French had lost the colony of Saint-Domingue (Haiti) to a revolutionary slave uprising led by the legendary Toussaint Louverture. 'The present state of things cannot go on much longer,' wrote Lord Howick, parliamentary undersecretary at the Colonial Office and son of the prime minister Earl Grey, to the governor of Jamaica, 'emancipation alone will effectually avert the danger'.[20]

Convinced that Jamaica was a tinderbox that could explode again at any moment, in 1833 the ruling Whig government passed the historic Slavery Abolition Act. It was, however, far from a clear victory for the abolitionist movement or enslaved peoples themselves. The West India Interest managed to obtain extraordinary financial compensation for their 'loss of property', equivalent to 40 per cent of annual government expenditure or £340 billion in today's money (an amount that was not fully paid off by the British government until 2015). The Legacies of British Slave Ownership project at University College London has documented 47,000 recipients of compensation – including ancestors of former prime minister David Cameron – revealing just how deeply the institution of slavery had penetrated into society. The idea that enslaved people themselves should be compensated was not on the agenda. Quite the opposite: the Interest secured a provision in the Act forcing them to stay on as unpaid 'apprentices' for a minimum of four years before they were legally liberated. It is a history of injustice that galvanises the contemporary moral case for reparations for the descendants of the transatlantic slave trade. As Kehinde Andrews writes, 'as the wealth of Britain, and the wider Western world, was built on the back of slavery it therefore follows that a debt is owed to those descendants of the enslaved'.[21]

The story of abolition challenges the mythology that emancipation was primarily due to the benevolence of a wise white elite – people such as the parliamentarian William Wilberforce. Instead, it was far more the product of popular protest and struggle. Some of this was peaceful and legal, such as the mass meetings, public petitions and sugar boycotts led by British campaigners including Elizabeth Heyrick and Thomas Clarkson. But what really made the difference, argues historian Adam Hochschild, were 'the huge slave revolts, especially the final great rising in Jamaica that so clearly hastened the day of freedom', which 'were anything but peaceful'.[22] Although it is important to recognise the multiple causes of abolition – including factors such as the declining importance of sugar for the British economy – it is clear that disobedience and resistance created a crucial tipping point of change.

Yet there is a vital part of the story that remains to be told. Why was it that Parliament had enough MPs willing to support the Abolition Act, when for decades it had been stuffed full of politicians who were in the pockets of the West India Interest?

Once again, rebellion provides the answer. But this one was home-grown.

On the night of 28 August 1830, a group of agricultural labourers in east Kent, near the ancient pilgrimage site of Canterbury, sneaked into a farmyard and smashed to pieces one of the most divisive inventions of the Industrial Revolution: a threshing machine. At the time, rural Britain was in crisis, with high levels of unemployment and low wages for farmworkers causing acute levels of poverty. Threshing machines became the symbol of their oppression. Over the following nine months, hundreds of them were destroyed in a rebel uprising that spread swiftly across the country. Agricultural workers turned on large landowners, breaking machinery, burning down farmhouses and demanding higher wages and the restoration of common lands that had been 'enclosed' by powerful landlords. With nearly 3,000 recorded cases of revolt, it remains the greatest instance of contagious insurrection in Britian's history.[23]

Their leader was the infamous and elusive Captain Swing. Labourers typically made their demands and threats of arson in a handwritten letter sent to the landowner, which was signed with the flourishing autograph of 'Captain Swing'. But the captain in question did not exist. He was a political invention, a larger-than-life mythological rebel who struck revolutionary terror into the hearts of the rural elite.

AN ORIGINAL PORTRAIT
OF
CAPTAIN SWING

In many places, public support for what became known as the Captain Swing Riots or Rebellion was widespread. In Otmoor, Oxfordshire, disguised workers tore down fences to reclaim farmland enclosed by a local aristocrat, Lord Abingdon. More than 40 of them were arrested by the county yeomanry, but while being escorted to Oxford Castle, a crowd of revellers celebrating St Giles's Fair managed to wrest them free from the soldiers. Yet the greatest support for Captain Swing came from urban radicals such as the journalist William Cobbett, who saw the rebellion as an expression of the social and political exclusion of rural workers, and the need for an overhaul of the country's political system. Top of the agenda was expanding the electoral franchise to include more working people and eliminating the system of 'rotten boroughs' – parliamentary constituencies that enabled MPs to be elected by a tiny number of voters, and which were largely controlled by the Tory establishment.

An unexpected result of the Swing uprising was to rapidly accelerate the emerging movement for parliamentary reform. A hysterical fear of revolutionary unrest swept across the ruling political class, who had already been set on edge by nationalist revolts taking place in cities throughout Europe in 1830.[24] Prominent politicians, including Prime Minister Earl Grey, argued that reform was the only way to quell the danger of further rural rebellion. 'The principal of my reform is to prevent the necessity of a revolution,' he argued, 'reforming to preserve and not overthrow.'[25] In critical elections the following year, the greatest support for reforming Parliament was precisely in those regions that had been directly impacted by the revolts. According to scholars of the period,

> The reform-friendly Whigs would not have obtained a majority of seats in the House of Commons in the 1831 election had it not been for the violence of the Swing riots. Without such a majority, the reform process would almost certainly have come to a stop.[26]

But how is this all connected to the movement against slavery? The newly elected Whig government, fortified by the impact of the Swing uprising, was able to pass the Reform Act of 1832, the most far-reaching overhaul of the political system in more than a century. By eliminating the rotten boroughs, dozens of Tory politicians who supported the West India Interest's pro-slavery stance were swept from power in the subsequent election of December 1832. Now controlling more than two-thirds of Parliament, the Whigs were in a powerful position to pass the Slavery Abolition Act the following year.[27]

This tale of two rebellions – which are often downplayed in

standard accounts of British abolition – is a message for today. The Jamaica revolt and Captain Swing protests were tipping-point events, an unlikely conjunction revealing how popular uprisings and radical resistance can be accelerators of fundamental political change. For all its complexity and multiple causes, the story of abolition cannot be told without recognising the essential role played by grassroots disruption and disobedience that went far beyond the usual political strategies of lobbying, petitions and public demonstrations.

This raises a potentially controversial question. What role should such extra-parliamentary action play in today's struggle to abolish carbon emissions? Perhaps these two uprisings of the early 1830s are exceptions, and today's environmental activists would be wiser to play strictly by the book, pursuing reform within the legal boundaries of the existing system. But as the following section argues, they were not exceptional at all. In fact, they were early examples of what is termed the 'radical flank effect' – one of the most transformative social innovations devised by humankind.

The Hidden History of the Radical Flank

What exactly is a 'radical flank' and how does it work to create disruptive change? Over recent decades, social movement scholars have recognised that some of the most successful protest movements in history fighting for basic rights and social justice have benefited from having more radical organisations or factions engaged in struggle alongside them. These radical flank groups take more extreme positions than the mainstream moderate movement, making the latter's demands appear more palatable or 'reasonable' to those in power. In effect, the radicals change the terms of the debate, helping to shift the so-called 'Overton window' (named after the American policy analyst James Overton) – the range of policies that governments consider to be politically acceptable among the public at any one time. They can also create a sense of political crisis that is to the advantage of the moderates – a belief among elite actors that if they don't give in to the moderates' demands then the radicals will only grow stronger, and the situation could spiral out of control. Without the presence of the radical flank it can be all too easy for politicians to ignore popular movements for change. The radical flank is a key for unlocking political will.[28]

That's the theory – often described as the 'radical flank effect' – in a nutshell. What about the historical evidence? The struggle to abolish slavery in British territories was a striking instance of the radical flank effect in action: the mainstream reformist movement in Britain could have been campaigning for decades longer had it not been for the Jamaica Rebellion and Captain Swing revolts, which instigated a political crisis that helped accelerate the pace of change. Yet the theory itself was first developed in relation to the US civil rights movement of the 1960s.

The civil rights movement under the leadership of Martin Luther King Jr is often celebrated in the popular imagination as a triumph of peaceful sit-ins, bus boycotts and other forms of non-violent civil disobedience. But it is increasingly recognised that this is a sanitised version of history that underplays the importance of the Black Power movement. This was the radical flank of the racial justice struggle, involving key figures such as Malcolm X, Kathleen Cleaver and Angela Davis, and organisations such as the Nation of Islam and the Black Panthers. Their tactics were more confrontational and their demands more radical than the mainstream movement: many Black Power activists called for the creation of a separatist Black state and revolutionary insurrection, while openly carrying arms for self-defence and being involved in violent encounters with police.[29]

Establishment politicians feared that if they didn't give in to the demands of the comparatively moderate civil rights movement, then more and more African Americans would be drawn towards the militant organisations. As one senior government official warned President Kennedy, unless major concessions were made, 'Negroes unquestionably will look to untried and less responsible leaders' – such as Malcolm X.[30] It was a fear that King himself was well aware of, writing from his cell in Birmingham Jail in 1963 that if the channel of non-violent protest was not permitted, 'millions of Negroes, out of frustration and despair, will seek solace in black nationalist ideologies' and then 'the streets of the South would be flowing with floods of blood.'[31] As the decade wore on, his words seemed increasingly prophetic: more than 400 urban race riots broke out in 1967 and 1968, perhaps the greatest wave of social unrest in the USA since the Civil War.

The Reverend King may have preached 'the excellent way of love and nonviolent protest', but the success of the civil rights movement depended on the countervailing pressure of the Black Power organisations. As the social historian Andreas Malm argues, the legislative gains of the mainstream movement in the 1960s – such as ending segregation – were won 'because it had a radical flank that made it appear a lesser evil in the eyes of state power.'[32]

It turns out that many movements that have traditionally been depicted as peaceful, moderate and playing by the rules have benefited from a radical flank. Take the campaign for votes for women in Britain. Initially it was organised around the National Union of Women's Suffrage Societies (NUWSS), which adopted a peaceful and non-confrontational strategy. But in 1903, frustrated with the lack of progress, Emmeline Pankhurst founded the more radical Women's Social and Political Union (WSPU), which critiqued 'respectable' NUWSS methods such as petitions and public meetings, adopting the motto 'Deeds Not Words'. Over the following decade, WSPU members chained themselves to railings, disrupted public meetings, broke the windows of government offices, set fire to post boxes and went on hunger strikes while imprisoned. The WSPU was a classic radical flank organisation, which relied on a mixture of non-violent and more militant tactics, especially targeting property. As Pankhurst argued, 'to be militant in some form, or other, is a moral obligation.'[33] While there is some debate over the extent of its members' impact, according to historian June Purvis their actions helped turn women's suffrage into one of the foremost political issues of the era and raised feminist consciousness across the political spectrum, galvanising the broad movement for women's voting rights.[34]

Slavery, civil rights and women's emancipation are just some of the examples where radical flank movements have played a decisive role. The list could also include the Iranian Revolution, the Arab Spring in Egypt, the fall of the Nepalese monarchy, the gay rights movement and many more.[35] Together, they raise a crucial and politically sensitive issue: should today's climate movement be tapping more into the power of the radical flank?

Turning Up the Low Flame of Gradualism

In the winter of 2018, I found myself in a crowd of hundreds of people in Parliament Square in London, some of whom were busily digging a hole in the pristine lawn in order to bury a black coffin with 'Our Future' written boldly on the side. It was an early action by a new movement called Extinction Rebellion (XR). The police were out in force and began encircling the crowd, squeezing us closer and closer together – a tactic known as 'kettling'. Finding our way through the police cordon, we all then began to move out of the square, following the coffin, which was now being carried out in a mock funeral procession. The crowd then split up to take part in a series of 'swarm' roadblocks, sitting down to block major bridges and traffic intersections, and calling on the government to declare a climate emergency and rapidly accelerate the drive towards net zero carbon. Cars were honking angrily, with drivers shouting abuse at protestors for disrupting their journeys. The police were busy arresting those who refused to move, and struggling with activists who had glued their hands to the ground.

I had been engaged in mainstream climate politics in the past, writing reports for international NGOs and briefing politicians and government officials on the issues. I had also been on plenty of climate protest marches over the years, some involving tens of thousands of people – though most felt like they were doing little to shift the political dial, much like the previous decade's demonstrations against the war in Iraq. But this was the first time I was taking part in 'direct action' that pushed the boundaries of legality. And the truth is that I didn't really want to be there. I have no desire to disrupt people's lives. I'd far rather be in an old library beavering away doing research on a book. But like many others, I had come to realise that the government's chronic failure to take substantive action on the climate crisis was going to cause far more disruption to the lives of future generations and the planet they live on than I would to today's commuters. Frustrated with the slow – and deadly – pace of change, the most effective option left, I had decided, was to join the radical flank. It was the best way I could think of to be a good ancestor.

The mainstream media excels at demonising the more radical organisations that campaign on climate change, from Extinction Rebellion's 'die-ins', where thousands of protestors lie on the street disrupting traffic, to Just Stop Oil's eye-catching tactics such as throwing orange paint over famous works of art (being careful not to damage them). Activists are often branded 'idiots' at best and 'terrorists' at worst, with thousands having been arrested for their actions. Whether their methods are justifiable or not is a complex issue, which requires addressing both strategic and moral arguments.

The main strategic argument made against radical flank movements is that they typically don't work. According to this view, they not only alienate the public but also taint more moderate movements with their confrontational tactics, causing reputational damage through association – what is sometimes referred to as the 'negative radical flank effect'.[36] This is what arguably occurred in 1961 when Nelson Mandela founded uMkhonto we Sizwe (Spear of the Nation), the armed guerrilla wing of the African National Congress (ANC). Although Mandela said at his trial that they only took this militant route because 'all else had failed' and 'all channels of peaceful protest had been barred to us', it enabled the South African government to discredit the ANC's parallel non-violent civil resistance campaign.[37] A climate movement example took place in October 2019, when two Extinction Rebellion activists climbed on top of a London tube train during the morning rush hour, disrupting the commute of people from a relatively poor, multiracial part of the city, who turned in anger on the rebels. The action produced outrage across the political spectrum, including from many XR activists themselves who believed they should be targeting the privileged and powerful rather than people just struggling to get by and travelling on public transport.

This negative radical flank effect appears to be backed up by evidence suggesting that militant movements tend to have relatively low success rates. In a study of 323 social and political movements since 1900, Erica Chenoweth and Maria Stephan found that 'nonviolent campaigns were nearly twice as likely to achieve full or partial success as their violent counterparts'.[38] Movements that take up arms – such as the Fretilin guerrillas in East Timor or the Shining Path in Peru – generally fail, whereas those based on peaceful mass participation, such as the People Power Revolution that deposed Ferdinand Marcos in the Philippines in 1986 or Czechoslovakia's Velvet Revolution in 1989, which brought half a million people onto the streets to overthrow the discredited Communist government, are more likely to accomplish their goals. The critical tipping point for success, they argue, is getting 3.5 per cent of the population to support your cause. The implication is clear: radical flanks engaging a relatively small number of militant activists are a misguided strategy. So forget the guns and forget the orange paint too.[39]

The curious thing about Chenoweth and Stephan's study – which has been quoted repeatedly to justify climate protests based on non-violent mass mobilisation – is how irrelevant it is.[40] The authors were specifically looking at movements attempting to achieve regime change (such as toppling a dictatorship), rather than those focused on specific policy goals such as women's right to vote, racial equality or environmental protection. That explains why the suffragettes and the US civil rights movement – two of the most successful social movements of the modern era – are not even included in their dataset. In addressing climate change, radical flank organisations like Just Stop Oil in the UK, Ende Gelände (Here and No Further) in Germany or Climate Defiance in the US are not taking up arms and trying to overthrow governments wholesale – they are typically campaigning for policy changes such as ending state subsidies and licences for fossil fuel exploration. So it makes little sense to compare them to guerrilla groups fighting in the hills and to therefore condemn them as likely to fail.[41]

The more relevant comparison is precisely with social movements focused on policy change such as the suffragettes, civil rights and anti-slavery campaigns. In these and many other movements, radical flanks have played essential roles in achieving successful outcomes. The evidence so far suggests that the global climate movement is similarly benefiting from their disruptive presence.[42] Extinction Rebellion activists may have been criticised for climbing on a train, but such 'negative' radical flank actions have been far outweighed by the positive public response to their direct-action campaigns, which have spread to 84 countries, including in the Global South. Survey data reveals that XR actions have pushed the proportion of people for whom the environment is a top priority issue up to record levels.[43] More than 40 national governments and over 2,000 local government bodies have responded to their demand to declare a 'climate emergency'. XR's power to shift public agendas is also recognised by parts of the mainstream environmental movement such as Fridays for Future and Friends of the Earth, who have expressed solidarity with them. Radical flank organisations such as XR have helped to open the political space for transformative policy initiatives: in 2023, roadblocks by Dutch climate activists forced the government to hold a parliamentary vote – which was successful – to rapidly phase out fossil fuel subsidies.[44] The constructive dissent of such groups has shifted the Overton window, widening the policy possibilities, even at the cost of alienating some members of the public. Such is the inevitable price of their success.[45]

Similarly, Just Stop Oil may have upset some gardening enthusiasts by throwing orange vegan dye over plants at London's exclusive RHS Chelsea Flower Show, but its members keep using such tactics because they calculate that the media hit they get has a net positive impact on public consciousness, making it worth the risk. Despite the fact that the majority of UK citizens are opposed to the organisation's provocative methods, the most comprehensive study of its actions shows that 'there was no evidence that protests reduced support for climate policies or the goals of Just Stop Oil'. On the contrary: the data suggests that as a result of its protests, 'the number of people saying that they were willing to take part in some form of climate activism increased from 8.7% to 11.3% of the UK population, equivalent to approximately 1.7 million additional people'.[46] Just Stop Oil is now even getting the backing of major public figures: top Formula 1 racing driver Lewis Hamilton supported its disruption of the British Grand Prix, while BBC sports commentator Gary Lineker – who has more than 8 million followers on X (formerly Twitter) – has publicly defended its supporters storming the tennis courts at Wimbledon. As Lineker commented, 'history kind of tells you the only demonstrations that really work are the disruptive ones.'[47] When you start getting sporting heroes on your side, something is changing.

Strategically, the case for radical flanks in the climate movement is, on balance, convincing. What about morally? One argument that appears constantly on social media concerns inconvenience: protestors have no right to undertake actions such as blocking roads that delay innocent commuters on their journeys to work. But this can hardly compare to the far more drastic 'inconvenience' of a future where your children have to flee wildfires, millions of people have their homes flooded and there are a billion climate refugees.

A second argument is that it is morally wrong to break the law and that the 'rule of law' should be treated as sacrosanct. But where would we be without the illegal sit-ins of the civil rights movement or the law-defying general strikes called by Mahatma Gandhi that brought colonial India to a halt? If nobody ever broke the law, we would be unlikely to enjoy many of the basic human rights that we take for granted today. Politicians may often dismiss radical flank groups as 'extremists' or 'lawbreakers', but this represents an acute failure to understand how progressive political change happens and what gives democracy its meaning and vitality. As the social activist Abbie Hoffman quipped: 'My critique of democracy begins and ends with this point. Kids must be educated to *disrespect* authority or else democracy is a farce.'[48] The great irony is that the walls of my children's school history classrooms are covered with pictures of heroic lawbreakers such as Gandhi, Martin Luther King Jr and Emmeline Pankhurst. Should they really all be torn down?

A third ethical argument against radical flanks is that the use of violence is wholly unjustifiable. The underlying fear here is some kind of descent into ecoterrorism, like the fictional Children of Kali,

Mural at my children's school showing Emmeline Pankhurst, founder of
the radical Women's Social and Political Union, being arrested by police,
flanked by militant suffragettes including the figure of Emily Davison
(in the hat on the far left), who died in 1913 after being knocked down by
King George V's horse during a protest action. Mural by Soham De,
courtesy of the Rumble Museum.

a clandestine organisation based in India that sends up drones to
swarm around the private planes of oil company executives, causing
them to crash, in Kim Stanley Robinson's sci-fi novel *The Ministry for
the Future* (2020). Yet this argument misses the mark too. Virtually
every radical climate organisation explicitly rejects the use of violence. Hence their dedication to non-violent tactics such as gluing
themselves to the doors of oil companies, disrupting intergovern-
mental meetings, occupying coal-fired power plants and stopping
fuel trucks leaving their depots, as well as more carnivalesque actions
such as holding street parties on traffic roundabouts and guerrilla
gardening.

One might respond that such actions, which often involve the
destruction or violation of private property, themselves constitute
acts of violence. This is a common view advocated by many politicians and some scholars, including Chenoweth and Stephan, who

define violence broadly as 'physical harm of people and property.'[49] Such reverence for property has deep historical roots, going back to seventeenth-century thinkers such as John Locke, who considered the protection of individual private property as a fundamental right. But why should property be as sacrosanct as a human life? Surely there is a difference between a terrorist group assassinating a politician and climate campaigners pouring red paint on the steps of a bank that invests in fossil fuels, or racial justice activists toppling over the statue of a slave trader.

Take the case of the Tyre Extinguishers, an anonymous group with a singular aim: 'To make it impossible to own a huge polluting 4x4 in the world's urban areas. We are defending ourselves against climate change, air pollution and unsafe drivers.' Their method is to target SUVs, particularly in wealthy neighbourhoods, and let down a single tyre by unscrewing the cap, placing a lentil in the valve, then screwing the lid back on again, causing the air to slowly escape. Each vehicle then has a polite notice stuck to it – a little like a Captain Swing letter – informing the owner about the flat tyre and explaining the colossal CO_2 impact of their cars: 'If all SUV drivers banded together to form their own country, it would rank as the seventh largest emitter in the world.' This campaign against the 'luxury emissions' of the rich (rather than the 'subsistence emissions' of the poor) began in the UK in 2021 and spread virally to 18 countries within just a few months. At the latest count, more than 12,000 tyres have been deflated.[50] Does it cause inconvenience? Yes. But is it violent? Hardly. Lentils are not bullets. The actions of the Tyre Extinguishers should make us question the ideological fixation with the sacredness of private property, especially when that very property is helping to destabilise the ecological systems on which all life depends.

'The crucial problems of our time no longer can be left to simmer on the low flame of gradualism,' wrote the historian Howard Zinn.[51] The purpose of radical flank climate organisations is to turn up the heat. With effective, targeted action, they have the power to help transform the ecological crisis into a political one and create a tipping point of change. A major challenge of the climate emergency is that most people, especially in the rich countries that are responsible for the highest emissions, do not experience it as a crisis. It doesn't touch their personal lives closely enough unless they have had to escape a summer fire or are a drought-struck farmer. The slow violence of climate change doesn't strike fear like the bombing of Pearl Harbor or a pandemic that suddenly sweeps the globe and kickstarts governments into instant action. Most of the impacts are too gradual, so we get boiled alive like the frog in the pot of water whose temperature is rising only bit by bit. Radical flank movements prod us to jump out of the pot before it is too late.

This doesn't mean that other strategies should be abandoned. Just as the anti-slavery movement also benefited from moderate protestors gathering signatures for petitions and reformist politicians trying to change the system from within, the global climate movement requires citizen engagement at every level, from political lobbying to using the courts. But given the overwhelming failure of mainstream strategies over the past three decades to shift the CO_2 dial at the pace and scale required, and the continuing intransigence of the fossil fuel industry and most governments, it is simply too risky *not* to pursue the radical flank pathway too. We must accept the political virtues of disruption and disobedience at this critical pivot point in the human story (an issue explored further in Chapter 10). The activists committed to it join a distinguished historical tradition stretching back through some of the most renowned movements for human rights and social justice of the past two centuries, which pursued radical strategies when all else had failed.

Who is more likely to be remembered as a good ancestor by future generations: fossil fuel executives and the politicians supporting them, or the activists worldwide who have dedicated their lives to preserving our precious living planet? The answer is increasingly clear. 'Climate activists are sometimes depicted as dangerous radicals. But the truly dangerous radicals are the countries that are increasing the production of fossil fuels,' remarked UN Secretary General António Guterres. 'The world's biggest polluters are guilty of arson of our only home.'[52]

We should not be too quick to judge those who are putting themselves on the line for the climate crisis. The radical flank is a vital technology of survival in a world on fire. It has history on its side, from slave rebels to suffragettes. And its time has come. As the nature author Jay Griffiths writes, 'Only when it is dark enough can you see the stars, and they are lining up now to write rebellion across the skies.'[53]

2

Nurturing Tolerance

Living Together in a Medieval Islamic Kingdom

On Friday, 13 November 1951, an 18-year-old from Poland arrived by boat in Melbourne, Australia, with over a thousand other European migrants. He came with no family and no possessions, except for a few silk shirts he had won playing poker and a fez he had picked up on the journey. He arrived instead with memories – of watching his village being burned to the ground in the war, of begging for food door-to-door with his aunt, of long days wandering the rubble-strewn streets of post-war Berlin, scavenging cigarettes and waiting for his immigration papers from the International Refugee Organization. Finally they came. The price of his passage was two years working wherever the Australian government sent him. He spoke five languages and was a gifted mathematician and musician, but he was sent to work nights as a cleaner and orderly in a Sydney hospital. By day, he slept in a corrugated tin hut in the hospital grounds with a dozen other workers – Czechs, Hungarians, Poles, Lithuanians. One of his colleagues had been a Polish cavalry officer who had charged the German tanks; another had shovelled dead bodies in Auschwitz. He chose to stay on an extra year, saving money and using the dark hours on the ward to study English and bookkeeping, while the night sister turned a blind eye. In 1954, nearly a decade after the end of the Second World War, he stepped out of the hospital grounds into his new life, joining the millions of other migrants who hoped to make it good in the so-called 'lucky country'.

My father's story is his own. But it is also the story of humanity. We are a migratory species. Ever since *Homo sapiens* made their first journeys out of Africa towards the Middle East over 50,000 years ago, we have been a people on the move. We have occupied every environmental niche on every continent, along the way turning forests into fields, building cities, colonising and enslaving one another, fleeing wars and famines, travelling the seas and searching for safe havens to work and raise families. We may no longer be nomads but we never stay still. Our nature lies in restlessness; we are *Homo viator*, the wandering species. Whether by choice or force of circumstance, large swathes of humanity have always been seeking out new places to call home.

I see the traces of these great migrations written in my own DNA: 24 per cent Ashkenazi Jewish, 23 per cent Irish, 17 per cent Eastern European, 9 per cent Croatian. My maternal genetic haplogroup H6a1a takes my family tree back to Central Asia over 5,000 years ago.

Almost nobody can claim to possess a genetic ancestry that does not cross boundaries of nation or ethnicity. The story of migration runs through all of us, even if we are not aware of it or don't want to know. Go back far enough and the borders begin to break down: there is no 'us' and 'them'.[1] Patriotic pride has its origins in imagined communities. By all means cheer for your national football team. Just know that your scarf should be woven through with the colours of many others, even your rivals.

The coming century heralds a new age of migration that will far exceed the scale of the momentous shift from the countryside to the city during the Industrial Revolution, or the mass exodus from Europe in the late nineteenth century. Since the 1960s, the level of international migration has been surprisingly constant at around 3 per cent of the global population. That figure is fast becoming outdated. Today there are about 280 million people on the move, of whom 35 million are refugees compelled to leave their homelands by persecution or war.[2] By some estimates, however, the number of migrants will reach 1 billion people by 2050 – one in ten of the human population – most of them climate refugees fleeing the impacts of droughts, rising sea levels and the resulting political turmoil.[3] Some people will just move to the nearest big town or city, hoping for better prospects: most migration is internal, happening within, not between, countries. Yet many will seek to cross borders and even continents – on foot, by dinghy, hidden in trucks – taking the long and risky path of their migratory ancestors, often with little hope of success. Central Americans heading north to the United States. North Africans crossing towards Europe. Bangladeshis and Indians to the Persian Gulf states.

As the number of people on the move continues to grow, so will the social impacts. Anti-immigrant sentiment is rising sharply in many countries, with right-wing parties and media feeding the fires of xenophobia and preying on the twin fears that immigrants 'steal our jobs' and 'threaten our way of life'.[4] Such persecution is also directed towards citizens with immigrant backgrounds whose families may have arrived generations ago. None of this will halt the phenomenon of escalating migration as environmental crises hit, automation forces people to seek jobs in new places, and some wealthy countries actively seek more migrants to reinvigorate labour markets as their populations age and even decline.[5] And that raises a question: how are hundreds of millions of people, often from extremely diverse cultural backgrounds, going to find ways to live together in relative harmony?

Here I explore the challenges and possibilities of nurturing what migration scholars call 'conviviality' – the idea of living together with difference in multicultural communities.[6] This requires searching the past for the conditions that create tolerance not just of new immigrants but also of established citizens who may still be considered 'outsiders' due to their ethnic and religious backgrounds. History offers no golden ages where this kind of peaceful coexistence has easily emerged. Discrimination and violence plague the annals of migration. As the historian Theodore Zeldin observes, 'the West has for most of its history been intolerant'.[7] But through journeys across the last thousand years, from Europe's forgotten Islamic kingdom to post-colonial Ghana and Singapore, we may find clues for generating human connection rather than fractured societies. To gain perspective on the problem, we begin with the brutal story of Chinese immigration to the United States.

Chinese Americans and the Threat of the 'Yellow Peril'

Dozens of Hollywood films feature European migrants arriving at Ellis Island in New York in the early 1900s, queuing up with bulging suitcases and wailing children, ready to begin a new life in the land of opportunity. Few of them show Angel Island on the other side of the country.

In 1910, the Angel Island Immigration Station was opened in San Francisco Bay, primarily to enforce draconian policies banning most Chinese people from entering the United States. Chinese and other Asian immigrants were subject to intense interrogation and often detention – for weeks, months and sometimes years – as they awaited their fates. Some of them carved poetry about their ordeals onto the walls, which can still be seen today. 'Imprisoned in a wooden building day after day, my freedom withheld – how can I bear to talk about it?' reads one inscription. Their words reveal one of the darkest chapters of US immigration history.[8]

Prejudice and violence against Chinese people had been taking place since the 1850s, when the first large waves of immigrants began to arrive, fleeing the turmoil of the Taiping Rebellion and lured by the Californian gold rush and the prospect of jobs on the railroads. Almost immediately, white workers were turning on those they referred to as 'John Chinaman', accusing the Chinese of being 'coolies' willing to work for slave wages. In a notorious 1854 legal case, in which a white man was accused of murdering a Chinese miner, the California Supreme Court ruled that Chinese could not testify as witnesses against a white defendant on the grounds that they are 'a race of people whom nature has marked as inferior, and who are incapable of progress or intellectual development beyond a certain point.'[9] Like African Americans and Native Americans, who were subject to similar legal discrimination, the Chinese then became an easy target, with the ruling unleashing a wave of lynchings, torching of homes and destruction of businesses.

The anti-Chinese fervour escalated following the economic downturn of 1873. The Chinese quarters of small towns were burned down. New anti-Chinese trade unions were formed, such as the United Brothers of California, while in 1876 an anti-Chinese

Workingmen's Party won a third of the seats in the state legislature. In 1877, ethnic violence swept San Francisco's Chinatown, with white mobs setting fire to Chinese laundries and killing their proprietors, a repeat of a similar rampage a few years earlier in Los Angeles's Chinatown, when 15 Chinese people were found hanged.[10]

Opportunistic politicians across the nation – both Republicans and Democrats – began to realise that demonising the Chinese was a sure way to win the white working-class vote and tip the electoral scales in their favour. By the early 1880s, public campaigns were calling for a halt to Chinese immigration, not just in California – where they were 10 per cent of the population – but throughout the country. The result was the 1882 Chinese Exclusion Act, the first ever federal law to restrict immigration explicitly on the basis of nationality or ethnicity. All new immigration of Chinese workers was banned (with some exceptions such as diplomats). Existing migrants could remain but they would not be permitted citizenship, no matter how long they lived in the United States.[11]

The persecution of Chinese migrants found its cultural expression in a single phrase: the 'yellow peril'. By the turn of the century, anti-Chinese prejudice was represented in a whole genre of novels, artworks, cartoons, plays and newspaper stories that depicted the Chinese as an uncontrollable horde that might overrun the white race. The 'yellow peril' was portrayed as a virus that would infect Western civilisation, sapping it of its life force and economic might. This deep fear was personified in Sax Rohmer's 1913 fictional character Dr Fu Manchu, a fiendish master criminal who was 'the yellow peril incarnate in one man', possessing 'all the cruel cunning of an entire Eastern race'.[12]

The discrimination continued for decades until an unexpected turn of events took place on 7 December 1941. Few could have foreseen that the Japanese bombing of Pearl Harbor would be a liberation for Chinese immigrants. Japan was now the arch-enemy whereas

THE ONLY ONE BARRED OUT.

An American magazine commenting on the recent passing of
the Chinese Exclusion Act of 1882.

China, which had been at war with Japan for the previous four years, converted into an ally of the US. Racism against people of Japanese descent escalated rapidly. Around 120,000 Japanese Americans – more than half of them children – were sent to internment camps behind barbed wire for the duration of the war. On the other hand, over 10,000 Chinese Americans joined the US military, taking up roles in combat units, intelligence and logistics. Racist slurs remained common in the armed forces, but oral histories of Chinese American soldiers reveal that the non-segregated units in which most of them served helped to break down cultural barriers. According to historian Kevin Scott Wong, 'Many of those who saw combat recalled that facing the enemy under fire equalised everyone in the unit regardless

of rank, race, or ethnicity.'[13] Simultaneously, the shortage of industrial workers on the home front during the Second World War opened
the labour market to Chinese women, who now found themselves
working as riveters in San Francisco shipyards alongside white and
African American women. With Chinese Americans increasingly
being seen as patriotic 'good Asians', in 1943 the US government
finally removed the 15 pieces of anti-Chinese legislation on the stat-
ute books, including the Chinese Exclusion Act. The Angel Island
detention centre, which burned down during the war, was consigned
to historical memory.

By the 1960s, Asian Americans – especially those of Chinese
heritage – were starting to be described as a 'model minority' whose
children studied hard and set their sights on middle-class profes-
sions such as law and medicine.[14] Yet this was, in many ways, just
another stereotype. Back then, as today, many Asian American teenagers were struggling at school and feeling an oppressive pressure to
live up to expectations. The label also failed – and continues to fail –
to recognise the variety of Asian American communities in the US,
which includes not just high-achieving professional families but
poor immigrant labourers from China and other countries working
for poverty wages, and refugees from more than a dozen Asian
states.[15]

The history of Chinese immigration to the US speaks from the
past to the migration challenges of our time. It is, most obviously, a
stark reminder of just how long it can take for the green shoots of
tolerance to emerge. In this case, it took more than a century, and
may have taken even longer if not for the impact of Pearl Harbor.
Even after all this time, racism and discrimination persist.[16] It also
reveals deep continuities in attitudes to immigrants. Donald Trump's
controversial decree banning travellers from seven Muslim-majority
nations, issued in his first week in office in 2017, was not just a product of post-9/11 Islamophobia but had its precedent in the ethnic

targeting of the Chinese Exclusion Act.[17] Similarly, his accusation that Mexican immigrants are 'criminals' and 'rapists' who are 'taking our jobs' was a modern reprisal of the 'yellow peril' menace.[18] Comparable language has been used by far-right politicians in Italy, France, the Netherlands, Australia and other countries.

The scapegoating of Chinese workers, particularly during economic downturns such as in the 1870s, illustrates how underlying economic factors can be a major barrier to the emergence of conviviality. As the sharp increase in anti-immigrant sentiment following the 2008 financial crash equally demonstrated, when jobs are scarce or insecure, when rent or mortgages can't be paid, people are quick to blame immigrant 'outsiders', even when there is little evidence of their culpability.[19] Indeed, a stream of studies shows that migration produces much greater economic benefit than harm. Migrant workers are typically net contributors to government finances, providing far more in tax revenues than they receive in health or housing benefits: in the UK, migrants contribute £2,300 more annually than the average adult, and make a net positive contribution of £78,000 over their lifetimes.[20] Regarding employment, migrants and locals are rarely in one-to-one competition for jobs: migrants generally take up jobs that locals are not prepared to do, from waste collection to picking fruit, or compete for jobs with the previous generation of migrants. Rather than pushing down wages, 'immigrants have a negligible, or even positive, impact on natives' earnings', according to migration expert Marco Tabellini.[21] They can also supercharge economies with skilled labour. None of this, of course, prevents populist politicians from targeting them. Migration issues are much more about fear than facts.

In a world of both rapidly rising migration and increasing job insecurity, we are set to witness further discrimination and persecution directed at migrants from a variety of backgrounds. Is there any way to avoid this tragic trajectory? The Enlightenment ideal of progress that prevails in the West has us believe that human morality has expanded through the ages and that we have become increasingly tolerant and open-minded over time. We no longer burn witches at the stake, run our economies on child labour or exclude women from the vote.

But history has never been bound by such linear narratives. Sometimes we need to travel far into the past to discover the most illuminating moments of human possibility. Now is the time to journey back a thousand years to the ancient kingdom of al-Andalus, where there are glimmers of radical hope for the creation of a more tolerant future.

Al-Andalus: Tolerance and Turbulence in a Medieval Islamic Kingdom

Imagine you could be born anywhere in Europe in the year 1000 but that you had no idea which strata of society you would be born into – neither your class, religion, ethnicity nor gender. Where would you choose? You could be forgiven for feeling this was an unfair choice. It is a year that typically conjures up barbaric images of the Dark Ages – a bloody era of violence, warfare, poverty and pestilence reminiscent of *Game of Thrones*. Yet there is more on offer if you look in the right places. One of your best options would have to be the city of Córdoba in the south of Spain, known across the continent as 'the ornament of the world.'

At the time, Córdoba was the epicentre of the Muslim kingdom of al-Andalus, which in various forms covered much of the Iberian peninsula from the reign of the Umayyad prince Abd al-Rahman I in the eighth century to the final surrender of Granada to Christian rule in 1492. Córdoba was a city of wonders, with well-lit streets, bustling markets, hundreds of bath houses and running water from its aqueducts, all enjoyed by a population of over half a million people (while both London and Paris had around just 20,000 inhabitants). It was also famed as a centre of knowledge and learning. In *The Decline and Fall of the Roman Empire*, Edward Gibbon exclaimed that its main library had 'six hundred thousand volumes, forty-four of which were employed in the mere catalogue', including Arabic translations of ancient Greek texts by Aristotle, Euclid and Hippocrates.[22] Nowhere in Europe could compete with such cultural riches.

But what really set Córdoba and the kingdom as a whole apart was that it appeared to achieve an almost miraculous civilisational feat: to have very different communities living in the same place, in relative peace, for long periods of time. Generally known as the *Convivencia* (which literally means 'living together' or 'coexistence' in Spanish), it was an era during which, according to historian María Rosa Menocal, 'Jews, Christians and Muslims lived side by side and, despite their intractable differences and enduring hostilities, nourished a complex culture of tolerance'.[23] It is a controversial thesis that has, ironically, ignited intense academic debate among medieval historians for over half a century. How much truth is there in it?

Al-Andalus was a stratified society where Muslims were in a position of authority. But under the Islamic legal doctrine of *dhimmi*, 'people of the book' – Christians and Jews but not pagans – were granted the right to practise their own religions as long as they did not worship in public and paid a special tax for the privilege. While many Christians felt oppressed by their Muslim conquerors and threatened by the number of Christians converting to Islam (often to avoid the tax), for Jews it was a reprieve after long periods of persecution by Christian rulers, where they were shunted to the bottom of the social hierarchy.[24] In fact, attracted by its tolerant attitudes, Jews migrated to al-Andalus. They eventually comprised around 5 per cent of the total population, alongside other migrants, including Muslim Berbers from North Africa.

Although Muslims, Jews and Christians often lived in segregated neighbourhoods they were 'all the time being thrown together in the cities and towns, intermingling as they went about their daily business', writes historian John Elliott.[25] They traded with each other in the markets, often washed together in the same bath houses, played music together, and sometimes had illicit sex. Muslims were even known to slip into Christian monasteries for a forbidden glass of wine.[26] 'In many day-to-day contexts', notes medieval historian Brian Catlos, 'people saw themselves as Andalusis first and treated their fellow citizens as such, regardless of their faith'.[27]

Social interaction revolved around their shared language, Arabic, the lingua franca in which they gossiped, negotiated, laughed and argued. 'All talented young Christians read and study with enthusiasm the Arab books', complained the Christian theologian Paul Alvarus,

> For every one who can write a letter in Latin to a friend, there are a thousand who can express themselves in Arabic with elegance, and write better poems in this language than the Arabs themselves.[28]

In 1360, when the Jewish community leader Samuel Halevi Abulafia built a synagogue in the city of Toledo, he not only did so in the extravagant Islamic Nasrid architectural style, but he covered its walls in beautiful carved script in both Hebrew and Arabic – which was still the language of the cultured Jews of Castile nearly 300 years after Toledo had fallen to the Christians.[29] Arabic was a cultural glue that enabled al-Andalus to become one of the most cosmopolitan societies the world had yet seen. Perhaps its closest contemporary rival was Sicily under the rule of the Norman king Roger II

Cultural exchange on the Iberian peninsula in the thirteenth century.
Above, a Muslim and Christian jamming together on lute-like instruments.
Below, a Jew and a Muslim playing chess.

(1095–1154), who created a multicultural court including Muslims, Christians and Jews, promoted the use of Latin, Greek and Arabic, and whose architectural legacy included buildings incorporating Arabic, Norman and Byzantine design.[30]

Among the most celebrated figures of al-Andalus was a Jewish poet and political leader named Samuel HaNagid. When Córdoba was sacked by the Berbers in 1013 and the Umayyad kingdom began to split into a number of competing *taifas* or Islamic city-states, Samuel's family fled with other Jewish refugees to Málaga, where they opened a spice business. The story goes that a maidservant of a local official visited the shop and, noticing Samuel's exquisite Arabic calligraphy skills, asked him to write letters for her. Word about his literary abilities spread and he was soon appointed as personal secretary to the vizier of Granada, the most powerful political official apart from the king. By the age of 34, the brilliant Samuel had himself been appointed vizier. It is hard to imagine, but this Jewish scribe now found himself as a trusted diplomat of a Muslim king, even leading Muslim soldiers into battle riding an Arabian stallion. He simultaneously rose to become the leader of Granada's Jewish community. Samuel is also remembered for developing a new form of Hebrew poetry that drew on Arabic literary style and metre – a fine example of the innovation and riches that migration can produce through cultural fusion.[31]

While some scholars consider Samuel HaNagid as an exemplar of the culture of tolerance found in al-Andalus, for others he is an exception. These critics point out that the so-called *Convivencia* was punctuated by periodic outbreaks of ethnic and religious violence. In the mid-ninth century, nearly 50 Christians in Córdoba were executed for their beliefs. In 1066, there was a massacre of Jews in Granada, with Samuel's own son Joseph – who had succeeded his father as vizier – being torn limb from limb by an angry Muslim mob. From the twelfth century, violence against Jews began escalating across the Iberian peninsula, just as in other parts of Europe.[32] It is important not to romanticise *Convivencia*: Islamic Spain's culture of tolerance was fragile and could easily flare up into acts of violence and cruelty, especially at times of economic and political crisis. Yet it is also difficult to deny the reality of the widespread peaceful coexistence of Muslim, Christian and Jewish communities, even amidst the simmering tensions.[33] 'Popular religious violence was exceedingly rare' in al-Andalus, observes historian Brian Catlos.[34] Moreover, al-Andalus appears all the more tolerant when compared to the Christian rule that increasingly extended across Spain from the fourteenth century: an estimated 100,000 Jews were killed by Christians in the pogroms of 1391 and a similar number forced to flee.

What made it all possible? Certainly a shared language and freedom of religious practice. But above all it was the forced intimacy of city life. 'These independent cities,' writes David Levering Lewis of the *taifa* period, 'produced a great upswell of commercial activity and an even greater *Convivencia*.'[35] Urban living fostered personal relationships across community lines and created webs of economic interdependence that sustained a culture of tolerance and mutual respect: a Muslim leatherworker might depend for supplies on a Christian tanner, or a Jewish physician might want the services of a Muslim master builder (and vice versa).[36]

It is true that cities can be full of intolerance, discrimination and inequality, as those facing ghettoised housing and racist policing in the banlieues of Paris or the barrios of East Los Angeles know only too well. Yet cities are also one of humanity's greatest social innovations, a technology that excels at mixing together people of diverse backgrounds on a mass scale. Cities help turn us into citizens. Studies of urban living reveal that the bigger the city, the more tolerant of outsiders its residents are likely to be, especially if people have a common language in which to communicate with one another.[37] That may be why, in the 2016 Brexit referendum – which to a large degree centred on immigration issues – London voted overwhelmingly against leaving the European Union while rural England voted for it. Like in Córdoba a thousand years ago, local inhabitants and migrant newcomers were in constant contact with each other in the city's shops, schools, workplaces, parks, sports clubs, buses and cafés. The face-to-face jostle of city living can help people recognise what they share in common and consider cultural variety as normality rather than a threat.

The underlying psychological phenomenon behind this urban tolerance is known as 'contact theory'. Its central thesis is that if different groups are brought into contact with each other in conditions of relative equality, where they have to regularly interact and cooperate together, the typical result is to reduce prejudices, stereotypes and other divides between them. An analysis of over 500 different studies showed that intergroup contact reduced prejudices and increased tolerance in over 94 per cent of cases, whether it was kids from different ethnic and religious backgrounds playing in a football team together, or soldiers in a racially diverse regiment under enemy fire (as took place when Chinese Americans fought alongside their white counterparts in the Second World War).[38]

The towns and cities of al-Andalus provide a remarkable example of large-scale contact theory in action, grounded in the complex realities of a long period of medieval history. Ultimately, writes Brian Catlos, the coexistence of different communities in Islamic Spain teaches us that 'as humans we have a tremendous capacity to get along, despite our differences and our failings'.[39] That's history as a message of hope.

Designing Conviviality in the Cities of Tomorrow

In an age of growing migration, it makes sense to look to cities to generate cultures of conviviality: migrants naturally gravitate towards them and by 2050 more than two-thirds of the global population will be living in urban areas.[40] While cities have a strong record of nurturing tolerance, how is it possible to minimise the kind of periodic violence that broke out in al-Andalus and which affected Chinese immigrants in the US? There is a crucial ingredient that can improve the chances that cities forge unity rather than sow division: convivial design. By this I mean initiatives by governments and planners to create the conditions that help human relationships to thrive.

Three countries offer inspiration for what this might look like in the cities of tomorrow. One of those is Ghana, whose first post-independence leader, Kwame Nkrumah, feared that differences between ethnic groups such as the Akan, Ewe and Ga-Adangbe could fracture the country following its liberation from British colonial rule. 'If we tolerate the formation of political parties on regional, sectional, or religious bases', he warned in the mid-1950s, 'we shall not only be heading for political chaos but, worse still, we shall be sowing the seeds of the destruction of our national existence.'[41]

When independence came in 1957, Nkrumah embarked on a series of policies and programmes to create a unifying Ghanaian national identity that would simultaneously encourage the country's ethnic and religious communities to coexist peacefully with one another. A new national anthem and flag, national monuments, banknotes and postage stamps all celebrated and symbolised the birth of Ghana: outgoing British officials were furious with the first stamp, which replaced Queen Elizabeth II with a bust of Nkrumah together with an African palm-nut eagle breaking chains fastened to its legs. In a controversial decision, English was made the language of national education, in an effort to prevent divisions in a country with a large number of language groups. Nkrumah wasn't attempting to eradicate cultural differences but rather promote unity within diversity. At a personal level, he often wore a northern tunic at political rallies despite not being from that part of the country, and fasted during Ramadan in solidarity with the minority Muslim population even though not being one himself.[42]

These foundational actions of nation building are among the key factors explaining the relatively low levels of intercommunal violence in Ghana since independence. Although there have been some serious outbreaks of violence – such as the 1994 Konkomba–Nanumba conflict in Northern Ghana – and inter-ethnic disputes over land and other issues continue to arise, Ghana is generally considered, according to conflict researcher Paul Kwame Asamoah, 'a peaceful nation amid an otherwise unstable sub-region.'[43] This is borne out in survey data: Ghana ranks as having among the highest levels of tolerance of people from different ethnicities and religions on the continent.[44]

The Ghanaian state has not acted alone in its efforts to promote cultural coexistence: grassroots civic and religious organisations have played a significant role, especially in urban areas. Every Sunday afternoon in the town of Ashaiman, local residents gather for meetings in dozens of different multi-ethnic and inter-religious self-help organisations, ranging from women's development groups to youth clubs. They bring out chairs, hang out banners and wear colourful matching T-shirts in a vibrant display of boundary-crossing communal solidarity. Reflecting such attitudes, in 2019 Ghana's chief imam, Sheikh Osmanu Nuhu Sharubutu, attended a Catholic Church service as an act of inter-faith harmony during the celebrations of his one-hundredth birthday.[45]

While a sense of shared national identity can help foster social inclusion and tolerance, it can just as easily be used as a tool of exclusion: for a populist politician such as Donald Trump, immigrant Mexicans do not qualify as patriotic Americans, no matter how long they have lived in the country. In this sense, national flags have the potential to divide as much as unify. So what other strategies can be used to design conviviality and neighbourliness into diverse urban communities?

Here we can turn to Singapore, whose post-colonial dilemmas in many ways echoed those in Ghana. When the Asian city-state gained full independence in 1965, after more than a century of British rule, its first prime minister, Lee Kuan Yew, was similarly confronted with the question of how to create a unified republic. At the time, Singapore was experiencing acute ethnic tensions among its population, where there was a Chinese majority (around 75 per cent) living alongside large Malay (15 per cent) and Indian (7 per cent) minorities. 'We are going to have a multi-racial nation in Singapore,' Lee adamantly declared. 'This is not a Malay nation; this is not a Chinese nation; this is not an Indian nation.'[46]

One of the most innovative attempts to turn this multicultural dream into reality has been in the area of public housing. During a recent trip to Singapore, one of the city's former development planners lured me away from the glitzy central district to visit an outlying residential area on the edge of the metro system. We emerged into a world of uniform tower blocks – some of the oldest in the city – surrounded by neatly clipped lawns on which seniors were doing their morning tai chi and women in saris were talking in the shade. We then took a lift up to the fifth floor of one of the towers, where I found myself on a long balcony – more like an outside corridor – containing drying washing, children's bikes, pot plants and the doorways into several flats. 'This is what makes Singapore different,' my guide announced triumphantly. I gave him a quizzical look and he began to explain.

Following race riots in 1964 and 1969, Singapore's Housing Development Board endeavoured to design a housing system to promote 'racial harmony'.[47] One of its key elements became an ethnic quota system – still operating today – where each housing estate must reflect the national percentage of Singapore's main racial groups to ensure that housing does not become ethnically segregated or ghettoised. The corridors themselves are part of this system and function to encourage neighbourly encounters, often having a mix of Chinese, Malay and Indian residents. Most apartments do not have private balconies, so the corridors act as common areas where children play, neighbours chat and small intercultural gifts are often exchanged, such as speciality sweets during religious festivals. On the ground floor of each building is a shared public space that might be used for a Malay Muslim wedding or a Chinese funeral, as well as for residents' committee meetings. 'The public spaces within Singapore's high-rise public housing estates, which are home to more than 80% of Singaporeans, are spaces of everyday conviviality', concludes one study.[48]

As we went back down in the lift, I commented to my host that Singapore's ultra-designed multicultural harmony all seemed a little too good to be true. Although genuinely proud of the government's achievements promoting inter-ethnic coexistence, especially through housing policy, he was also ready to admit its failings. Tens of thousands of temporary migrant labourers – many from southern India, Bangladesh and Vietnam – who are employed in construction and other manual jobs, are typically left out of the system, shunted away in poor dormitory housing and facing low wages and racial discrimination. At the other end of the spectrum, there was increasing recognition of the problem of 'Chinese privilege', referring to the way that the Chinese population dominates certain realms of public life, such as top positions in the civil service – in stark contrast to official government discourse about racial equality.[49] Singapore may hold an annual Racial Harmony Day and have left the era of race riots long behind, but the lived realities of conviviality – like in al-Andalus – remain full of complexity and contradiction.

The biggest challenge of the Singapore model is political: its semi-authoritarian system of government has enabled the ruling party – which has been in power uninterrupted since independence – to impose its policies with minimal opposition. But what if you would prefer to live in a democracy rather than what might be best described as a benevolent dictatorship?

Let's return to Spain, which has developed a very different approach to promoting convivial cities in a more democratic context. In the first decade of this century, Spain underwent a seismic demographic transformation: over 6 million immigrants arrived in the country, especially from Morocco and Latin America, bringing the foreign-born population to 14 per cent of the total. While this has contributed to the rise of far-right, anti-immigrant political movements such as Vox, environmental journalist Gaia Vince points out that 'Spain hasn't seen significant anti-migrant backlash' on the scale of other countries such as France and Germany.[50] Why not?

The main reason, she argues, is due to smart government management and planning to help create a new generation of multi-ethnic cities. Turning standard immigration policy on its head, Spain started by granting citizenship rights to all migrants in full-time employment – including 'illegal' undocumented workers – which gave them access to public services such as healthcare, and brought them into the tax system where they could become contributors to public finances. It also granted one-year work permits to tens of thousands of African migrants – keeping them out of the underground economy – with the incentive to become permanent citizens if they could stay in employment. Over 2 billion euros were additionally funnelled into migrant support programmes to help them find jobs, learn Spanish and take part in citizenship classes.

The results are clear to see in towns such as Mataró in Catalonia. On a Sunday afternoon in the public park in the neighbourhood of Cerdanyola – where one in four people were born outside

Spain – Catalans and Castilians intermingle with Senegalese and Moroccans, while children play football in ethnically mixed teams. Through the system of *empadronament* (residency registration), all migrants register with the local council, giving them the same social service benefits as other residents. In the free, voluntary classes for 'new citizens', they are introduced to the term *convivencia* – an echo of medieval al-Andalus – which promotes the ideals of cultural tolerance and neighbourliness. Anthropological studies of the town reveal that while neighbourhood disputes across ethnic lines certainly take place, the general picture is one of cordial respect and coexistence.[51]

Yet as befits the historical record, *convivencia* in Mataró – and in Spain as a whole – is potentially fragile: the growing prominence of far-right political parties may make the country's immigration policies far less welcoming. On the other hand, with its population set to decline due to a low birth rate – by as much as 50 per cent by 2100 – Spain will be in desperate need of more immigrants to sustain its economy and pay taxes to support its pension system. As in many other European countries, immigration may become a necessity not a choice.

Living together has never been easy. The examples of Ghana, Singapore and Spain reveal the variety of ways to design conviviality into urban life, providing the invisible scaffolding that helps cities do what they have always done best: mixing together people of different cultures and backgrounds. These three cases are not strict models or blueprints to follow – ethnic quotas for public housing might work in Singapore but could be unworkable in places where state housing is limited and the ethnic mix more fragmented. But they do suggest that if we want people to live together peaceably, while respecting cultural differences, intentional planning and design can improve the chances of success.

We know that human history is a catalogue of intolerance – of prejudice, discrimination and violence against those deemed to be 'outsiders'. But I hope to have shown that history teaches us just as much about what a tolerant society looks like and how we might get there. Over the last 1,000 years, our forebears have, through turbulence and turmoil, found ways to bridge their differences and flourish side by side. With the past as our guide, we have the insights and knowledge to create the convivial cities of the future and nurture a new choreography of human relationships.

3

Kicking the Consumer Habit

Preindustrial Japan and the Design of
Regenerative Economies

> Our enormously productive economy demands that we make
> consumption our way of life, that we convert the buying and use of goods
> into rituals, that we seek our spiritual satisfaction, our ego satisfaction,
> in consumption ... We need things consumed, burned up,
> replaced and discarded at an ever-accelerating rate.
>
> – *US economist Victor Lebow, 1955*[1]

Shopping, as we know it today, was invented in Paris in 1872. That was the year Aristide Boucicaut opened the doors of the grand new building of Bon Marché, the world's first department store. Designed by the upcoming architect Gustave Eiffel, it was soon hailed by novelist Émile Zola as 'the cathedral of modern trade'.[2] Bon Marché – 'the good deal' – pioneered shopping as an all-embracing wraparound entertainment experience. People went there not just to shop in its sumptuous hallways surrounded by cascading fine silks and oriental rugs, but to meet friends, have lunch served by liveried waiters, enjoy free newspapers in its reading room and attend art exhibits and even opera performances in its opulent atrium. Until the eighteenth century, 'consumption' was the term for a potentially fatal wasting disease. Bon Marché transformed it into an addictive pleasure.

Behind the silken curtains, the store was also a hard-nosed capitalist enterprise whose marketing innovations became a model for the expanding retail industry across Europe and North America. Walk through its entrance on the Rue de Sèvres and you would immediately be squeezed between its bargain counters, where the frenzy of jostling shoppers gave the impression that there were deals not to be missed. Continuing your journey through its spacious departments and up the elegant, curved stairway, you could calmly peruse the plethora of household and luxury goods all under one roof, try on clothes with the help of trained assistants and enjoy the certainty of fixed prices rather than haggling in the city's specialised shops. If you were lucky, you might be there for the famous February White Sale, when all white-coloured items – towels, sheets, curtains – were sold at a discount. Today's Black Friday shopping hysteria is the mutant descendent of the seasonal sales invented by Bon Marché.

The historian Keith Thomas writes of the culture of 'limitless desire' that emerged in eighteenth-century Europe, as rising incomes enabled the growing middle classes to move beyond satisfying basic needs, and social status was increasingly expressed through displays of wealth.[3] Bon Marché's greatest innovation was to tap into this desire by getting people to buy things they had never imagined they needed. The company's enticing advertising and mail-order catalogues suggested to the aspiring bourgeoisie that they didn't need just one coat, but a different one for every season, and a special coat for travel, and another for visiting friends and going to the theatre. A respectable home should have different forks for every purpose: eating fish, meat, olives and strawberries. Matching linen serviettes. Patterned curtains. Sailor suits for the children and new outfits for holiday trips. Bon Marché turned the manufacture of desire into a highly profitable art form.

The birth of the department store was just the beginning. The fixation on economic growth that took hold of Western societies in the early twentieth century required insatiable consumerism to power it. Consumer culture was supercharged in the 1920s by PR

Gentlemen's coats for every occasion. From the
Bon Marché catalogue, 1920.

gurus such as Edward Bernays – the nephew of Sigmund Freud –
who convinced women to start smoking cigarettes because they were
liberating 'torches of freedom' and who dreamed up bacon and eggs
as a hearty American breakfast on behalf of the pork industry.[4] It was
ratcheted up by the Mad Men advertising executives of post-war
America, and by Nike telling us to Just Buy It.[5] Now we are lured by
the algorithms of online shopping emporiums whose individually
targeted ads and Buy Now buttons promise immediate satisfac-
tion of our genuine needs and fabricated desires. Onion goggles,
anybody?

There was nothing inevitable about this process. Consumerism is
a historical invention – like democracy or organised religion – that
has been so successful it has redefined the meaning of the good life.

In preindustrial society, people typically gained esteem and status from being a great warrior, pious priest or fine scholar. Today, it is more likely to come from the clothes we buy, the car we drive, the luxury holidays we take. I shop, therefore I am. Our material aspirations continue to rise in a process sociologist Juliet Schor calls 'upscale emulation', where we increasingly compare ourselves to the lifestyles of the rich and famous we see on our screens rather than to our friends, family and local community.[6]

The challenge of consumer culture is not only that it typically fails to deliver higher levels of wellbeing once our basic needs have been satisfied: above a certain point, more stuff doesn't make us much happier. We must also contend with its devastating planetary impacts.

The well-off shoppers of the Global North are the frontline troops of an ecological plundering that our preindustrial forebears could barely have imagined. The e-waste mountains filled with discarded iPhones and their rare earth metals. The microplastics found in the stomachs of dolphins, sea turtles – and children. The toxic chemicals in the water we drink and air we breathe. The forests ravaged by cattle ranches to put meat on our plates. This is about far more than climate change: even if we had 100 per cent renewable energy, our intensive resource use would still be sending us across dangerous thresholds of biodiversity loss, air pollution and soil degradation. Humanity's material footprint is almost double what the planet can safely sustain – we are using up the resources of two planet Earths annually – and it is continuing to grow. Moreover, as economic anthropologist Jason Hickel notes, 'virtually all of this overshoot is being driven by excess consumption in high-income nations'.[7] The rich are devouring the world.

The Earth is not an endless frontier with inexhaustible resources. It is a closed system, powered by the Sun, spinning through the blackness of space – what the economist Kenneth Boulding called 'spaceship Earth'.[8] We don't need a crystal ball to tell us that, in the long run, the limitless desires of consumer culture are incompatible with life on a finite planet.

If history has bound us to consumerism, how might it also liberate us? Can it help humankind – especially citizens in the wealthy Global North – kick the consumer habit and stop trashing the planet? When I walk through my local shopping centre, which is constantly buzzing with people buying, chatting, eating and parading – a true Bon Marché experience – I often think that the juggernaut of consumer capitalism cannot be stopped. It is too entrenched. It is too powerful. It is too enjoyable.

Yet history reveals that another path is possible. It is not simply about individuals changing their habits to become 'green consumers'. Rather, it requires a more profound systemic shift: the embrace of regenerative design. This means designing our economies to operate within the ecological limits of our delicately balanced planetary home, so we don't use more resources than the Earth can naturally regenerate, and we don't create more waste than it can naturally absorb. Regenerative design is an ideal of deep sustainability rooted in many indigenous cultures, which has also become central to the field of ecological economics since its birth half a century ago.[9] It constitutes an invaluable – yet largely unacknowledged – innovation of human societies. Exploring histories of consumerism, from colonial America to feudal Japan, offers crucial insights for creating a regenerative future.

The Extreme Sport of Simple Living

Few people have heard of John Woolman. Born in New Jersey in 1720, Woolman was a member of the Religious Society of Friends, a radical Protestant sect more commonly known as the Quakers.

Quakers distinguished themselves by rejecting the idea of ordained clergy so they could have a direct relationship with God, and through being committed advocates of social justice. But they were also champions of simple living or what they referred to as 'plainness', embodied in a set of rules still operating today called the 'Testimony of Simplicity'.

Quakers such as Woolman wore dark clothes made from undyed cloth and shunned showy adornments such as buckles, lace or ribbons. They minimised their material possessions, favouring sparse wooden furnishing over puffed cushions and velvet curtains. They ate plain food and even spoke plainly, avoiding honorific titles and naming the days of the week 'First Day', 'Second Day', and so on.

In the early eighteenth century, many Quakers were disturbed by the growing number of their brethren who were breaking the rules – exemplified by the founder of Pennsylvania, William Penn, who lived in a stately home and had a penchant for fine wines and thoroughbred horses. In the 1740s, Woolman spearheaded a movement to return Quakerism to its spiritual and ethical roots in plainness and piety. He travelled the country tirelessly, preaching the virtues of simplicity and urging his fellow Quakers to confront injustices such as slavery, a subject on which he published numerous essays.

Neither a great orator nor brilliant intellect, his main claim to fame, according to one historian, was being 'the noblest exemplar of simple living ever produced in America'.[10] Woolman turned simple living into an extreme sport. After establishing himself as a cloth merchant to earn a subsistence living, he found himself making so much money that he tried to reduce his profits by requesting that his customers buy less cloth and cheaper cuts – not something they teach you at Harvard Business School. In the end, he switched to tending an apple orchard instead. Woolman was also a pioneer of fair trade, boycotting cotton goods produced on slave plantations and insisting on directly paying pieces of silver to enslaved servants in homes he visited. He was a practising vegetarian too. Once, when offered poultry, he replied, 'What, would you have me eat my neighbours?' When travelling as a missionary to England in 1771, Woolman was so troubled by the luxury of his ship's cabin that he chose to sleep for the next six weeks in the damp and filthy steerage with the sailors. Upon arriving in England, he decided to visit York, where he planned to observe the country's poor social conditions first hand. But upon hearing that he would have to travel in a horse-drawn carriage, Woolman decided to avoid such cruelty to his equine brothers by choosing to walk instead – more than 200 miles. He finally reached York but never managed to leave. While there he caught a deadly dose of smallpox and was buried in a pauper's grave.

Eccentric? Undoubtedly. Crazy? No. Woolman was a clear-headed radical changemaker. He was ready to sacrifice creature comforts and convenience knowing there was a greater reward: the luxury of a life observing his religious principles. It was about expressing his freedom of choice in more fulfilling ways than mere materialism – by choosing to oppose slavery, respect his fellow creatures, help the poor and spread his beliefs far and wide. Quaker simplicity was the foundation of it all, freeing him from the pursuit of earthly pleasures.

While John Woolman deserves to be in the pantheon of history's most inspiring examples of simple living, he is not alone. There was the ancient Greek philosopher Diogenes, son of a wealthy banker, who downsized to live in an old wine barrel. St Clare of Assisi, who in the thirteenth century founded an order of nuns – the Order of Poor Ladies – who took vows to live in poverty. Henry David Thoreau, who built his New England log cabin with his own hands and declared, 'A man is rich in proportion to the number of things which he can afford to let alone.' And there are figures such as Mahatma Gandhi, who inspired millions to live a simpler life, spinning their own clothes and living on ashrams. 'Live simply, so others may simply live', he reputedly said.

But how many people really want to live penniless in a barrel or make their own clothes? In a consumer-driven society, simple living can easily come across as frugal extremism that involves too much sacrifice, too much abstinence, too much giving things up. Yet that is not how advocates of simple living see it. They have almost always been guided by larger ideals that are core to their identities, such as religious belief, social justice or ecological stewardship. It is an existential exchange where the comforts of a new sofa are swapped for a value-driven life that is 'outwardly simple, inwardly rich', to borrow a phrase from today's Voluntary Simplicity movement.[11] It is about expanding the free, moneyless spaces of your life, whether through singing in a community choir or growing vegetables on your allotment. It is about being rather than buying.

Despite all the potential benefits, the real problem with simple living is not so much that it is an extreme sport but that it is a minority sport. Since the rise of the consumer age, simplicity has remained a fringe activity. There are just not enough Gandhis or Thoreaus, Quakers or St Clares, to keep the forces of materialism at bay. We know that more stuff is unlikely substantially to boost our wellbeing, yet most of us with the economic means (or at least a credit card) keep on accumulating more clothes, more shoes, more gadgets, more clutter. We have so internalised the advertising messages linking material goods to personal fulfilment that few other options seem viable or even thinkable. We choose what futurist James Wallman calls 'stuffocation'.[12]

Even those who are aware of the ecological quandary we are in are largely unwilling to alter their lifestyles. A survey of ten high-income countries revealed that three-quarters of people believed more environmental regulations were important but almost half felt there was no real need for them to change their personal habits, and only a fifth thought it necessary for people to fly less or reduce their meat consumption.[13] The reality is that it is difficult to resist a whole culture geared towards buying rather than being. The new iPhone is too enticing, Amazon Prime is too convenient, the holiday flight is too good a bargain, the burger is just too tempting.

There are, of course, people who have made the decision to step away from mainstream consumer culture to pursue another path – and their actions can make a difference. In the UK, for instance, 16 per cent of 18 to 24-year-olds are now vegan or vegetarian.[14] Every time they ask for non-meat options at their local cafés, more get put on the menus, nudging the whole population towards the normality of plant-based diets. A tipping point of change may soon be reached. Yet the global meat industry remains a formidable opponent. In Britain alone, over a billion chickens are slaughtered each year. By 2050, at current rates, our planet will have to support around 120 million extra tonnes of humans but 400 million extra tonnes of farm animals – and all the environmental waste and destruction they produce.[15]

This raises an acute dilemma: individual actions such as voluntarily changing your diet can make an impact in some sectors, but are unlikely to be enough by themselves to create the broad-based regenerative economies we urgently need, at the scale and pace required. The cultural drives of consumer capitalism, and the vested interests behind it, are too deeply entrenched. The result would be too little, too late. So we must also seek solutions at the systemic level. The philosopher Herbert Marcuse once wrote that Western society is trapped in 'the consumer machine'.[16] The question is how to dismantle the machine, or at least fundamentally alter how it works.

John Woolman was moving in the right direction. He wasn't just trying to change his own habits: he was intent on galvanising the whole Quaker community across North America to embrace radical simplicity. But undertaking this task in twenty-first-century Western nations with millions of shoppers is an even more ambitious prospect. Does history offer any instances of such large-scale simplicity in action? Is it possible to keep the forces of consumer culture under control and create complex urban societies that operate within ecological limits? It so happens that one of the world's earliest sustainable economies was in full operation just when Woolman was preaching his gospel of simplicity – but on the opposite side of the globe.

Edonomics: Deep Sustainability in Preindustrial Japan

Imagine standing on the old wooden Nihonbashi Bridge in the commercial heartland of Edo, the ancient Japanese city now known as Tokyo. It is some time around 1750 during the Edo period, the era from 1603 to 1868 ruled by the Tokugawa shoguns. You are surrounded by a bustle of chattering locals twirling their umbrellas, seafood traders rushing across the bridge, balancing brimming baskets on their shoulders, and labourers carrying rice and cloth to the market stalls on either side of the riverbank. The smell from the famous Nihonbashi Uogashi – the fish market – wafts through the air. You gaze into the distance to the rising sun on the horizon of Edo Bay.

Japan under the Tokugawas was cut off from the rest of the world: in an effort to protect itself from the influence of Christian missionaries and Western powers, the regime severed most of its international trade links and banned travel to foreign lands. But that didn't stop Edo from becoming a colossal city with over a million inhabitants. It was dominated by Edo Castle and the residences of samurai and regional lords or *daimyō*. The *shomin* – the 'common people' – lived mostly east of the castle, with much of the rest of the city given over to shrines and other religious buildings. After having been devastated by the Meireki fire of 1657, when an estimated 100,000 people

The bustling Nihonbashi Bridge in the city of Edo (Tokyo)
during the Tokugawa era.

died, Edo was still a city of wood, from houses to temples, from boats
to bridges.

But, looking closely, there was something even more remarkable
about Edo: it was a city without waste. Almost everything was reused,
repaired, repurposed or in the last instance recycled – what we would
today call a circular economy. The Edo economy 'ran as a very effi-
cient closed loop system', argues sustainability historian Eisuke
Ishikawa.[17] A traditional *yukata* – a simple summer kimono made of
cotton – would be used until the cloth began to wear out, at which
point it had become soft enough to be turned into pyjamas. Its next
stage of life was as nappies, which could be washed again and again,
after which it might become a floor cloth before finally being burned
as fuel. Cotton was so precious that a tradition of patchwork called
boro – literally 'tattered rags' – was developed in parts of Japan, with
poor villagers collecting fragments of discarded cloth and sewing

them into coats and other garments, which would be passed on from generation to generation. Everything was collected for reuse – the drippings of candle wax were remoulded, old metal pots were melted down, human hair was sold to wigmakers. Modular house design meant that floorboards could be easily removed, planed down and used again in new buildings. Samurai down on their luck repaired umbrellas. The leftover straw from growing rice was used for making sandals and rope, wrapping up household goods, and finally as fertiliser and fuel. Paper recycling was a huge industry – they even recycled used toilet paper, which was made from the tough fibres of bark. You didn't pay nightsoil men to take away human waste – they paid you, then sold on the precious load as agricultural fertiliser. While this circular economy operated across Japan's islands, it was most highly developed in the city of Edo, which was home to over a thousand refurbishing and recycling businesses.[18]

Edonomics in action: traditional *boro* patchwork kimono.
Image courtesy of the Trey Trahan Collection.

This culture of deep sustainability was reinforced by extensive regulations to manage resource scarcity, especially for timber. Japan's economy was as dependent on wood as we are today on fossil fuels. When the Tokugawa shoguns took power, they were facing an acute shortage of this precious resource: ancient woodlands had been so severely depleted – partly due to population growth – that there was a genuine threat of economic collapse. According to environmental historian Conrad Totman, 'Japan today should be an impoverished, slum-ridden, peasant society subsisting on an eroded moonscape, rather than a wealthy, dynamic and highly industrialised society living on a luxuriant green archipelago.'[19]

The Tokugawa's regulatory regime, which enabled them to avoid this fate, started with bans on logging, including limits on felling trees of certain sizes and species, to allow for forest regeneration. Fines were substantial and in some regions breaking the rules was punishable by death. There were also restrictions on the types of tools that could be used for logging and the amount of firewood villagers could gather. These measures were combined with a wide-ranging system of timber rationing. Edicts were introduced that limited the type, size and number of pieces of wood that could be used in the construction of houses and other new buildings. The rationing rules were closely linked to status: those higher up the social hierarchy, such as samurai and lords, were permitted greater use of scarce timbers and could build larger homes – but they too faced restrictions. Although timber rationing rules were sometimes flouted, they were a crucial policy instrument that 'bought time' for woodland regeneration, argues Totman.[20]

These 'negative' demand-side restrictions were combined with a 'positive' supply-side approach: the Tokugawas embarked on one of the most extensive programmes of plantation forestry the world had ever seen. Although a top-down policy imposed by the ruling shogunate, it was highly dependent on involvement from local rural populations. While some regional lords used forced labour, over time a series of incentive structures evolved, such as villagers being offered cash payments for planting new trees. Rental forests became more common, often in the form of *nekiyama*, in which a villager planted a site and sold the timber in advance to a merchant. The villager nurtured the trees and when the trees were harvested after several decades, the villager could replant and re-lease the land. Village assemblies also developed new rules to administer their communal forests, known as *wariyama*, to help manage them sustainably and avoid disputes, and planted new woods to protect their lands from erosion and flooding. Over a period of a century, beginning around 1750, tens of millions of trees were planted, reafforesting the denuded landscape.[21]

This combination of sustainable circularity and resource regeneration was the essence of what has been called the 'Edonomy' that emerged in preindustrial Japan. The Edo period remains one of the best historical examples of what a regenerative economy operating within safe ecological limits might look like.[22] It was, writes environmental scientist Eiichiro Ochiai, 'a small-scale model for spaceship Earth' that took 'every possible step to maintain the principles of zero-waste, zero-emission, long before such terms came to be appreciated.'[23] It is also notable for sustaining its low-footprint economy over a long time period of more than two centuries. Moreover, it did so while producing an extraordinary era of cultural flourishing. While life was hard for poor rice farmers and women confined by patriarchal oppression, the Edo period also gave birth to the poetry of Bashō, the artworks of Hiroshige, and a thriving culture of street theatre, sumo wrestling, pottery, calligraphy and flower arranging. Edo may have been lacking the steam engines of industrial England but it made up for it in sophistication and beauty.

To sum up, what explains the emergence of the Edonomy? Some historians stress the strong sense of intergenerational connection in

Japanese society, which encouraged long-term policies such as tree planting, where the benefits would mainly be enjoyed by people's descendants. Others highlight cultural factors such as the ideal of *mottainai* – a sufficiency principle of not being wasteful and having 'just enough'. As a visiting diplomat noted in the 1860s, even the homes of powerful lords were relatively sparse and lacking in material luxuries, unlike the overstuffed parlours of the Victorian middle classes. Quality mattered far more than quantity.

A more common explanation, however, is the isolationist no-trade policy of the Tokugawa regime.[24] By maintaining a closed economic system, or autarky, the country was compelled by scarcity to become hyper-efficient in the use of its own resources, particularly with respect to commodities such as timber and cotton. The dictatorial power of the ruling shoguns to impose their economic policies, such as timber rationing and tree planting, was also a key factor in the operation of the Edonomy. But their policies would never have functioned effectively without the engagement of local populations who responded to scarcity with ingenuity and commitment: it was everyday citizens who sewed together the patches for their *boro* kimonos, who started up businesses recycling candlewax, and who planted trees on their communal village lands. The success of state regulation was firmly grounded in, and enabled by, local participation.

The result was what may be the world's first large-scale ecological civilisation. But it was not to last. Following the fall of the Tokugawa regime in the late nineteenth century, Japan reopened itself to foreign trade and began its trajectory to becoming an ultra-modern, high-consumption, high-carbon society. Unsurprisingly, many of its environmental experts and organisations look back to Edo as an instructive model for creating a sustainable, regenerative economy today. But what would it take to create an Edo 2.0 that is fit for the ecological realities of the twenty-first century? What insights might we draw from the past?

Redesigning Choice for a Regenerative Future

The path towards a regenerative future for humankind can be usefully approached by thinking about it as a problem of design. It is about 'designing out' (or 'editing out') certain consumer choices that push us beyond the biocapacity of the planet, so that they no longer appear on the menu of options, while simultaneously 'designing in' (or 'editing in') alternative options that bring us safely within ecological limits.[25] In an age when our everyday consumer decisions can have devastating – and often unseen – environmental impacts, we must recalibrate the architecture of human choice. Edo offers two fundamental insights for doing so to produce the regenerative revolution we so urgently require.

The first is that we should follow Edo's lead by striving to create a no-waste circular economy. As the sustainability writer Azby Brown observes, 'The circular economy mode adheres so closely to the Edo-period environmental and design principles that Edo can serve as a prototype and inspiration.'[26] In practice, that means designing out linear industrial systems based on planned obsolescence and throw-away 'take, make, use, lose' processes, and designing in cyclical systems where most products and materials are continually used again and again through being repaired, refurbished, repurposed and recycled. It is an idea familiar to those who have experienced periods of extreme resource scarcity: many people who lived through the Second World War recalled how they darned every sock, repaired every gadget, saved every scrap of cloth and never wasted an ounce of food. In preindustrial Japan, this zero-waste mindset was deeply embedded into the normality of everyday life, generation after generation.

While we might marvel at how the inhabitants of Edo gave a cotton kimono multiple lives by turning it into pyjamas, then nappies and then floor cloths, the context in Japan was very different to the one we are currently facing. Circularity emerged in the Tokugawa period primarily due to resource shortages, whereas many of today's most harmful resources – such as the petrochemicals used to make single-use plastics – are in plentiful supply. So we need to deviate from the Japanese model and simulate scarcity through strict regulations to ensure that products are designed based on circularity, and enterprises integrate it into their business models. A regenerative economy would edit out standard resource-intensive phones from the landscape of choice, so that we can only choose between a range of sustainable models. These would likely resemble the Dutch Fairphone, which uses recycled plastic and copper, and has a modular design so that every component part – from screens to batteries – can be easily repaired, or replaced by the owner.[27] If our phones lasted twice as long, we would only need half the number. In policy terms, it might require giving companies a five-year regulatory lead time where they know when new restrictions will come into force, leaving them plenty of time to phase out their old models and bring in new ones that meet the regenerative standards. These are precisely the kinds of targeted policies that are already being used in many countries to edit out the use of fossil fuel cars: Paris, for example, is banning them from the streets from 2030.

Just as it is wishful thinking to believe that enough individuals will voluntarily switch to products such as the Fairphone, it is equally wishful to believe that enough companies will voluntarily make the switch to circularity. We need a whole circular economic ecosystem like in Edo.[28] The Dutch government is leading the way by pledging to have an economy that is 50 per cent circular by 2030 and 100 per cent by 2050, with cities such as Amsterdam having already introduced circularity regulations into food, textile production and construction (such as the reuse of building materials).[29] In France, manufacturers are now legally required to provide 'repairability scores' for electronic goods – similar to energy-efficiency ratings on fridges – to show how easily they can be repaired, inducing companies to compete on their circular credentials. Similarly, the EU has introduced 'right to repair' legislation, making it mandatory for many goods such as televisions (and soon smartphones) to be repairable for up to ten years. Only 7.2 per cent of the global economy is currently circular.[30] If we hope to boost that figure to Edo levels, companies like Apple, Samsung, Tesla and Holcim (the biggest cement company in the world) will need to be legally obligated to up their circular game. Governments have long banned the sale of products, such as asbestos, that are dangerous to personal health. Why should they not phase out and eventually ban the sale of products that are dangerous to planetary health?

Critics rightly argue that circularity is far from enough for an effective regenerative economy. For a start, many products, from polystyrene and aerosol cans to mattresses and disposable nappies, cannot be easily recycled, while recycling itself can be highly energy intensive. Moreover, spaceship Earth cannot easily absorb the environmental impacts of another 10 billion phones, laptops and electric cars, even if their designs were largely circular: the material footprint of producing, selling and powering them would be simply too great and outstrip the gains of circularity.[31]

So we also need to do something about the growth of consumer demand itself. How do we go about ratcheting down consumption to sustainable levels, especially in wealthy countries where retail therapy has become a way of life? Many cities, among them Geneva and Grenoble, have started to ban the 'visual pollution' of advertising billboards in an effort to edit advertising messages out of sight. Others have introduced charges for driving fossil fuel vehicles in congested areas to reduce private-car use and edit in cycling and walking – though these are often controversial, as debates about the enlargement of London's Ultra Low Emissions Zone in 2023 demonstrated.[32] Edo pursued the more radical option of rationing, which extended beyond timber to include other goods such as silk cloth. This is the second insight from Edo, asking us to consider whether we should be introducing rationing today – in our case for major ecological culprits like carbon and red meat.[33]

Rationing has a long history in human affairs, with Tokugawa Japan being just one of many examples. In the Western world, the last time it was introduced on a widespread scale was during the Second World War. In Britain, wartime rationing of everyday items such as tea, meat and petrol helped reduce consumption as a share of national expenditure from 87 per cent to 55 per cent. The United States also introduced rationing, together with price control regulations, driven both by the need to divert resources to the war effort and the fear of inflation caused by an overheating war economy. Just 16 months after Pearl Harbor, there were 13 major rationing programmes in operation, covering products such as tyres, petrol, sugar, coffee, meat and cheese. At the same time, the Office of Price Administration – which had the economist John Kenneth Galbraith as its deputy administrator – established maximum prices for hundreds of basic consumer goods, affecting more than 3 million businesses. This 'General Max' regulation was enforced by over 250,000 volunteers – mostly women – who worked alongside 5,000 local War Price and Rationing Boards, regularly checking prices in their neighbourhood stores to make sure retailers were not cheating the system.[34] It is hard to imagine that the world's most ardently capitalist economy largely suspended the operation of the free market for the duration of the war. But it did.

Rationing has always faced several difficulties. First, the rules can be hard to enforce. Just as timber-use restrictions were often contravened in Japan, in the US as much as 40 per cent of meat was being sold on the black market by 1944.[35] Second, the rules are often perceived as unfair. In Edo they were skewed towards favouring the social elite, while in Britain, although aristocrats and factory workers

US government rationing poster, Second World War.

received equal rations, the rich could still use their wealth to buy expensive unrationed goods such as pheasant and eat in pricey restaurants. Third, they are typically introduced by authoritarian means or only in exceptional circumstances. In Japan, rationing was imposed by what was, in effect, a military dictatorship, while Britain and the USA were experiencing a wartime crisis that gave governments the power to enforce emergency measures.

All of this makes rationing a very hard sell today. For most people – and governments – ecological challenges such as biodiversity loss, climate change and chemical pollution simply don't prompt the same crisis response as the Luftwaffe dropping bombs on the nation, or public health emergencies like the COVID pandemic, when countries rapidly brought in restrictions on travel, work and socialising. Rationing is also often associated with drab wartime austerity – people queuing up with ration cards for meagre handouts of butter and sugar. It can additionally conjure up visions of an overbearing government taking away our freedom: why shouldn't I be allowed to fly to Thailand for a well-earned holiday break? As a result, most politicians steer clear of supporting rationing, fearing it is a sure way to scare off voters at the ballot box.

Yet there is a growing movement of policymakers, think tanks and public figures in favour of rationing as a viable – even necessary – response to the global ecological emergency. Much of the discussion so far has focused on the energy sector. 'Developing a system of individual carbon cards,' writes the French economist Thomas Piketty, 'will certainly be part of the indispensable institutional tools for meeting the climate challenge.'[36] The Hot or Cool Institute in Berlin has similarly made the case for rationing – or what has been skilfully rebranded as Personal Carbon Allowances (PCA). Their research highlights the success of trials in the Finnish city of Lahti (where residents had carbon allowances deducted from their digital accounts via a smartphone app) and Australia's Norfolk Island (where they used a swipe card system), both of which led to substantial emissions reductions. They advocate not just equal shares for all but also allow people to trade their unused carbon allowances on digital platforms, so the high polluter pays while the low polluter is rewarded. They point to survey evidence showing that such schemes have the potential for public popularity, as long as there is a genuine sense that the system is administered fairly and protects low-income households, while also noting that many cities around the world already have successful rationing policies that go by other names, such as the use of parking permits in residential zones.[37]

There are critical voices on this issue too, who argue, for instance, that rationing carbon in rich countries may not even be necessary if the price of renewables drops low enough to make the demand for fossil fuel energy disappear. But on our current trajectory, where we are failing to rein in our use of carbon and other important planetary resources, rationing will almost certainly need to be considered among the policy options, as it was in eighteenth-century Japan under the Tokugawas. In our more democratic age, let us at least have a vigorous public debate about rationing rather than treat it as taboo.

We also shouldn't forget figures from the past like John Woolman. His example suggests that as well as supporting public policies such as rationing and the circular economy, we should additionally be taking action in our personal lives to live lightly on the earth. One option might be to join a grassroots citizens' movement such as Take the Jump, which offers six principles for adopting a 1.5°C lifestyle:

End clutter: keep electronic items for at least seven years.
Holiday local: take short-haul flights only once in three years.
Eat green: adopt a plant-based diet and leave no waste.
Dress retro: buy at most three new items of clothing a year.
Travel fresh: don't make use of private cars, if possible.
Change the system: act to nudge and shift the wider system.[38]

If the first five principles seem too intimidating, Take the Jump recommends trying them out for a month as an experiment. But the sixth principle is just as crucial: voluntarily editing your consumer choices is a start, but ultimately there is no substitute for systemic change when so much is at stake. We need to support citizen initiatives that help put regenerative policies like the circular economy firmly on the political agenda. These policies will also need to be supplemented with other changes to forge a regenerative future, such as finding new metrics to replace the outdated focus on GDP growth, and promoting innovative business models like steward ownership and cooperatives that provide alternatives to the short-term extractivism of shareholder capitalism (see Chapter 9).

Edo, however, remains a beacon of radical hope, calling on us to expand our imaginations with inspiration from the past. Perhaps the greatest value of the Edo experience is to remind us that it may be possible to move beyond the idea of mere sustainability – where something is maintained in its current state – to the more profound notion of regeneration. A truly regenerative economy is one that recovers and renews, that creates ecological abundance, that leaves the world in a better state than it was found. And that is what happened in Japan, where the response to an acute deforestation emergency was a monumental tree-planting effort driven by government policies but powered by citizen participation, which transformed the country into a green archipelago. Human societies have an enormous capacity to respond effectively to crisis. The memory of Edo can help us confront the crises of our own age and chart the journey towards an ecological civilisation.

4

Taming Social Media

Print Culture and the Invention of the Coffeehouse

We are today as far into the electric age as the Elizabethans had advanced
into the typographical and mechanical age. And we are experiencing the
same confusions and indecisions which they had felt when living
simultaneously in two contrasted forms of society and experience.

– Marshall McLuhan, 1962[1]

In *The Decline and Fall of the Roman Empire*, Edward Gibbon high-lighted some of the great technological innovations of the ancient Romans, from the aqueduct system and public sewers to road building and stone arches. But he failed to mention that they also pioneered what we now call social media.

Social media can be broadly defined as a communications technology enabling peer-to-peer exchange of information, which can be shared through distributed networks and communities. Flick through the 900 letters that the Roman philosopher and politician Cicero left behind and you will see how it worked. Cicero didn't just write copious letters to his friends. As was common among members of the literate Roman elite, he also shared copies of and extracts from letters he had received from others – naturally adding his personal comments to the various discussion threads – and sent multiple copies of his own letters to different people so they could be widely distributed and read out in public. In a typical letter Cicero writes, 'I sent you on the 24th of March a copy of Balbus' letter to me and of Caesar's letter to him'. In another he notes, 'You say my letter has been widely published: well, I don't care. Indeed, I myself allowed several people to take a copy of it.' The Romans were, in effect, writing social media posts, sharing messages and retweeting content but without the benefit of an electronic 'share' button. Instead they typically used enslaved people to convey their messages: 'slaves were the Roman equivalent of broadband', according to technology historian Tom Standage.[2] They also had a craving for constant updates. As Cicero wrote imploringly to a friend, 'whether you have any news or not, write something.'[3]

The resemblances to modern digital communication don't end there. Like today's text messages, the Romans used abbreviations such as SPD, short for *salutem plurimam dicit* ('sends many greetings'), and SVBEEV, which stood for *si vales, bene est, ego valeo* ('if you are well, that is good, I am well'). Messages sent over short distances were often written with a stylus on wax tablets embedded in a wooden frame – an ancient form of iPad – which the recipient could then erase with the end of the stylus to write their reply. Each day when the government posted its gazette of official information, the *Acta Diurna* ('Daily Acts'), on a board in the Forum, hired scribes would descend and copy key extracts for distribution to far-flung provinces. These condensed news digests were frequently accompanied by the kind of trivia found in social media feeds, such as the divorces of famous people or the story of a loyal dog that swam after the corpse of its executed master as it floated down the River Tiber. In an early version of Facebook's message walls, the walls of city buildings operated as public message boards and were rife with personal commentary and graffiti – everything from 'Atimetus got me pregnant' to the rather more mundane, 'On April 19, I made bread.' One message in Pompeii read, 'Oh wall, I am amazed you haven't fallen down, since you bear the tedious scribblings of so many writers.'[4]

Social media in the Roman Empire was slow compared to our

fibre optic networks: without any formal postal service, it could take more than a month for letters from Rome to reach the outer edges of the empire in Britain and Syria. With circulation limited to the estimated 10 per cent who could read, messages rarely went viral (St Paul's Letter to the Romans was one exception). Despite such limitations, the Romans' early use of communications technology is a reminder that the digital media revolution may not be quite as revolutionary as we think. Ever since the invention of writing, humankind has been exploring ways to amplify our voices and spread information and ideas, whether for good or ill. Our suite of digital communications technologies – social media platforms, websites, texting, email, blogs, podcasts, video streaming – is part of a much older story.

This raises questions about what we might learn from history for tackling the challenges of the digital age, especially to counteract the toxic impacts of social media, from political polarisation and fake news to malicious trolling, election hacking and the manipulation of human attention. Underlying this is a larger question about whether the digital technologies at our disposal are simply neutral tools – as the tech industry likes us to believe – or if there is something inherent in their design that is likely to mould human society and the human mind in particular ways, independent of the content. In other words, was the 1960s media theorist Marshall McLuhan right to argue that 'the medium is the message'?[5]

No technological innovation offers greater insights into these issues than the printing press, whose invention represents the most significant shift in the production and dissemination of human knowledge prior to the rise of digital communication. It is important to recognise the immense benefits that printing produced, but if we wish to learn from its history, we first need to explore some of its more destructive consequences, many of which were unforeseen when the technology first emerged.

How the Printing Press Inflamed Polarisation, Persecution and Violence

When Johannes Gutenberg built the first mechanical printing press in Mainz, Germany, in the 1440s, and published an initial print run of 180 Latin bibles, his invention was hailed as a gift from God that could help spread the teachings of the Roman Catholic Church.[6]

Yet the papal blessing given to the press soon turned out to be a curse. As the old scribal culture of hand-copied manuscripts gradually disappeared, the new printing presses that spread rapidly across Europe also spread heretical religious doctrines that were a direct challenge to the authority of the established Church. What exactly happened? Martin Luther went viral.

In October 1517, the German priest nailed his famous Ninety-Five Theses to the door of the castle church in Wittenberg, a Latin text that criticised Church corruption such as the sale of 'indulgences' (financial payments that could be made to absolve people of their sins). Within two months, printed copies in the form of pamphlets and broadsheets had appeared in Nuremberg, Leipzig and other cities, financed by Luther's supporters. It was then translated into German – hugely widening its potential readership – and became an instant publishing sensation. In just two weeks, his theses were known throughout Germany; within a month, they had reached every corner of Europe. 'It almost appeared as if the angels themselves had been their messengers', reported one contemporary.[7]

Luther realised that it wasn't angels but the printing press that made the difference. Like politicians today who understand the power of social media, Luther swiftly took advantage of the power of print technology, especially to reach audiences unversed in Latin, the language of the scholarly elite. He translated the New Testament into German for the first time so it could be read by ordinary people in their homes without the need for priestly intermediaries, and also began publishing cheap pamphlets in simple German with cartoon-like woodcuts ridiculing the religious establishment (including the Pope with a donkey's head and fish-scale skin). Catholic theologians attempted to counter his arguments, but their obscure Latin prose could not compete with Luther's mass media campaign. More than a quarter of the different pamphlets published in German-speaking territories between 1520 and 1526 were editions of Luther's works. Of the total 6 million pamphlets printed in the first decade of what became the Reformation, one-third were by Luther, who outsold his Catholic rivals by a factor of five to one.[8] James Patterson and J.K. Rowling would be envious.

An unflattering portrait of the Pope, from one of Martin Luther's pamphlets printed in 1523. Satirical illustrations such as this helped Luther's anti-Catholic message reach illiterate audiences.

It is unlikely that the rise of the Protestant faith could have happened at such pace and scale without the printing press. More than a century earlier, renegades such as John Wycliffe in England and Jan Hus in Bohemia had criticised the Church, but they didn't have a mechanical press to amplify their ideas. Luther was lucky to be born into a different technological era. His actions inspired a whole generation of religious reformers: in 1522, William Tyndale received a copy of Luther's German New Testament and promptly began the deeply subversive and illegal act of producing an English translation of the Bible. Protestantism, writes the renowned historian of printing Elizabeth Eisenstein, became 'the first movement of any kind, religious or secular, to use the new presses for overt propaganda and agitation against an established institution.'[9]

In this sense, the printing press acted as a liberating force that challenged the entrenched authority of the established Catholic Church. But at the same time, it unleashed turmoil, helping to generate an intense period of religious upheaval and social polarisation across the continent. The Protestant–Catholic divide, fuelled by the print revolution, tore Europe apart over the following two centuries, leading to theological schisms and, moreover, tragedies such as the Wars of Religion (1562–98) and the Thirty Years War (1618–48), in which an estimated 8 million people died. As Eisenstein argues, 'Gutenberg's invention probably contributed more to destroying Christian concord and inflaming religious warfare than any of the so-called arts of war ever did.'[10]

The printing press no longer appears so innocent: it had polarising effects similar to today's social media technologies. Yet its destructive impacts go even further, as it also helped to inflame the witch-hunt craze that swept across Europe during the Reformation.

Magic and sorcery had always been a part of European culture, but between around 1530 and 1650 the victimisation of so-called 'witches' became a hysteria that gripped the continent. While some

500 people in England were sentenced to death for witchcraft, the heartland of the frenzy was Germany, where an estimated 25,000 people were executed, around 80 to 90 per cent of them women.[11] As historians such as Lyndal Roper have documented, they were accused of cannibalism and infanticide, of having sex with the Devil and worshipping him in nocturnal assemblies, of making wax models of their victims to induce death or illness, of killing livestock and flying on goats and broomsticks.[12]

One of the main explanations for the rapid spread of this ferocious wave of persecution is none other than the printing press. 'It's said that without print, the Reformation could not have happened, but I suspect that the witchcraft phenomenon would not have happened without print either,' writes historian Charles Zika.[13]

Particularly in Germany, sensationalist news stories that make today's fake news seem tame appeared in illustrated pamphlets and broadsheets, the precursor of modern newspapers. An early example concerned the 'terrifying story' of the Maid of Schiltach. According to reports from the time, on Maundy Thursday in 1533 a devastating fire destroyed the town of Schiltach in the Black Forest. The next day a maidservant who had worked at a local inn was accused of using witchcraft to perpetrate the crime. At first, she claimed innocence but soon admitted to the offence – probably under torture – confessing that she had been helped by the Devil himself, with whom she had been having sexual relations for the previous 18 years. The maid, who remained nameless in the reports, had apparently flown to the town on her oven fork to set it alight, and had also been using her witchcraft skills to inflict harm on locals long before the fire (as had her mother). She was put on trial and promptly burned at the stake on Easter Monday.

The story was published and republished by eager printers far and wide, who imaginatively sexed it up with racy coloured illustrations depicting the woman topless among the surrounding flames.

Clickbait from the year 1533: the Maid of Schiltach being burned alive, while the town she allegedly set on fire goes up in flames. The headline reads, 'A Terrifying Story of the Devil and a Witch'.

Even the Dutch philosopher Erasmus heard all about it in distant Rotterdam, pointing out that there were so many reports of the Devil's involvement that 'it cannot be considered invented'.[14]

Reports of witchcraft were spread by both Catholics and Protestants, who saw them as a means of teaching moral lessons about the dangers of sin and temptation in an apocalyptic age when the Devil was believed to be wreaking havoc in the world. But they were also part of the commercial strategy of the expanding printing industry: attention-grabbing 'true crime' stories of alleged witches were a huge seller, which the historian Natalie Grace describes as 'the early modern equivalent of clickbait'.[15] The term 'fake news' may have been popularised only in recent years, but the phenomenon itself can be traced back at least to the witchcraft accounts that flew off the printing presses of sixteenth-century Europe.[16]

Printers were simultaneously mass-producing demonology

manuals such as the bestselling *Malleus Maleficarum* (The Hammer of the Witches), which was used by papal inquisitors in Germany and other countries to identify, track and prosecute those suspected of witchcraft. In effect, printing helped create a standardised code for a regime of terror that resulted in hundreds of thousands of women living in a state of constant fear, especially spinsters and widows, who were among the most common targets.[17]

What should all this history of printing mean to us today? The parallels with contemporary digital media are all too clear. Accusations of witchcraft may have largely disappeared, but the clickbait culture remains in the sensationalist stories and 'alternative facts' that litter our social media news feeds.[18] The witch hunt has now shifted to groups such as 'illegal immigrants' and 'Muslim extremists' – outsiders who, like the 'witches' of the past, are used as scapegoats for the economic problems and other ills that blight our societies. 'The history of the European witch-hunt', concludes Charles Zika, reflecting on such contemporary persecution, is 'a history from which we can and need to learn.'[19]

The religious polarisation of the Reformation is also disconcertingly familiar. We often talk with shock and surprise about the acute social and political polarisation caused by social media platforms – thanks to their algorithms that trap users in echo chambers where their beliefs are continually reinforced by shared posts and news feeds. Common divides include liberals vs conservatives, pro-choice vs pro-life and climate change deniers vs climate change believers. But there is a clear historical precedent in the impacts of print technology over four centuries ago, which helped drive a wedge between Protestants and Catholics.

Moreover, just as the printing press served to unite disparate Protestant radicals into a powerful community that could challenge the supremacy of the Catholic Church, digital networks have enabled anti-establishment movements and politicians to unite and mobilise disaffected citizens against mainstream parties and the state. Right-wing populists such as Donald Trump, India's Narendra Modi and Brazil's Jair Bolsonaro have been savvy social media operators, as have the USA's Bernie Sanders and Spain's Podemos movement on the left. Similarly, anti-authoritarian uprisings including the Arab Spring and Hong Kong's Umbrella Movement were kickstarted and sustained by social media posts and campaigns.[20]

There is evidence, however, that social media particularly plays to the advantage of far-right extremists: the medium suits their message.[21] First, it provides an unrestricted and little-regulated platform for spreading overtly racist and xenophobic views and conspiracy theories, which are generally given little airtime in traditional media, where there are usually stricter editorial codes of conduct. Second, it is an effective tool for gathering their scattered supporters into a cohesive online community, enabling them to punch above their weight. The US House Select Committee investigating the January 2021 Capitol attack made clear that the insurrection to prevent the inauguration of Joe Biden and keep Donald Trump in power was fuelled by platforms such as Facebook and Twitter (now X), whose algorithms spread false claims about the illegality of the 2020 election and promoted extremist groups such as the Proud Boys and QAnon.[22]

In the 2020 docudrama *The Social Dilemma*, Silicon Valley tech entrepreneurs innocently claim that social media was designed to be a force for good to unite friends and connect the world, and that they had no idea it would inflame social divides and benefit groups who wanted to undermine democratic institutions. As Jeff Seibert, a former top executive at X (when it was still Twitter), put it, 'Nobody, I deeply believe, ever intended any of these consequences.' Perhaps that is true. But if any of them had read books on the history of print technology, they might have realised that their well-meaning communication tools could have the potential to create social polarisation and political violence. If I could go back in time to the early days of the tech boom, I would give each of them a copy of Elizabeth Eisenstein's classic text *The Printing Revolution in Early Modern Europe*, just like John F. Kennedy handed out copies of Barbara W. Tuchman's *The Guns of August* to his officials.

At least some of them may be beginning to realise what they have done. Towards the end of the film, Tim Kendall, former CEO of Pinterest and ex-head of monetisation at Facebook, is asked what he is most worried about in relation to the impacts of social media. 'I think, in the shortest time horizon, civil war,' he replies.[23]

At first it sounds alarmist. But the religious wars that ravaged Europe in the wake of the print revolution suggest that he might be right. The digital revolution could fuel violence on a similar scale over the years and decades to come – and the unprecedented speed of data networks might bring it on much faster than in the past. The Capitol attack may be just the beginning of a descent into societal breakdown and political fracturing. I wouldn't be surprised if there were half a dozen nations in North America by the end of this century. If it happens, future historians will no doubt not only pinpoint factors such as growing wealth inequality and the climate crisis but place blame on the tech barons and the polarising algorithms on which they built their fortunes. Wilful myopia may turn out to be their greatest crime.

Coffeehouse Culture and the Birth of the Public Sphere

The history of the printing press is a cautionary tale for our social media age, revealing how easily communication technologies can become tools of violence and persecution. Yet it would be unfair to deny the transformative benefits it eventually bestowed. By the late seventeenth century, printing was starting to spread rationalist thinking that challenged superstitions such as witchcraft. It under-pinned the development of mass literacy and amplified the pleasures and liberations of reading. It enabled the scientific advancement of the Enlightenment: astronomers and cartographers, for instance, could now easily share and compare their findings to make more accurate maps of the stars and continents.[24] More unexpectedly, during the eighteenth century printing played a foundational role in the emergence of modern democratic culture and human rights. How so? By creating a new, invisible continent called the public sphere. But it couldn't do so without the help of another revolution-ary invention: the coffeehouse.

Just down the road from where I live in Oxford is the site of Eng-land's first coffeehouse, founded in around 1650. Today, it is filled with students wired into the web, tapping silently on their laptops with headphones in their ears, but a few centuries ago it would have been a vibrant hive of conversation. Having originated in Turkey, coffeehouses spread with remarkable rapidity throughout the coun-try: by 1700 there were more than 2,000 in London alone. Walk into one such as Manwarings off Fleet Street and you might be greeted by the owner with a friendly 'What news have you, master?' or 'Here's fresh news from all parts.' For only a penny you would be given a bowl or cup of coffee, which you were free to nurse for hours. You might take your seat at a private table or booth, or more likely sit at a communal table, which was a defining feature of the English coffeehouse – 'a table of an acre long covered with nothing but tobacco-pipes and pamphlets', as described by one enthusiastic cus-tomer.[25] There you would while away your time reading newly arrived periodicals, debating the latest news with friends and stran-gers, and perhaps leave copies of your own writings for others to read. Long before email, you could also have your post sent to a cof-feehouse, with customers often dropping in several times a day to see if they had received new messages.

Will's Best Coffee Powder at Manwarings Coffee House in Falcon Court over against S.t Dunstans Church in Fleet Street

An advertisement from around 1700 for Manwarings Coffee House, where coffee, conversation and the latest journals were all on offer at the communal table.

'Coffee houses were an alluring social platform for sharing information,' argues Tom Standage, functioning as an operating system for the exchange of news, opinion and gossip. According to an account from 1707, 'The Coffeehouses particularly are very commodious for a free Conversation, and for reading at an easy Rate all manner of printed News.'[26] Critics worried that they promoted trivial chatter and timewasting (sound familiar?). But they were even better known for their intellectual vitality. There were coffeehouses that specialised in scientific discussion, art and literature, business and trade. Meetings at Lloyd's Coffee House, which was popular with merchants and shipowners, famously led to the establishment of the London insurance market. But above all they were hubs for political talk – or as one poet put it, 'coffee politicians does create'.[27] Some establishments even published their own political journals while others became a source for journalism: the *Spectator* magazine, founded in 1711, is said to have grown out of reports of conversations overheard in coffeehouses such as Will's, Child's and St James's.[28]

It was the prevalence of political conversation that later prompted the German social theorist Jürgen Habermas to locate the origins of what he called the 'public sphere' in the coffeehouses of eighteenth-century London.[29] This term referred to a social space where people from diverse backgrounds could freely converse about public affairs, criticise the government, and debate new ideas such as republicanism or the abolition of slavery. The public sphere, in effect, acted as a school for democracy. What made it all possible was not just that the printing press furnished the coffeehouses with streams of information and opinion for discussion, but that differences of social status were generally left at the door, encouraging the expression of multiple points of view. The typical owner, reported one observer, 'admits of no distinction of persons, but gentleman, mechanic, lord and scoundrel mix, and all are of a piece'.[30] While it is easy to romanticise the inclusive nature of the coffeehouse – most customers were educated men from the emerging bourgeoisie – these 'penny universities', as they were sometimes called, were the most egalitarian institutions of their day and provided an ideal setting for the exercise of free speech and free thought.

This is what made them so potentially subversive. Charles II recognised the dangers early on, attempting to ban them in 1675 on the grounds that they were 'places where the disaffected met and spread scandalous reports concerning the conduct of His Majesty and His Ministers'. Radical writers such as Daniel Defoe and the republican firebrand Tom Paine, who held court at London's coffeehouses, helped give them this reputation for dissent and sedition. In reality, however, the liberties of the coffeehouse could be limited by the prevailing political context. During the turbulent period of the French Revolution, London solicitor John Frost – a close friend of Paine's – was heard to say, 'I am for equality and no kings', in the Percy coffeehouse. He was not just hissed at by outraged customers but later reported to the police and imprisoned for six months.[31]

Although coffeehouses went into decline in the early nineteenth century, the public sphere they had nurtured became increasingly broad in scope. In the 1830s and 1840s, Britain's radical press flourished despite government attempts to tax it out of existence, with publications such as the militant *Northern Star* and the *Poor Man's Guardian* reaching millions of working-class readers who made sure copies were stocked by union branches, political clubs and local pubs. The radical press, wrote the Chartist leader Feargus O'Connor, was 'the link that binds the industrious classes together'.[32]

Yet over the following 150 years the pluralism of the public sphere was gradually asphyxiated by the rise of mass media. First came mass-circulation newspapers such as the *Daily News* and *Daily Mail*, which used their advertising revenues to under-price and outcompete smaller publications, pushing them out of business. The establishment of the British Broadcasting Company (which soon became the British Broadcasting Corporation) in 1922 then ushered in the era of state broadcasting corporations, which centralised and homogenised the provision of public information. A third key development was the exponential spread of television after the Second World War: by the 1970s, 99 per cent of Western households had a set in their homes with the occupants watching, on average, more than three hours per day.[33] The heady days of early print culture, with its proliferation of pamphlets and periodicals and spirited debates in the coffeehouses of Georgian London, had been replaced by a culture of passive home entertainment, largely devoid of human agency and social intercourse, except for occasional discussions about whether or not to switch channels.

The explosion of the internet in the 1990s was supposed to change all of this. Here was a chance to revive the public sphere with free-flowing digital information. Netizens could now bypass the creaky purveyors of mass media and become active content creators themselves. Discussion forums, blogging, independent news sites and niche e-magazines would create a cornucopia of borderless communities sharing ideas from multiple perspectives. 'Information wants to be free,' as the digerati triumphantly proclaimed.[34] It all promised so much. But we know what happened: social media monopolised by a few Big Tech firms, the scraping of our personal data to sell to advertisers, filter bubbles, fake news, conspiracy theories, election hacking, binge watching, doomscrolling, the dark web, angry trolls, selfies, FOMO, cute emojis, thumb up or thumb down. The public sphere, observed Habermas in 2022, 'has been stripped down to "like" and "dislike" clicks.'[35]

The public sphere was one of the greatest social innovations of the eighteenth century. How can we win it back in the digital age? With the help of an historical caffeine fix, where we learn from the coffeehouses that brought it to life.

One notable feature of coffeehouse culture was the healthy competition between diverse establishments. They were small businesses. There were no chains. If you didn't take to one particular coffeehouse, you could probably find half a dozen others within walking distance. Social media, of course, is dominated by a few giant platforms such as Facebook, TikTok and X: open-source, ad-free alternatives such as Mastodon and Signal have only a relatively small share of the market. Taking history as a guide, it might be wise to consider breaking up the Big Tech companies using anti-monopoly laws, similar to the way that the Rockefeller family's Standard Oil was split into 43 companies in 1911, as a way to end its stranglehold on the US oil market.[36] This is a policy increasingly favoured by progressive politicians such as US senator Elizabeth Warren, who argues that, just as anti-trust laws were used to prevent Microsoft from controlling web-browser technology in the 1990s, today's dominant digital players should be broken up to promote market competition and stop them 'from throwing around their political power to shape the rules in their favour.'[37] Governments could simultaneously broaden the eco-system of firms by supporting the development of alternatives to standard profit-driven enterprises, such as digital cooperatives (see Chapter 9). We need more options, not fewer. Imagine if the only coffee on offer was from Starbucks.

Among the challenges is that social media is prone to 'network effects': the sector tends to develop a small number of dominant networks because people want to stick with platforms that their friends and family are using, such as WhatsApp, and are averse to checking messages on multiple apps. That is why it may be necessary to supplement breaking up Big Tech with other approaches, such as taking the largest firms into public ownership to overcome the dominance of commercial monopolies. A precedent has already been set by the EU's European Open Science Cloud, which operates as a publicly run digital cloud service. Just as we may think of water supply or railways as essential public utilities that should be provided by government, the same could be said of digital infrastructure. Another suggestion, from tech analyst Azeem Azhar, is that when a digital firm hits a specified threshold of market share (say 10 or 15 per cent), they must permit users to transfer their profiles and data easily to other networks with a single click.[38] It would be like switching your patronage to the coffeehouse down the street if the coffee or conversation becomes too bitter for your taste.

A second feature of the coffeehouse, and a key component of the public sphere, was vigorous table talk with strangers whose views might differ from your own. Online chatrooms such as Reddit could be considered our modern equivalent. It is no secret, however, that they are prone to becoming polarising dens of intolerance, where abusive users hide behind the shield of anonymity, while poor (or absent) moderation fails to hold them to account. One major study of Reddit, looking at 3.5 billion posts from 25 million users over a ten-year period, found that people were 35 per cent more likely to use offensive language in political discussion forums than in non-political ones, and that around one in ten political comments were offensive. Based on sophisticated vocabulary analysis software, it also discovered that the typical political chat on a Reddit thread looks like it was written by a six-year-old.[39]

Yet there are some positive models for digital conversation between strangers, which are reminiscent of the most celebrated coffeehouses of the eighteenth century. You won't find much abusive behaviour on a discussion site like MetaFilter. This is partly because it has a very clear set of guidelines for its community of users, such as 'be considerate and respectful', 'be aware of your privilege' and 'be mindful of microaggressions', which helps nurture a culture of respectful disagreement.[40] When offensive comments are made, conversations are flagged and paid moderators quickly step in, acting like the speaker of the House of Commons, who has presided over parliamentary debates in Britain since the thirteenth century and ensures that MPs act with decorum. MetaFilter has the added feature of being largely funded by its 12,000 active users (who pay a one-off $5 joining fee), who have an interest in maintaining a safe, shared conversational space, rather than being financed by venture capital or shareholders who are more interested in a healthy balance sheet than healthy and balanced discussion.

If we hope to revive the conversational culture of the Georgian coffeehouse, however, we can also turn to bricks-and-mortar coffee shops themselves, which over the last two decades have experienced a growth in popularity not seen since the eighteenth century. But rather than focusing on boutique beans and perfect pastries, they should be bringing back the communal conversation tables of the past. Imagine walking into your local café knowing that the long table covered with magazines and newspapers was a place where you could freely talk to strangers about the issues of the day. No laptops or phones. No anonymity. Just human beings having face-to-face discussions. There are now around 30,000 coffee shops in the UK alone. If there were just ten conversations between strangers per day in each of them, that would be over 100 million conversations per year.[41]

No doubt certain establishments would become known for their speciality topics, perhaps looking for inspiration to the Death Café movement which, since 2011, has organised more than 15,000 discussions about death in existing cafés in 83 countries. I would suggest that the tables also have printed Menus of Conversation, containing intriguing questions to spark an exchange of thoughts and experiences between strangers. For several years, I worked with the historian of conversation Theodore Zeldin doing exactly this: curating discussions in cafés, parks, community centres and other public spaces between people of different backgrounds, using conversational menus.[42] The questions, covering 24 universal topics, included, 'What have you learned about the different varieties of love in your life?', 'In what ways do you wish to become more courageous?', 'How have your priorities changed over the years?' and 'How do you think about the future?'

We should never underestimate the power of conversation between strangers, which can flower even in the most politically charged contexts. In 2002, the Parents Circle – which brings together Israelis and Palestinians whose family members have been killed in the conflict – launched a project called Hello Peace. A freephone number was posted on billboards in major towns and cities: any Israeli who called it was put through to a Palestinian volunteer who they could talk to for up to half an hour on any subject, while Palestinians who called were likewise put through to Israelis. Within its first five years of operation, there were over a million conversations between the two sides.[43] While they occasionally resulted in arguments, more often they led to mutual understanding and even lasting friendships. The grassroots dialogue projects promoted by the Parents Circle are considered so subversive (partly because they highlight deaths caused by the Israeli Defence Forces) that the Israeli government has branded the group as 'terrorists' and attempted to ban it on multiple occasions.[44] It continues its work even in the midst of the renewed conflict that broke out in late 2023, holding dialogues that bring 'enemies' together to share their grief and find common ground.

Conversations between strangers are a powerful antidote to the polarisations that divide us from one another, and can help shake us out of entrenched views and stale thoughts. Not always, but at least sometimes. Whether taking place in well-moderated online chatrooms or face-to-face in your local coffee shop, they are a crucial constituent of a healthy and vibrant public sphere. To discover the minds of others is a way of expanding our own. As Theodore Zeldin puts it, 'A satisfying conversation is one which makes you say what you have never said before.'[45]

From Typographic Mind to Digital Mind

As we look towards the digital future, there is one final reason why we need to look back to the history of the printing press: to understand what might happen to the human mind.

Let's return to Marshall McLuhan's pithy sixties slogan, 'The medium is the message.' It invites us to move beyond focusing on the content of communication technologies – like the ways in which the printing press fed the witchcraft craze, or how social media platforms have become forums for political abuse. 'The "content" of a medium,' he wrote, 'is like the juicy piece of meat carried by the burglar to distract the watchdog of the mind.'[46] What really matters, in his view, is not the message that the medium conveys but the subtle ways in which the medium itself shapes the deep structures of our psyches. This is the subject of a new field known as 'cognitive history', which concerns not what we think but how we think.[47] So how has the printing press shaped the cognitive evolution of the human mind? And what does this suggest about the likely impacts of digital media?

One major consequence of Gutenberg's invention, according to McLuhan and scholars such as Walter Ong, was a sensory shift from a predominantly oral culture that gave primacy to the ear, towards a written culture where the eye became far more dominant.[48] Rather than learning about the world through communal experiences of storytelling and conversation, we increasingly absorbed knowledge through looking at words on a page, which we typically read in silence and isolation. Our thought processes became more internal and self-reflective, to an extent that was scarcely known in pre-printing societies. The result, writes technology historian Neil Postman, was that 'printing vastly enhanced the importance of individuality', transforming it into a core element of the emerging typographic mind.[49]

Printing also introduced new forms of order and standardisation. Innovations included ordering information alphabetically (for example, in reference works), and providing indexes and page numbers for books – practices that had been largely absent from the handwritten manuscripts of the medieval age.[50] When Robert Cawdrey published the first English dictionary, the *Table Alphabeticall*, in 1604, he had to carefully explain to the reader, 'Nowe if the word, which thou art desirous to finde, begin with (a) then looke in the beginning of this Table, but if with (v) looke towards the end? The printed word and the accompanying rise of mass literacy also created linguistic uniformity, diminishing the importance of local dialects in favour of a standardised written language that could be understood by all and which, argued McLuhan, contributed to the growth of nationalism.[51]

As our eyes learned systematically to scan words running across a page, line by line, printing additionally encouraged a linear mode of thought. Books and pamphlets had beginnings, middles and ends. They were sequential, taking our minds in a straight line and reinforcing a causal and mechanistic worldview where A leads to B. Such linear thinking underpinned the rationalist logic of Enlightenment science and ideas of perpetual progress, contrasting sharply with notions of circularity and balance that remained prevalent in many indigenous cultures, such as the idea of humanity living in balance with Mother Earth, or the symbiotic relationship between yin and yang in Taoism.[52]

We are the inheritors of the typographic mind, which has wormed its way so deeply into the Western psyche that we barely notice it. And now we face the prospect of it being rewired by the technologies of the digital age. The shift from *Homo typographicus* to *Homo interneticus* will generate profound changes in our understanding of self and world, representing a new stage in the cognitive history of humankind.[53] How will search boxes and hyperlinks affect the way we connect ideas, organise information and discover meaning? Will digital social networks alter the human personality and create new political ideologies or religions? What effect will our electronic existence have on our perception of time and our relationship with the rest of the living world? How will the nature of love and family life transform as we begin to develop relationships with personalised AI chatbots and robots? It remains far too early to answer such questions – it would be like trying to predict the impacts of the printing press just a few decades after its invention. But let's speculate for a moment.

Imagine teenagers in the year 2100 confronted with the following question in a multiple-choice history test:

Tick the statement that is true (you may select more than one answer).
The digital revolution of the early twenty-first century had which of the following effects?

a. It induced a fundamental decline in human attention spans that diminished educational attainment levels across many subject areas.

b. Its interconnected network structure fostered holistic system-level thinking that resulted in breakthroughs in quantum computing and the understanding of human consciousness.

c. It revived anarchism as a political ideology by promoting a new culture of horizontal peer-to-peer relationships that challenged the hierarchical and centralised organisation of politics and business.

d. Its addictive AI-enhanced virtual reality technologies contributed to an epidemic of depression and a detachment from worldly affairs that hindered action on the climate crisis.

e. It was partly responsible for the rise of dictatorships across Western Europe and fostered civil conflict that split the United States of America into multiple nations.

f. It enabled the spread of post-growth regenerative economies that accelerated the demise of capitalism.

Any or all of these statements could well be true by the end of this century. I offer them as a reminder that we would be unwise to think we can already see the digital future. All major technologies have unintended consequences, which are sometimes not visible for decades or even centuries – as the history of the printing press so clearly reveals. Some might be destructive, like the polarising violence inflamed by print technology during the Reformation. Others may prove beneficial, like the development of a democratic public sphere in the coffeehouses of the eighteenth century.

The history of printing can help us see more clearly what is already beginning to emerge in the age of digital communication, shining a light on both the dangers and possibilities. That is why we should act to mitigate the polarisations that are fuelled by social media, and do our best to nurture conversations between strangers, in a concerted effort to expand the realm of tolerance and mutual understanding.

We need a new public conversation – informed by history – about how we can best work with and manage digital technology. So let's put our phones away, take a seat at the coffeehouse table and start talking. Perhaps we should begin by discussing a quote attributed to Marshall McLuhan: 'We shape our tools and, thereafter, our tools shape us.'

5

Securing Water for All

Water Wars and the Genius of the Commons

We are a civilisation heading towards aquacide.

It is not just that a billion human beings currently don't have access to clean drinking water, with ten times more people dying from dirty and contaminated water each year than in all wars put together.[1] It is the future that is hurtling towards us. Droughts brought on by climate change. Expanding industrial agriculture that depletes the life-giving aquifers, which store water in permeable rock deep beneath the ground. Population growth taking water consumption far beyond the point of sustainability. More than one in every four people will be affected by increasing water scarcity over coming decades – maybe you, maybe your children, but mostly people you will never know. In 2018 Cape Town, a coastal city with nearly 5 million inhabitants, was just weeks away from running out of fresh water – the ominous Day Zero – before miraculous rains broke a four-year drought. A top-ten list of other cities likely to face critical water shortages includes Cairo, Jakarta, Los Angeles, Beijing, Melbourne, Mexico City and São Paulo. As the environmental scientist Vandana Shiva starkly puts it, 'The water crisis is the most pervasive, most severe, and most invisible dimension of the ecological devastation of the earth.'[2]

Our Blue Planet may be 70 per cent covered in water, but the name is deceptive. Only 2.5 per cent of the total is fresh water, and over 99 per cent of this is trapped in glaciers, soil and underground aquifers. Of every 10,000 drops of water on Earth, less than one is

Countries facing severe water scarcity by 2040

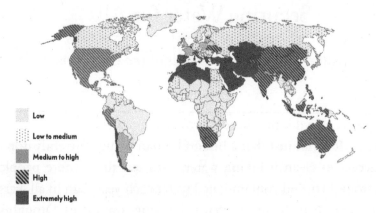

Fifty-nine countries, including global superpowers China and the United States, will experience high or extremely high levels of water stress by 2040. Source: World Resources Institute.[3]

accessible fresh water found on the surface, in rivers and lakes.[4] Remember Samuel Taylor Coleridge's *The Rime of the Ancient Mariner* (1798): 'Water, water every where, Nor any drop to drink.'

The only place where water seems truly abundant is in history. It appears on virtually every page in the chronicles of humankind. No civilisation has been able to flourish without it – to parch the thirst of its people, to irrigate its fields, to flush away sewage, to power its machines, to harbour its ships, to enable trade. It is no wonder that almost every culture has worshipped water deities: the ancient Greeks had over 50 water gods, goddesses and spirits.

This is precisely what we have lost touch with today: a reverence for water. We urgently need to recover it if we hope to tackle the crisis on the horizon. You know the country you are from, the street where you live, but do you know the name of the water catchment you live within? Most of us, especially in the wealthy countries of the Global North, are largely disconnected from water: we turn on the tap, go to the toilet, have a shower, make some tea, put on a wash, largely unaware of just how much the precious elixir of life streams through our daily existence. History holds stories and examples that can help us reconnect before the taps run dry. Through journeys to ancient China, medieval Spain and the incendiary water wars of the Middle East, this chapter reveals how we can grant water the reverence it deserves, treating it not as a commodity to be bought, sold and exploited, but as a common treasury that can be democratically managed for the benefit of all.

How Water Makes and Breaks Civilisations

The Chinese character for political rule or 'to govern' – zhì 治 – derives from the root meaning 'water control' or 'harnessing the rivers'.[5] The struggle to tame and manage water has been central to China's history for thousands of years, from dealing with the devastating floods of the Yangtze and Yellow rivers to transporting water from the wet rice-growing south of the country to the dry and barren north. The legendary emperor Yu the Great, who may have lived in around 2000 BCE, was a skilled water engineer who supposedly toiled alongside his workers for 13 years to build the irrigation canals and dykes that alleviated a destructive deluge known as the Great Flood (he was helped, it is said, by a channel-digging dragon). Still today, many of China's leading government officials are trained hydraulic engineers.

The completion of the monumental Grand Canal in the early seventh century contributed to China becoming one of the world's most powerful empires over the next 500 years. Far more impressive than its Venetian namesake, it remains humankind's longest artificial waterway, connecting south to north and covering a distance from Florida to New York. Thanks to the efforts of several million conscripted labourers – more than were required to build the Great

Wall – the thirsty northern plains suddenly had the water needed to irrigate their rich soils, with the canal fuelling rapid growth in agricultural production, population and trade. Military garrisons now had the water and food necessary to sustain their troops and fend off northern invaders. Central government expanded its dominion and economic growth was accompanied by a literary and cultural awakening. Water was a secret ingredient that helped to make it all possible, symbolised by the construction of a 40-foot-high water-driven clock in the capital Kaifeng in 1090. China became the exemplar of what historian Karl Wittfogel called a 'hydraulic civilisation', a controversial thesis contending that a centralised, authoritarian government is necessary to manage the water resources required for sustaining a large-scale agrarian society (for instance, to requisition labour to build canals and dams).[6]

If there is one figure who embodies China's hydraulic achievements, it is Chen Hongmou, a government official who presided over water management in the glory days of the Qing dynasty in the mid-eighteenth century. Chen's career was a Chinese version of the American Dream. Born in rural poverty in 1696, through sheer hard work and academic acumen he rose through the imperial ranks to become such a successful provincial governor that the emperor himself repeatedly refused to let Chen retire. Chen was, reputedly, not much fun to be with. He was utterly humourless and had a strong puritanical streak, being a vocal opponent of drinking, smoking and recreational sex. Although his daughter was a published poet, he despised poetry and ridiculed the literary pretensions of his fellow officials.

But when it came to water, Chen was a technocratic wunderkind. Driven by Confucian ideals of the public good – and memories of his own impoverished childhood – he was totally committed to helping the rural poor. For four decades, he skilfully managed the building of irrigation and drainage systems, and kept a watchful eye on emergency grain stores. He championed the construction of water wheels and ensured regular repair work on ditches, dams and polders. In just one province, he ordered the digging of over 30,000 wells. He took personal command of famine relief efforts during the droughts of the 1740s, ensuring that the imperial government provided welfare for those in need, including soup kitchens and direct cash handouts – an achievement no European country at the time could match. He also successfully lobbied for long-term state investment in flood control infrastructure despite the huge upfront costs. Chen was an icon of Chinese statecraft and remains a model for the virtues of cool-headed technocratic expertise.[7]

Yet not even Chen could have saved the Qing dynasty from the tragedies of the nineteenth century. Under pressure from the Opium Wars with Britain and France, the Taiping Rebellion and declining tax revenues, the Qing state began to fall apart. Its bureaucracy crumbled into corruption and ineptitude. Irrigation ditches and dykes were left unrepaired and grain stores unfilled. The vital lifeline of the Grand Canal silted up. Then came climate disaster. Between 1876 and 1878 a major El Niño – one of the key weather systems determining global climate – wrought worldwide havoc, bringing unprecedented floods to some regions and even more severe drought to others. India and Brazil had it bad, but no country suffered more than China.

Accounts of the famines in Shanxi and Shandong provinces in the north are the stuff of nightmares. When the rains failed, hungry peasants began eating grass and tree bark. They then sold the timber from their homes and ate the rotten reeds from their roofs. Millions of refugees fled south and to the coasts. Those who remained slowly starved, while government relief was pilfered by corrupt officials. According to one eyewitness:

In the ruined houses the dead, the dying, and the living were found huddled together ... and the domestic dogs, driven by hunger to feast on the corpses everywhere to be found, were eagerly caught and devoured ... Women and girls were sold in troops to traffickers ... and suicide was so common as to hardly excite attention.[8]

Some sources suggest that over 100,000 women and children were sold into servitude to southern labour contractors. It didn't stop there: as occurred in medieval Europe at times of famine and Ukraine in the early 1930s, people resorted to eating human flesh, digging up and cooking the corpses of their neighbours. Qing officials reported that 'children abandoned by their parents ... were taken to secret locations, killed and consumed'. In some places, human flesh was sold openly on the streets, rolled up into macabre meatballs.[9]

Victims of El Niño: children for sale in Shandong province, 1877.

These are not the stories you will find in most histories of the nineteenth century, which are more likely to describe the arrival of the steam train, the invention of the telephone and the first cricket test match between England and Australia. The Chinese famine – in which between 10 and 20 million people died – is a neglected history that should be etched into our memories. Environmental historian Mike Davis called it a 'late Victorian holocaust'.

These glimpses into China's struggles with water – and its absence – tell a larger historical story: that water makes and breaks whole civilisations. In some countries this is deeply understood. China is one, which is why it continues to build gargantuan canals and dams, and jealously guards the precious water sources it controls in Tibet. The Netherlands is another, where a quarter of the land is below sea level and flooding has been a major threat for centuries. Equally in Ethiopia and Sudan, which are among the most drought-prone nations in the world. But in most countries, water remains a casual afterthought that rarely merits serious public attention or debate. As we head towards a world of acute water crisis, we should be learning from China's history, especially the way that a combination of state negligence and extreme climate events brought on the calamity of the 1870s. It is a salutary warning for our own climate future – a future for which most nations are scarcely prepared.

China's hydraulic civilisation also raises questions about the most effective means to govern water. Some analysts view China as a model, arguing that the best way to manage water resources is with a top-down, centralised and authoritarian state – a form of benevolent hydro-dictatorship that can undertake monumental projects such as the Three Gorges Dam, completed after nearly two decades in 2013. Yet clearly this offers no guarantees. As Chinese history reveals, such a system can succumb to corruption, corrosion and incompetence, especially when faced with crisis. Might there be a more effective – and possibly more democratic – approach that brings the governance of water closer to the very people who rely upon it for survival? It is a search that takes us back to the water culture of medieval Spain.

Hydro Democracy and the Promise of the Commons

The ancient bell strikes 12. It is Thursday noon and outside the Door of the Apostles of St Mary's Cathedral in the Spanish city of Valencia, nine black-cloaked figures – one wearing a banded cap and with a ceremonial harpoon by his side – gather for their weekly meeting, as they have done for hundreds of years. This is the Tribunal de les Aigües – the Tribunal of Waters – the oldest institution of justice in Europe. Tourists crowd around to watch the proceedings. Each of the members, who represents one of the local irrigation canals of the city's rich agricultural hinterland or *huerta*, sits in attendance as the steward with his brass harpoon calls forth farmers who have been accused of violating the water laws, such as by syphoning off water out of turn for their fields. The tribunal discusses the cases in the open and then issues a fine or dismisses the case. Often there are no cases to hear, but the ceremonial gathering still takes place as the stone Apostles stand solemnly in the background.

The origins of the tribunal are shrouded in mystery. Sophisticated water management systems emerged in Valencia following the Islamic conquest of Spain in the eighth century, with Moorish farmers digging irrigation canals to grow olives, nuts, aubergines and fruits. Their agricultural practices were inherited almost wholesale by Christian settlers following the reconquest of the region in 1238, including locally agreed rules to settle water disputes, especially in times of drought. By the fifteenth century, there was an elected water tribunal meeting outside the Door of the Apostles, and by the early nineteenth century the regular Thursday hearing was firmly

History in the present: Valencia's Tribunal of Waters has been meeting weekly outside the city's gothic cathedral for centuries.

established. So it remains today, with the continued use of Arabic terms such as *azud* (weir) attesting to its medieval Islamic heritage.[10]

The tribunal ranks among the most remarkable examples of democratic resource self-management in the world, with some 20,000 local farmers electing their canal representatives every two years (the first female member was elected in 2011). Its longevity as an institution is matched by its success: thanks to help from hired guards, farmers rarely ever steal water from their neighbours. If you are looking to counter Wittfogel's thesis about the need for top-down, centralised water management, just visit the weekly tribunal hearings. And every time you bite into a juicy Valencia orange, remember that you are the beneficiary of a thousand years of dedicated communal water governance.[11]

The Valencia tribunal was of special interest to Elinor Ostrom, winner of the Nobel Prize in Economics in 2009, becoming a cornerstone of her pioneering work on the idea of 'the commons', one of the most important – and least understood – social innovations developed by human communities.

Ostrom, a political scientist by training, gained her international renown for challenging the widespread economic model of *Homo economicus* – the assumption that human beings are primarily motivated by individual self-interest to maximise their personal utility. Based on decades of empirical research, she revealed a far more cooperative picture of who we are through exploring a neglected economic realm known as the commons, which refers to the practices by which communities successfully self-manage resources such as land or water without recourse to the market or the state. Ostrom refuted the pervasive idea that local communities would naturally overuse shared resources like grazing land, with individuals scrabbling to get as much as they could for themselves – an outcome known as the 'tragedy of the commons'. Instead, she argued that many communities developed systems of democratic self-governance of what she called 'common pool resources'.

In searching for evidence, she found herself turning to history and dedicated a significant portion of her pathbreaking 1990 book, *Governing the Commons*, to the ancient water management system in Valencia, describing its origins and workings in intricate detail. She also explored examples such as West African communities that had sustainably managed fish stocks for centuries, and how the villagers of Törbel in Switzerland had communally managed their alpine forests, meadows and irrigation waters since 1224. Ostrom, a convinced practitioner of applied history, then used their rules to develop her celebrated model of the eight essential design principles for effective collective management of scarce resources, which included: participation of community members in making the rules; a graduated system of sanctions for rule violators; clear group membership boundaries of who can use the resource; ensuring governance rules matched local needs and conditions; making sure the rules are respected by outside authorities; establishing nested tiers of governance; developing systems for monitoring members' behaviour; and providing means for dispute resolution.[12] These were precisely the kinds of principles embodied in Valencia's Tribunal of Waters.

Ostrom had a kind of X-ray vision that helped her see that between the state and the market was another, almost invisible, sector of the economy called 'the commons', comprising shared resources that nobody individually owns and that can be sustainably managed by the users. It is a simple yet radical idea rooted – as Ostrom recognised – in indigenous practices of ecological steward-ship: no one should own the water, air, land or trees, just like no one owns the Sun or moon (at least not yet). They are gifts to be shared.

Such thinking is equally found in ancient legal traditions, for instance the public trust doctrine codified by the Emperor Justinian in 529 CE, which declared: 'By the laws of nature, these things are common to all mankind: the air, running water, the sea and consequently the shores of the sea.' Or as the Digger rebel Gerrard Winstanley put it in 1649 – while leading a movement to reclaim common lands stolen from the people through enclosure by rich English landowners – the earth is 'a common treasury for all.'

Partly thanks to her Nobel win, Ostrom is one of the most cited political scientists in the world (despite her death in 2012).[13] Her work, drawing on the deep history of community resource management, has not only contested the economics profession's gospel of self-interested rational economic man, but is now helping inspire the greatest surge of commons activism in human history: movements against water privatisation, from Greece to Ghana; community groups working to stop companies sucking water out of precious aquifers to sell as expensive bottled water; campaigns to give legal rights to rivers and to turn the Earth's oceans into a giant commons marine park; and the growth of local water cooperatives, such as in

Austria, where over 5,000 democratically controlled cooperatives supply water to rural citizens.[14] And there is much more commoning going on beyond the aquatic realm: growth of the digital commons, from Wikipedia and open-source software like Linux to open-access scientific journals; public trust litigation in the US to prevent fossil fuel firms pumping carbon into the air; and efforts to ban corporations from patenting the genetic code of medicinal plants. Many of them owe a debt of inspiration to Elinor Ostrom and the communal histories from which she learned.[15] As do I: it was only after two decades of studying social change – including a PhD in political science – that I finally discovered that the commons even existed when attending one of her lectures, not quite knowing who she was.

The commons, of course, has always been there, long before being championed by Elinor Ostrom and other commons thinkers and practitioners, operating largely unnoticed in the liminal space between state and market. But its recent 'rediscovery' ranks as one of the greatest historical findings of our time, more important than the unearthing of Tutankhamun's tomb or the Terracotta Warriors of Xi'an. Champions of the commons believe that local democratic water governance like in Valencia or other places such as Bali – where the *subak* system has been carefully sharing irrigation water between rice farmers for a thousand years – could help many of the world's water-stressed regions with the challenge of managing scarcity.[16] Moreover, it might ultimately be more effective than top-down solutions such as gigantic dams, which too often end up as costly and ineffective white elephants that displace whole communities and ignore local knowledge. Ostrom herself was damning of dams: 'We do not need any more engineering wonders that turn out to be institutional disasters.'[17] Rather than waiting for governments to bestow grand infrastructure projects, it may be wiser to tap into the power of community management in the commons.

Yet a sceptic might fairly argue that when it comes to water, small isn't always beautiful. Local water tribunals and cooperatives might sound attractive, but clearly we also need national-level policies to regulate agro-industrial pollution in rivers and large-scale coordinated responses to crises such as droughts and floods. As climate change and its global impacts speed towards us, isn't a decentralised model of commons management just a nice-to-have utopian ideal?

Before answering this question – which will take us back to the work of Elinor Ostrom and the Valencia tribunal – we first need to understand what water conflicts might look like in the coming century, particularly the prospect of water wars.

The New Age of Water Wars

Human beings have been fighting over water for centuries, a fact evident in the origin of the word 'rival', which comes from the Latin *rivalis*, meaning someone who uses water from the same river as another. Yet struggles over water rarely make front-page news. One exception from the recent past is what has come to be known as the Cochabamba Water War.

In 1999, the Bolivian city of Cochabamba privatised its water services under pressure from the World Bank and IMF. The new provider, a subsidiary of the US firm Bechtel, drastically raised prices by 35 per cent and even made it illegal for households to collect rainwater on their rooftops. In January 2000, tens of thousands of people took to the streets in protest, from factory workers and street children to peasant farmers worried about the destruction of their traditional communal water systems. After protracted clashes with police, the government declared martial law, which only fuelled the uprising – street blockades, tear gas, live bullets, hundreds of arrests and six deaths ensued. In April, the government finally backed down and returned the municipal water to its citizens.[18] Bolivia subsequently outlawed the privatisation of water and enshrined access to it as a human right in the constitution of 2009, while also giving it protection under its Law of the Rights of Mother Earth in 2010.

The global wave of water privatisation that took off in the 1990s has caused similar backlashes in several other countries – among them Nigeria, India and the Philippines – particularly because privatisation tends to push up the price of water, hitting the poor hardest.[19] But how common are water conflicts between countries, rather than within them? And are they likely to grow? Here, it is worth looking at inter-state water rivalry in the Middle East.

On 5 June 1967, Israel launched one of the most devastatingly successful military campaigns of the twentieth century. In less than a week, it obliterated the air and land forces of Egypt, Jordan and Syria, and gained the Sinai Peninsula, the West Bank and the Golan Heights.

Like all wars, the Six-Day War had a tangle of complex causes: the belligerence of Egypt's President Gamal Abdel Nasser, who was intent on destroying the Israeli state; the USSR, which allegedly sparked the conflict with false intelligence; the ongoing tensions around land since the establishment of Israel in 1948; and, of course, the deep divides of religion. Yet it was also, without doubt, one of the clearest historical examples of a water war.

Israel's victory not only quadrupled the land area of the fledgling state – it also vastly increased its strategic water reserves. Deep under the West Bank lay some of the largest aquifers in the region, while the Golan Heights contained the headwaters of the River Jordan. As former Israeli prime minister Ariel Sharon, who was a top military commander during the war, wrote in his autobiography:

People generally regard June 5, 1967, as the day the Six Day War began. That is the official date. But, in reality, it started two-and-a-half years earlier, on the day Israel decided to act against the diversion of the Jordan ... While the border disputes between Syria and ourselves were of great significance, the matter of water diversion was a stark issue of life and death.[20]

In 1964, with the support of other Arab states, Syria had begun a huge engineering project to redirect water from the River Jordan – which supplied one-third of Israel's water – into its own territory. For Israel, a desert country that dreamed of creating a green Zionist homeland for millions of Jewish immigrants, losing the Jordan waters was an economic and political catastrophe. It was only a matter of time before skirmishes over the diversion project – Israeli tanks had been firing at the canal construction site since digging began – transformed into a more serious military conflict.[21]

The legacy of the Six-Day War is still painfully visible today. While Israel has secured its water supply, the 2.9 million Palestinians living on the West Bank have not been so lucky. Israel not only limits their access to the precious waters of the Jordan, but under a skewed international treaty, around 80 per cent of the underlying aquifer waters flow into Israel. The result is that Palestinians have to buy back the water under their own feet from the Israeli state water company Mekorot at highly inflated prices. Nearly 50 per cent of Palestinians have access to running water fewer than ten days per month. Thanks to cheap water from Mekorot, Israeli settlers on the West Bank consume four times as much as Palestinians.[22] While some Israelis have swimming pools, Palestinian farmers live in permanent drought conditions. Almost nowhere on Earth is the deprivation of the human right to water more plainly evident. And almost nowhere is water more political: when conflict between Palestinians and Israelis flared up in October 2023, following the launch of a military assault by Hamas, one of the first actions of the Israeli government was to block water supplies to the Gaza Strip.

Some water historians view the Six-Day War as an anomaly since the historical record reveals few wars specifically over water. This 'water peace' school of thought points out that of the 412 interstate crises between 1918 and 1994, only 7 involved disputes about water.[23] In fact, you have to go back to 2500 BCE to find a full-blown water war, when the Sumerian city-states of Lagash and Umma fought over the Tigris–Euphrates basin. International water cooperation, these scholars argue, is far more common than conflict.

But it is unlikely to stay that way. There is a growing consensus that conflicts over water are set to increase this century, with the Six-Day War being an early warning sign of what is to come. While it is true that most wars in the past were not triggered by water, they were certainly often fought over resources such as land and oil. And in the twenty-first century, as we face the impacts of a changing climate and urban population growth, water will be the resource that really matters. As former UN secretary-general Kofi Annan warned in 2001, 'if we are not careful, future wars are going to be about water and not about oil.'[24] It was a prescient statement. The latest data reveals an enormous spike in international water conflicts since the turn of the century, bucking the historic trend (see below).[25]

The potential for conflict is built into the history of political geography. In 1978, there were 214 international water basins, where river catchment areas cross national borders. Today, largely due to the breakup of the USSR and the former Yugoslavia, there are 263, covering over half the surface of the globe and including two in every five people. The watershed of the River Congo encompasses 13 countries, the Nile 11 and the Mekong 6. China has effective control over the waters flowing into the Ganges–Brahmaputra–Meghna basin, home to 630 million people mainly in India and Bangladesh, making it the region's dominant hydro-power. Turkish dams at the head of the Tigris–Euphrates basin have contributed to water

Trends in Interstate and Intrastate Water Conflict Events

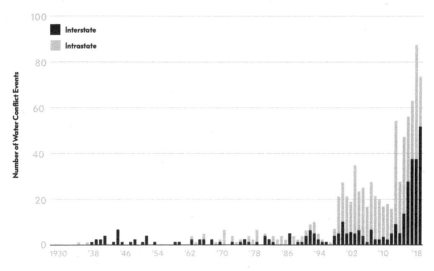

Water conflicts are already on the rise, both within and between countries.
Source: Gleick, Iccland and Trivedi (2020), World Resources Institute.[26]

scarcity in downstream Syria and Iraq, aggravating civil war and social unrest.[27] The construction of the Grand Ethiopian Renaissance Dam has prompted disputes with Egypt and Sudan, who fear their water supplies from the Nile may be cut off.

War and water are destined to become deadly accomplices in a thirsty world. Countries will still go to war for reasons less important than water. Yet water is likely to be an increasingly significant ingredient in the cocktail of factors causing future conflicts. It will equally cause tens of millions of people to flee across borders, hoping to escape acute water deprivation and the violence and instability it fuels (see Chapter 2 for discussion of these migration issues). Unlike oil, water has no substitutes. Every nation will be intent on securing its access to what the Canadian water activist Maude Barlow calls 'blue gold.'[28]

Governing Water in the Twenty-First Century
(with a Helping Hand from History)

There are no easy solutions to the waterborne geopolitical crisis that is starting to accelerate. But might history offer, at the very least, clues for diminishing the potential tensions?

Let's return to an unlikely source of inspiration: Valencia's Tribunal of Waters. It would be wishful thinking, wouldn't it, to suppose that a similar mechanism could help alleviate the water crisis in a hotspot such as the West Bank? One can hardly imagine Israeli settlers and Palestinian householders dressing up in matching gowns and amiably resolving their water disputes at a weekly meeting. But this is precisely what leading Palestinian hydrologist Abdelrahman Tamimi suggests. He believes that they should 'import and adapt the model of the Tribunal of Waters ... not only to resolve conflicts between farmers, but to reduce tensions between Israelis, Palestinians and Jordanians.'[29] In Tamimi's view, there will be no hope of reducing water conflicts in the Middle East without using such mechanisms, which can generate the dialogue and trust needed to underpin cooperation. 'We can fight for water or cooperate for it, it depends on us,' says Tamimi. 'The first step is to trust each other.'

This isn't pie-in-the-sky thinking. The organisation EcoPeace Middle East has created a Good Water Neighbours programme, which brings together Palestinian, Israeli and Jordanian mayors and residents for joint dialogues to manage collectively their shared water resources in the Lower Jordan Valley. In 2013, it succeeded in getting the Israeli government to release fresh water from the Sea of Galilee into the depleted Lower Jordan River for the first time in 49 years. Similarly, in 2022 the Arava Institute facilitated a dialogue between Israeli officials and the Palestinian Water Authority that resulted in the building of a new pipeline transporting water to Palestinian farmers in the Jordan Valley.[30] Such water diplomacy projects continue in the midst of an ongoing conflict, attempting to build peace at the grassroots one drop of water at a time.

If Elinor Ostrom were still alive today, she would be the first to support such initiatives and recognise their larger potential. Ostrom's work has been criticised for putting an excessive focus on local community management and avoiding complex issues such as the regional water struggles in the Middle East, but she was well aware of the bigger picture. Ostrom believed that an essential element of governing a shared resource like water is to create nested tiers of decision making – what she called 'polycentric governance'. It was a theory originally developed by her husband, political theorist Vincent Ostrom, who drew his inspiration from the self-governing ethos of Puritan settlers in New England, who made community decisions in local townhall meetings, as well as from the decentralised structure of nineteenth-century American politics, which devolved power from the federal down to the state level.[31] Elinor Ostrom argued that power needs to be spread across multiple levels, from the local to the national, regional and global, and not just imposed centrally from the top down (similar to the model of 'communal democracy' discussed in Chapter 6). So, just as there might be a body like the Valencia Tribunal of Waters at the community level, there could equally be a regional body to resolve interstate disputes in a shared water basin, or an international tribunal to manage the global water commons. Not just one council, but many, with autonomous yet overlapping spheres of influence.

What exactly might they look like? Some models already exist at the regional level. Most people have never heard of the International Commission for the Protection of the Danube River (ICPDR), but for 81 million people in 19 countries, it plays a vital role in managing the waters of the Danube River basin, flowing from the Black Forest into the Black Sea. Bringing together public officials, scientists and civil society organisations, it works quietly to prevent flooding, control pollution, and ensure that water is conserved and shared equitably in line with the European Union's Water Framework Directive. The ICPDR, whose roots go back to an 1856 international treaty establishing free navigation along the Danube, uses consensus decision making to forge a cooperative spirit among diverse nations, many of which – such as Croatia and Serbia – have an entrenched history of conflict. Among its achievements has been to help double the number of species in the Black Sea, which just two decades ago was considered effectively 'dead' due to its pollution levels.[32] The Great Lakes Commission in North America is a similar body, where officials from eight US states and two Canadian provinces jointly manage conservation of the five lakes, which together provide drinking water for 40 million people. Both these bioregional organisations display considerable technocratic expertise. What they lack, however, is a true commons design that integrates democratic citizen participation, which would help ensure accountability and the stewarding of water resources for both current and future generations.[33]

The biggest governance gap is at the global level. The UN Water Convention, which is supposed to adjudicate transboundary water disputes, is a toothless document with virtually no legal power, ratified by just 43 of the world's countries: national water sovereignty reigns supreme. An effective step forward, according to experts such as the Lebanese water law professor and politician Tarek Majzoub, would be the creation of a Universal Water Tribunal that is based – wait for it – on none other than the Valencia model.[34] This would be a kind of international people's water court, which tries countries – and ideally also corporations – for failing to uphold the human right to water and for violating the global water commons. Defendants would be held to account in public hearings for their actions such as diverting water from downstream countries, pouring toxic waste into rivers, subsidising fossil fuel companies whose CO_2 emissions contribute to drought and glacial melt, and for jacking up the price of water to unaffordable levels. A similar regional body, the Latin American Water Tribunal, has held public hearings across the continent and delivered over 250 advisory opinions since its foundation in 1998. Its work has been instrumental in mobilising communities from Mexico to Brazil to protest against dam building and water privatisation, and it has been especially effective in supporting the water rights of indigenous peoples.[35] With the idea of ecocide – the crime of destroying the living world – starting to gain traction in international legal circles, it is time we also developed mechanisms to prevent the crime of aquacide.

Tech enthusiasts see little need for such governance structures. They look to innovations such as desalination technology that allows harvesting of fresh water from the seas. Countries including Spain, Israel and China are already investing heavily in desalination facilities – many of them powered by the Sun – as is water-scarce California, where aquifers are rapidly being pumped dry and drought has become a way of life.[36]

The problem with this approach is not just that poor countries and their most water-deprived communities will be unable to afford desalination technology. It is also likely to put water increasingly in the hands of corporations, which typically operate the plants, further extending the shift towards privatisation that has proved so controversial in countries such as Bolivia. In England, where I live, the 57 million inhabitants are all compelled to buy their water from private companies that hold local monopolies – a fact that would have shocked the nineteenth-century citizens who fought so hard for municipal water ownership. Among them was the British statesman Joseph Chamberlain who argued in 1884, 'It is difficult, if not impossible to combine the citizens' rights and interests and the private enterprise's interests, because the private enterprise aims at … the biggest possible profit.'[37] He would probably not be surprised to discover that today's water companies are notorious for illegally dumping sewerage in rivers in an effort to cut costs and boost shareholder dividends. Across the political spectrum, there are now growing calls to put the ownership of water back in public hands.

That is exactly where it belongs. Water is not a commodity to be bought and sold but a commons to be governed for the public good. As the ecological emergency deepens, some countries will no doubt look to the top-down Chinese model as a way to navigate the water crises of the future. But as Elinor Ostrom so clearly revealed, there is just as much reason to look for inspiration in the communities throughout history that have democratically self-managed their water as a common treasury for all. The great unsung social innovation of the commons offers a powerful and ambitious vision worth fighting for, whether it is a water cooperative for the city we live in or a tribunal to settle international disputes. By doing so, we will be demonstrating the enduring relevance of historical examples like Valencia's ancient water tribunal, whose members will likely still be meeting every Thursday under the Apostles for generations to come.

6

Reviving Faith in Democracy

Rediscovering the Communal Democracy of the Past

The French archaeologist Raymond Mauny was disappointed. It was the late 1950s and he had travelled far to excavate an intriguing broad mound, around a kilometre wide, in the Niger delta region in today's Mali. After scrambling up its side, some 7 metres high, he cast his expert eye over the surface but saw nothing except random scattered debris – broken ceramics, tobacco pipes, crumbling mudbrick houses. It seemed to offer few prospects for archaeological discovery. There was no hint of monumental buildings, temples, palaces or grand statues. No suggestion of dynastic splendour, no evidence of wealth and power. This was not the great lost city he had hoped to find. 'We are on fickle land here,' he wrote, 'lacking any useful diagnostic artefacts.' Mauny left the mound in frustration, never to return.[1]

Little did he know that beneath his feet lay an extraordinary archaeological treasure: the ancient city of Djenné-Djeno. Between 250 BCE and 1400 CE, Djenné-Djeno was among the most flourishing urban civilisations in West Africa, a complex trading centre which, at its height, was home to more than 40,000 people.

What makes Djenné-Djeno so fascinating is how long it was ignored by Western archaeologists, who had been raiding potential sites across the continent for decades in search of riches. Mauny and his colonial-era predecessors simply assumed that any large-scale African city would have been ruled by some kind of king or chief and have the architectural trappings of a hierarchically organised society – an imposing citadel like the ancient cities of the Nile Valley with their towering obelisks, pyramids and burial chambers for exalted pharaohs.

Djenné-Djeno turned out to be the opposite. It was a city without a citadel.

When archaeologists finally stopped ignoring the mound and began sinking trenches into it in the late 1970s, they realised that they had stumbled upon a sophisticated urban culture producing high-quality pottery, innovative metalwork and refined sculpture.[2] But it completely lacked the expected structures of a centralised, authoritarian government. Roderick McIntosh, one of the earliest excavators, had no doubt about their biggest discovery: 'What have we found? Number one – no king. No hierarchy.'[3]

There is a long-standing Western assumption, dating back to the colonial era, that African societies are inherently hierarchical and despotic. As the Nigerian scholar Damola Adejumo-Ayibiowu writes, 'Eurocentrism denies Africa's democratic political history and projects Africa's culture as totally autocratic.'[4] Djenné-Djeno defied this assumption, displaying evidence of what McIntosh called 'heterarchy': a more horizontal system of self-governance, where different social groups – fishermen, blacksmiths, merchants – appear to have managed the affairs of the city themselves without the need for an elite caste of aristocrats, priests and kings. There are no grand buildings for the rulers or the rich. There are no audience halls or pleasure gardens. Rather, Djenné-Djeno is laid out in clusters where the various occupational groups lived and worked side by side with relative autonomy. Signs of wealth – such as fine ceramics – are spread throughout the city's 70 distinct areas, suggesting an egalitarian social structure to match the egalitarian politics.[5]

None of this should really be surprising. There is powerful evidence that collective forms of political organisation emerged across the African continent alongside more hierarchical systems. As the Ghanaian political philosopher Kwasi Wiredu observed, 'decision-making in traditional African life and governance was, as a rule, by consensus.'[6] Before the colonial slave trade erupted in the seventeenth century, the Ruund region (now in Democratic Republic of the Congo) was organised as a horizontal confederation. Rather than having a king, villages sent their elders and clan leaders to communal councils where decisions were largely made collectively. At the village level, decision making took place in popular assemblies open to most community members, and often in a 'palaver' hut or under a 'palaver' tree (from the Portuguese for 'talk' or 'speech' – hence the expression, 'What a palaver!'), which can still be found in many villages today.[7]

Similarly, Igbo communities in southeast Nigeria have a long history of communal decision making. When the British first entered Igbo lands in the nineteenth century, they could find no traditional rulers. Instead, there was a complex system of nested tiers of public assemblies, with power delegated upwards to higher levels for key

Elders meet at the *toguna* or 'palaver' hut in a Dogon village in Sangha, Mali.

decisions. This decentralised structure governed the lives of tens of thousands of people.[8] In an interview in 1973, an Igbo elder, Noo Udala – then aged 102 – recalled how it worked:

> Before the white man came we had no chief that saw to the affairs of the town. But we had several institutions that helped us organise our activities. During any cases affecting the whole town, the *ndi ishi ani*, village heads, would meet and discuss effectively the issues involved. They met as equals. But before any decision was carried, the issue must have been agreed on by all. All adult males and very aged women were entitled to attend the village level meetings. After taking the decision at village level, we then retired to the lineage or *umu nna* level. Here almost all adults, both men and women, were allowed to attend.[9]

This brief glimpse into African governance structures has deep personal resonance for me. Back in the 1990s, I spent a few years co-teaching a course on the history and practice of democracy at a well-known British university. Nowhere on the syllabus was there anything about these African democratic traditions: we simply assumed – wrongly – that democracy was a Western invention and a unique gift to be exported to a wider world full of dictators and despots. Alongside this flawed, colonialist worldview was an assumption that 'democracy' necessarily meant 'representative democracy' – professional politicians elected by their constituents in multi-party contests every few years. Alternative forms were not on the agenda, such as 'communal democracy', a model of decentralised self-government where community members openly discuss issues in local assemblies, and where decisions are often made by consensus rather than majority rule. Djenné-Djeno? The Igbo? To my shame, I'd never heard of them.

Yet it is precisely such examples – still glaringly absent from most mainstream democracy courses and textbooks – that are so crucial to the future of democracy. They open our imaginations to a different way of doing politics at a time when it urgently needs radical renewal.

The Western model of representative democracy is in crisis. Survey after survey shows faith in democratic institutions and trust in politicians plummeting across the Western world, especially among young people who are disillusioned by a system that seems to offer so little – a phenomenon described by political writer and historian David Van Reybrouck as 'democratic fatigue syndrome'.[10] Modern democracy's circus of media-driven elections, ego-driven politicians and corporate-driven policymaking is a catalogue of failures: three decades of inaction on the climate emergency, growing wealth inequality and job insecurity, unaffordable housing, crumbling health sectors, gun violence, terrorism. AI and the digital hacking of elections are compromising the integrity of democratic processes (see Chapter 10). At the same time, far-right politicians are gaining a stranglehold on parliaments and judiciaries, threatening the most basic civil and political rights, and heralding a return to the politics of the 1930s. The data is crystal clear: the number of authoritarian governments is on the rise. According to the respected Liberal Democracy Index produced at the University of Gothenburg, only 34 of 179 countries today can be classified as liberal democracies – the lowest number for 30 years – while more than half the world's population now live under dictatorships.[11]

Democracy as we know it is fragile and failing. Rather than trying to hang on to an existing system that shows little sign of being able to cope with our age of permanent crisis or crossing our fingers and hoping some benevolent dictator might come to our rescue, might there be other democratic possibilities buried in the history beneath our feet, which need unearthing like the ruins of Djenné-Djeno?

How Democracy Was Designed to be Undemocratic

It is time to tell a new story about the history of democracy. This is partly about discovering innovative democratic practices in Africa and other regions that have been ignored for too long. But it is also about dismantling the mythologies surrounding democracy in the West.

Let's get one thing straight from the outset: the much-prized ideal of representative government was invented to *prevent* democratic politics, not to enable it. The standard story – which, like many, I used to teach – locates the origins of democracy in classical Athens, and claims it was later revived, after a long gap, by the development of parliamentary politics in England and the democratic revolutions in France and America in the eighteenth century.[12] Nothing could be further from the truth.

The word 'democracy' comes from the ancient Greek *demokratia* – people's power. Yet the Founding Fathers in the United States were petrified by the idea of people's power, which they associated with mob rule that could threaten the privileges of the wealthy. James Madison, one of the chief architects of the US constitution of 1789, contrasted the Athenian model of direct democracy, where citizens took part in decision-making assemblies themselves, with the superior idea of electing representatives. The latter would 'refine and enlarge the public views by passing them through the medium of a chosen body of citizens, whose wisdom may best discern the true interest of their country' and 'be more consonant to the public good than if pronounced by the people themselves.'[13] Creating a balance of power between the executive, judiciary and congress – adopted from ancient Rome rather than the Greeks – was similarly designed to quell the mob, as was the limitation of voting rights to only white men with property.

This elitism was also evident in the French Revolution, where Emmanuel Joseph Sieyès (usually known as the Abbé Sieyès), author of the explosive 1789 manifesto *What Is the Third Estate?*, argued that politics should be put in the hands of a 'special profession' of elected representatives who could best secure 'the common interest.' As the contemporary political scientist Francis Dupuis-Déri concludes, 'the founders of the modern electoral systems in the United States and France were overtly anti-democratic.'[14]

So too in England, where the political elite constantly endeavoured to prevent the bulk of the populace from gaining the vote, or participating more directly in politics, by crushing grassroots political movements like the Levellers and the Chartists, and quelling radical voices such as Thomas Paine and Mary Wollstonecraft. The result was a fundamentally oligarchic system where political representatives, elected from a tiny, privileged class, were largely left to do as they pleased. The political philosopher Jean-Jacques Rousseau understood the essence of this system, writing in 1762,

> The English people believe themselves to be free; they are gravely mistaken; they are free only during the election of Members of Parliament; as soon as the Members are elected, the people are enslaved.[15]

Rousseau would probably be shocked to discover that politics across the Western world remains locked in this eighteenth-century representative model. We are enslaved to an inherently disempowering form of government that has been specifically designed to filter out the voice of the *demos*, the people. And this is the very root of the problem. Most professional politicians today are too distant from the lived realities of everyday people facing rising food and energy prices, public health cuts and devastating superstorms, to represent them effectively. Once elected, there is little to stop them pursuing their short-term career and party interests rather than the longer-term public interest.

But is there really any viable alternative in our complex, globalised world? Winston Churchill declared that 'democracy is the worst form of government, except for all the other forms that have been tried from time to time'.[16] Witty but wrong. Like most people, Churchill equated democracy with representative democracy. Yet there are other forms of democracy hidden away in the annals of Western history itself, which might be far better suited to our times.

An Unofficial History of Western Democracy

An alternative history of democracy in the West still needs to begin in Athens in the fifth and fourth centuries BCE. But instead of treating it as a distant antecedent of the representative system, we need to understand it as the predecessor of a more radical participatory democratic tradition – communal democracy – which has largely been sidelined by mainstream political history.

It is well known that Athenian democracy was not just based on direct participation but was fundamentally exclusionary – no women, slaves or immigrants could take part – with the consequence that politics was left in the hands of 30,000–50,000 male citizens, comprising no more that 20 per cent of the total population. But that's still a large number of people to coordinate. So how did they manage the affairs of the city-state and its outlying realms?

For a start, there was the People's Assembly (*Ekklesia*), which voted on laws and which any male citizen could attend. Up to 6,000 of them went to its almost weekly meetings on a hillside known as the Pnyx. But the real heart of government was the Council of 500 (*Boule*), which prepared the agenda for the *Ekklesia* and oversaw public finances and diplomatic relations. In order to distribute power fairly and prevent particular individuals or families becoming dominant, the *Boule*'s members were chosen by public lottery or 'sortition'. Names were thrown into a hat – in fact, a stone cut with slots called the *kleroterion* – with those selected being required to hold their paid positions for a year. Sortition was also used for picking most of the 600 magistrates (*Arkhai*) who implemented the laws, as well as for jurors in the People's Court (*Heliaia*), who were chosen by lot each morning for that day's court cases.[17]

It is difficult to imagine a democratic system more different from the paltry 'X' we scratch on a ballot sheet every four years or so. The male citizens of Athens lived and breathed politics: some 50 to 70 per cent sat on the Council of 500 at some point during their lifetimes (just envisage a similar level of political involvement today). And it worked. Although far from a perfect system – there was still plenty of corruption and power games, in addition to the glaring limits on citizenship – it managed successfully to administer public finances, construct civic buildings and survive through a turbulent period of warfare for nearly two centuries. Aristotle was among those who saw the virtues of random selection for public office, which broke down the barrier between citizen and politician, and prevented domination by elites. 'One principle of liberty is to rule and be ruled in turn', he wrote, making clear that 'the appointment of magistrates by lot is democratic, and the election of them is oligarchic'.[18]

Apart from the random selection of jury members, the wider participatory aspects of Athenian democracy have been largely absent from the Western democratic tradition since the representative system became dominant in the eighteenth century. Yet before this, for hundreds of years, the ancient Greek practices of sortition and direct participation were surprisingly common in the conduct of European politics.

Sortition was a defining feature of government in the city-states of the early Renaissance in the fourteenth and fifteenth centuries, such as the Florentine Republic that flourished in the age of Dante, before the Medici dynasty took power. Almost all major government positions were decided by lot, including the head of state, the legislative council and the executive (known as the *signoria*, equivalent to a cabinet today). Citizens were often first nominated by a guild they belonged to (an association of artisans or merchants), with some then eliminated if they had previously occupied positions of authority, at which point the drawing of lots would take place. As in Athens, appointments lasted no longer than a year, with the result that 75 per cent of citizens were nominated at some point to the 2,000 offices on offer. According to historian Piero Gualtieri this procedure, called *imborsazione* (placing names in a purse), was 'decisive in bringing stability to Florence's government' by reducing power grabs and factionalism among the city's elite families.[19]

Although limited, like in ancient Greece, to the male population who were deemed to be citizens, this system of selection by lot was considered so effective that it was adopted by other Italian city-states such as Siena and Perugia. It also expanded north to the German cities of Frankfurt and Münster, and then spread across the Iberian peninsula to Barcelona, Zaragoza and regions including Murcia, La Mancha and Extremadura. In 1492, the Spanish King Ferdinand II declared himself a convert: 'Experience shows that cities and municipalities that work with sortition are more likely to promote the good life, a healthy administration and a sound government than regimes based on elections. They are more harmonious and egalitarian, more peaceful and disengaged with regard to the passions.'[20] Quite an endorsement.

What about the other key Athenian practice of holding popular democratic assemblies, where community members could participate directly in decision making themselves, without having been selected through elections or sortition? Welcome to the Rhaetian Free State, also known as the Republic of the Three Leagues – one of the best kept secrets in the history of democracy.

Over a period of nearly three centuries, from 1524 to 1799, three alpine territories – known as the Grey League, the League of God's House and the League of the Ten Jurisdictions – in what is now Switzerland formed a political alliance to protect themselves against the territorial ambitions of the Habsburg Empire. But instead of being ruled by a duke or prince – the standard regime type at the time – they turned their backs on hierarchy and formed a confederation based on communal assemblies and collective decision making.

The newly minted Rhaetian Free State struggled at first, caught up in the turmoil of Europe's Thirty Years War and divisions between Protestants and Catholics (a topic explored in Chapter 4). Yet over time it developed an effective form of government for its 150,000 inhabitants.

At the base of its decentralised pyramid structure were 227 neighbourhood assemblies, in which all male residents had the right to take part. Picture them meeting in a cobbled town square – or perhaps a large tavern in the wintertime – making decisions on issues such as local tax rates, access to common farmlands, and which roads and mountain paths needed repairs. Each neighbourhood then sent delegates up to one of the 49 communes. These delegates were not elected representatives who acted independently but more like administrators or messengers who did the bidding of their neighbourhood and reported back to them. Above this was a federal assembly (*Bundestag*) with delegates from the communes, which met once or twice a year, and finally an executive comprising a delegate from each of the three leagues, who again reported back down the chain and had little power themselves. Layered on top was an unusual referendum system designed to avoid abuse or rash outcomes: instead of a simple Yes or No choice for the whole republic as a single unit, decisions – such as on foreign affairs – required agreement from a majority of the communes and each commune also had the right to modify the motion or accept it with conditions.[21]

'It would be difficult to find a more radical example of the thorough application of the principles of confederal decentralization,' observed the political historian Benjamin Barber.[22] The Rhaetian Free State was perhaps the most participatory form of democracy Europe had ever known, a system of bottom-up rather than top-down politics that prioritised face-to-face discussion and consensus building at the local level, and which gave a political voice not just to wealthy merchants but to almost all men including humble cobblers and poor cowherds – something that wouldn't happen in Britain for another 400 years. Although still excluding women and at times excessively complex, it generated enormous pride among the republic's citizens. There is a story about an obdurate farmer who encountered a foreign prince on an alpine path and refused to move his mules. 'Give way!' cried the prince. The farmer then hurled the nobleman from his horse, declaring, 'I am a Rhaetian freeman – and I too am a prince!'[23]

Unfortunately the Rhaetians were unable to unseat Napoleon Bonaparte from his horse, and their Republic of the Three Leagues was dismantled by the all-conquering French general in 1799. But its legacy lived on in Switzerland, which not only continues to hold local public assemblies – known as *Landsgemeinde* – in many regions, but also remains the most politically decentralised state in Europe through its canton system (which divides the country into 26 largely self-governing districts), and conducts more referendums than any nation in the world. The gender discrimination, though, lived on too: Switzerland, notoriously, didn't given women the vote in federal elections until 1971.

Although the Rhaetian Free State stands out for practising local assembly government on a large scale and over a long time period, it

Communal democracy in action. Some Swiss cantons – including in the
region of the old Rhaetian Free State – continue to hold open public
assemblies known as *Landsgemeinde*, which date back to the Middle Ages.
Thousands of residents often take part and voting is by a show of hands.

was a model that also appeared in other parts of Europe from the
early medieval period. Community assemblies were used to manage
shared grazing lands in the communes of rural France, surviving
into the nineteenth century despite growing state centralisation, and
played a fundamental role in the Paris Commune uprising in 1871,
when workers temporarily seized control of the city before being
brutally crushed by the French Army. They were part of the Russian
mir system of self-governing peasant communities, and appeared in
the Soviets or worker councils in the early days of the Russian Revolution. Local democratic assemblies later flourished in Republican
Spain in the 1930s, when anarchist workers took control of Barcelona and other cities.[24] They have a long history in the townhall

meetings of New England, having been imported by Puritan settlers in the early colonial period. And they still operate in local allotment associations in Britain, where the members communally manage their vegetable plots. Given half a chance, human beings have a powerful desire for the collective freedom to govern their own lives.

So we now have a new story about European democracy. To think of it simply in terms of *representative democracy* is a critical historical oversight. Ever since the Athenians first gathered at the Pnyx, there has been a hidden tradition of participatory politics that we can refer to as *communal democracy*, based on the '3 Ds' or three dimensions of decentralisation, deliberation and direct decision making.[25] This is a politics founded on horizontal rather than vertical relationships, which draws on mechanisms such as sortition and popular assemblies. The widespread nature of this alternative model in its various forms over the centuries is a reminder that there was nothing inevitable about the rise of centralised nation-states based on representative government during the eighteenth century. With a few different twists and turns in the tale, Europe might have ended up with a more varied political landscape, which included communal democracies that empowered everyday citizens more than professional politicians.[26]

Once we begin to imagine a different history, we can start to imagine a different future. But is it really feasible to envisage a more participatory form of democracy emerging today, which looks something like the Rhaetian Free State or Igbo communal governance, where a similar 3 Ds model of decision making developed independently of Europe? A sceptic might argue that such a system would never work at scale for nation-states with millions of inhabitants. It would be too cumbersome and inefficient, especially in times of crisis, and would lack experienced politicians and technocratic expertise.

I would like to suggest the opposite: that this might be the best form of government for our turbulent age of crisis. And it is already beginning to emerge.

How a Kurdish Revolutionary Embraced Communal Democracy

In April 2004, the American political philosopher and historian Murray Bookchin received a surprising letter. Then in his eighties, Bookchin had a reputation as a cantankerous old radical who had transitioned from Marxism in the 1930s, through several decades as an anarchist, to become the leading luminary of 'social ecology', a theory arguing that humans will only be able to live in harmony with nature if society becomes less hierarchical and shifts away from capitalist economic relations. He had a small, loyal following in left libertarian circles but was hardly a household name.

The letter that arrived at Bookchin's Vermont home was from the imprisoned Kurdish revolutionary leader Abdullah Öcalan. He was a charismatic figure who in 1978 had founded the Kurdistan Workers' Party (*Partiya Karkerên Kurdistanê*, PKK), a Marxist guerrilla organisation that aimed to create an independent Kurdish state, uniting the Kurdish people who were scattered across Turkey, Iran, Iraq and Syria. In 1999, Öcalan had been captured and jailed by the Turkish government for attempted armed insurrection, but had remained the undisputed leader of the Kurdish liberation movement despite his years in captivity.

His letter to Bookchin told an unlikely story. While languishing in prison, Öcalan had been given access to a library, where he had discovered Turkish translations of two key works by Bookchin, *The Ecology of Freedom* and *Urbanization without Cities*, which challenged traditional models of top-down politics and representative government. Their impact on him was electrifying. Öcalan underwent a Damascene conversion. He abandoned his Marxist belief in revolutionary armed struggle and seizing state power, and instead realised that the greatest hope for the Kurdish people lay in creating a new autonomous form of government *within* existing states, based on Bookchin's model of 'democratic communalism'. This was a system where local neighbourhoods organised popular democratic assemblies, which then formed confederations, with power delegated upwards to confederal councils in a series of nested layers – just like in the Rhaetian Free State. Öcalan was particularly drawn to Bookchin's deep historical analysis. 'It is vital that we search back into the past to find the elements of a true communalism', wrote Bookchin, while offering a detailed account of how it had been practised everywhere from the Swiss cantons and Puritan New England to Renaissance Italy and ancient Athens.[27]

Öcalan described himself as Bookchin's 'student', saying that he 'had acquired a good understanding of his work, and was eager to make the ideas applicable to Middle Eastern societies'.[28] He was serious. It turned out that he had already urged Kurds – from village mayors to freedom fighters – to study Bookchin's writings themselves and start putting his historically grounded model of communal democracy into action. When Bookchin died in 2006, the PKK honoured him as 'one of the greatest social scientists of the twentieth century' and promised 'to make Bookchin live in our struggle'.[29]

They remained true to their word. After Syria's civil war broke out in 2011, Kurds living in the northeast of the country managed to take control of three provinces where, remarkably, they established a *de facto* autonomous government based on Bookchin's model.[30] They set up hundreds of neighbourhood communes, where everyone was free to take part in discussions and decision making. Residents would gather in spartan village halls to discuss everything from the distribution of scarce medical supplies and organisation of local civilian defence units to children riding their bikes too fast around the village.[31] The neighbourhood communes then sent delegates up to councils at the district and regional levels for major decisions. Thematic committees were also formed, covering issues such as healthcare, education and finance. Unlike so many communal models in the past, Öcalan ensured that women's equality was given special priority: it was mandatory for all meetings to have both a female and a male chair, while any meeting had to have at least 40 per cent women present for voting to be valid. Right in the midst of a violent conflict, a new democratic society was being forged within the shell of the old, from the ground up rather than the top down.

Over the following years the Kurds occupying this renegade region, known as Rojava, expanded the local commune networks, formed worker cooperatives and made efforts to introduce sustainable

More inclusive than ancient Athens: a committee on women's issues meeting in Qamishli, in the Kurdish-controlled region of Rojava, Syria, in 2014. Photo by Janet Biehl.

agriculture in line with Bookchin's ecological ideals.[32] When a former British diplomat visited the area in 2015, he wrote, 'I found it confusing: I kept looking for a hierarchy, the singular leader, or signs of a government line, when, in fact, there was none: there were just groups.'[33] It soon became clear that this couldn't be easily dismissed as a small-scale experiment in radical democracy: Rojava was home to more than 4 million people, living in a region larger than Denmark or the Netherlands.

Critics of communal democracy are quick to point out its apparent defects, for instance that deliberative processes can be extremely time consuming (who has time to go to all those meetings?) and that delegates appointed by communal assemblies could turn out to be as self-serving as elected political representatives. But the evidence from Rojava and other communal processes, such as participatory budgeting in Porto Alegre in Brazil and digital democracy projects in Taiwan, challenge such views.[34] Citizens generally thrive on the sense of community that it offers, and they tend to make fairer, wiser and greener decisions than regular politicians, such as investing in public services and rooting out corruption. As the environmental and political writer George Monbiot argues, Bookchin's model 'works better in practice than it does in theory'.[35]

The Rojava Revolution is still going strong today, an island of possibility within the borders of the fragile Syrian state. Although it has struggled in the face of an ongoing civil war and the destruction wrought by earthquakes, it remains an outstanding example not just of the way that communal democracy can operate at scale, but also of the way that the insights of history can provide motivation for practical political transformation. Öcalan is still in prison and continues to write weighty political and historical tomes that draw on the ancient communal practices discussed by Bookchin, as well as traditional Kurdish forms of local clan solidarity.[36] If communal democracy can work for millions of Kurds, might it not have the potential to be integrated into the political systems of the Western world?

Citizens' Assemblies and the Deliberative Wave

Aside from Rojava's ongoing experiment in communal democracy, there is a second striking democratic development that echoes the politics of the past: the return of sortition. Over the last decade a 'deliberative wave' has swept the democratic world. This refers to the growing popularity of 'citizens' assemblies', which bring together a random selection of citizens to discuss topics of public interest ranging from same-sex marriage to the ecological crisis, and who then typically give policy recommendations to their national parliaments or local governments. Think of it, suggests political theorist Hélène Landemore, as a 'supersized version of the criminal jury'.[37] Perhaps the best-known example took place in Ireland in 2017, when a citizens' assembly recommended a constitutional change allowing the right to abortion, which was subsequently approved in a national referendum – a huge milestone in a deeply Catholic country. Since 2010, over 250 citizens' assemblies have taken place in the 38 nations of the Organisation for Economic Co-operation and Development (OECD) alone, with a large proportion of them focused on environmental themes.[38]

The rise of citizens' assemblies is one of the most significant developments in the history of democracy since the extension of the franchise to women in the early twentieth century. Their use of sortition is self-consciously modelled on past practices going back to the Greeks: one of Europe's most influential advocates of citizens' assemblies, David Van Reybrouck, has championed a model that 'takes its inspiration from ancient Athens'.[39] But how do they work? And how effective are they?

In 2022, I was lucky enough to be involved in one myself: Ireland's Citizens' Assembly on Biodiversity Loss – the first in the world on this crucial issue. In the selection procedure, 99 people were randomly chosen out of an initial pool of 20,000 randomly selected households that had received invitations, with an algorithm ensuring that they reflected the Irish population in terms of age, gender, ethnicity, geography and socioeconomic status.[40] After a field trip to environmental sites under threat, they met up in an old seaside hotel outside Dublin for the first of four intensive weekends of discussion and debate.

I was asked by the government organisers to give a talk to the participants on the opening weekend, encouraging them to regard themselves as 'good ancestors' – the theme of my most recent book – who were making decisions that would affect the lives of generations to come.[41] I reminded them that, unlike normal politicians who were caught up in the short-term cycles of elections and opinion polls, as a citizens' assembly they had the opportunity to do what was really best for the country – and the planet – in the long term. After I finished, each table – comprising around seven people and a facilitator – discussed the issues raised in my talk, after which I answered questions posed by the assembly members.

Afterwards came a succession of ecologists and policy experts, who briefed them on everything from the habitats of toads and the drastic decline of Ireland's fish stocks to the intricacies of EU biodiversity law, which the assembly would then take into consideration in their recommendations. At first, I was sceptical that the members would be able to deal with such a technical subject – especially since most seemed to have little prior knowledge of biodiversity issues – but within just a few hours they were having vigorous, informed discussions and asking penetrating questions. Their confidence seemed to grow rapidly and by the end of the first day, one in four members had stood up and asked a question to the experts.

I was likewise impressed by the sheer diversity of the group: I met, among others, a pig farmer, a shoe shop assistant, a pharmacist and a nurse, and members with Syrian and Ukrainian heritage. This was far from the privileged elite who seemed to dominate many national parliaments.[42] It was also refreshing to hear serious policy discussions without the usual bickering or braying politicians toeing the party line, and without sensing the presence of corporate lobbyists lurking in the background. As I sat watching this microcosm of Irish society, it struck me that citizens' assemblies have distinct advantages over referendums too. The latter are not just a favourite tool of dictators and demagogues but tend to reproduce the views that people absorb from their social media bubbles (as the UK's Brexit vote in 2016 so clearly revealed). Citizens' assemblies, in contrast, expose people to views different from their own, give them the opportunity to hear from top experts, and encourage the kind of considered and engaged deliberative discussions that might – just might – even make them change their minds.

Citizens' assemblies seem to embody the very best of the communal democratic tradition, while simultaneously providing a smart solution to the problem of representing the diversity of a whole nation by using a carefully designed random selection process. No wonder policymakers sometimes call them 'deliberative mini-publics'. Yet when I attended a conference of European experts on the topic – a mixture of academics and practitioners – I soon realised that they were far from perfect. I heard how assemblies are expensive to run, are often too rushed and sometimes lack diversity. They typically focused on relatively narrow policy issues, such as electoral reform or abortion, while failing to tackle systemic issues such as dependence on economic growth, or wealth disparities between the Global North and the Global South (an exception being the 2021 Global Assembly on the Climate and Ecological Crisis).[43] They could also be manipulated by politicians – French president Emmanuel

Macron established one on climate change in part to divert attention from his own political troubles.[44]

The most fundamental problem, as I saw it, was that they lacked genuine power. Citizens' assemblies had shown themselves capable of coming up with more transformative policies than regular politicians, particularly on ecological issues: several, for instance, had recommended making 'ecocide' – the destruction of the living world – a crime punishable by law.[45] Yet in most cases politicians were free to ignore them and treat their recommendations as merely 'advisory'. In one session at the conference I raised my hand and asked a renowned British expert what it would take for existing politicians to cede some of their power to citizens' assemblies. My question, they replied, was a 'red herring': the role of assemblies wasn't to replace representative democracy, I was told, but to be a consultative device to help invigorate it with more participation from the public.

That's where we parted perspectives. In fact, I soon realised that the whole room was split down the middle on this issue. I was in the half who believed that the representative system was unlikely to meet the urgent challenges of our time and that citizens' assemblies should therefore be given real decision-making power alongside elected politicians. A fellow believer mentioned how in the Polish city of Gdansk, the mayor had declared that he would implement any decision supported by 80 per cent of members of their citizens' assembly, and that in East Belgium, the regional parliament had established a permanent citizens' assembly. Someone else pointed out how climate campaigners, such as Extinction Rebellion, were calling for citizens' assemblies with real decision-making authority.[46] I then suggested that Britain's House of Lords should be replaced by a citizens' assembly based on sortition, becoming a House of Good Ancestors with the power to introduce and amend legislation, and to have veto power in key policy areas (such as those impacting future generations).[47] In other words, a hybrid system that combined communal democracy with representative democracy (by still retaining the House of Commons). Some people nodded. Others were clearly opposed to such a seemingly radical proposal.

The debates about the future of citizens' assemblies continue. One thing is certain: they remain one of our greatest practical hopes for reinventing democratic politics and escaping the confines of electoral fundamentalism.[48]

Let's be honest: representative democracy, in its current state, is no longer fit for purpose. If we really wanted to deal with a civilisational threat such as the ecological emergency, is this the political system we would freely choose and feel confident in, with all its party politicking, corporate lobbying and chronic short-termism? Now is the moment to open up our historical imaginations to alternatives such as communal democracy, with its three dimensions of decentralisation, deliberation and direct decision making, grounded in examples from ancient Athens and the Rhaetian Free State to Igbo governance practices in Nigeria. This does not mean that representative democracy should be dismissed outright. It will always be useful to have some elected politicians in the mix: at the very least, someone needs to make the rules for a more participatory system and be held to account if it isn't working effectively. The point is more that they should not hold such a monopoly of political power. We already have a long tradition of juries that entrust everyday citizens to make decisions on crucial matters such as criminal law. Why not extend this practice to a broader range of policy issues and put our trust in citizens, not just professional politicians, to uphold the public interest? Electoral fundamentalism needs to become a relic of the past.

7

Managing the Genetic Revolution

*The Shadow of Eugenics and the
Quest for the Common Good*

Picture yourself in the laboratory of a medieval alchemist. In the corner of the darkened room there is a glowing fire and bubbling cauldron. The table is covered with strangely shaped glass jars filled with coloured liquids, alongside leatherbound books containing secretive symbols. A cloaked, bearded figure is grinding yellow sulphur crystals with pestle and mortar, intent on making the fabled Philosopher's Stone, which is believed to have the power to transform base metals into gold.

Today, we view the alchemists as pseudo-scientists obsessed with magic potions and impossible dreams. But alchemy has a distinguished intellectual pedigree as a serious scientific pursuit grounded in deep philosophical ideals. It first emerged in ancient Egypt, then flourished in the Middle East between the eighth and tenth centuries, finally arriving in Europe on Friday, 11 February 1144 – the day the English monk Robert of Chester completed his translation of an Arabic text now known as *On the Composition of Alchemy*.[1] Its stature grew to such an extent that by the seventeenth century, its devotees included celebrated scientists such as Isaac Newton and Robert Boyle.

These early 'chymists' were primarily concerned with the transformation of matter. They noticed how adding a little vinegar to a barrel of wine could turn the whole quantity into vinegar, and that a small amount of rennet could turn gallons of milk into cheese. So why should it not be possible to add substances such as sulphur or mercury to copper or silver in order to transform them into gold? It was just about finding the right recipe.

The purpose of alchemy was not simply to produce riches. According to historian Lawrence Principe, alchemists saw themselves as having a theological mission to 'improve the natural world' and perfect God's divine creations.[2] This quest extended beyond turning raw materials into the 'noble' metal of gold. It also included using chymistry to make curative medicines and ultimately, for some alchemists, to generate human life itself. In his book *Of the Nature of Things*, the sixteenth-century Swiss alchemist and physician Paracelsus described how to create a Homunculus, a tiny superhuman baby (male, of course) endowed with extraordinary intellectual powers and artistic skills. All it required was some well-prepared sperm, horse dung and a little patience:

Let the Sperm of a man by itself be putrified in a gourd glasse, sealed up, with the highest degree of putrefaction in Horse dung, for the space of forty days, or so long untill it begin to bee alive, move, and stir, which may easily be seen. After this time it will be something like a Man, yet transparent, and without a body. Now after this, if it bee every day warily, and prudently nourished and fed with the Arcanum of Mans blood, and bee for the space of forty weeks kept in a constant, equall heat of Horsedung, it will become a true, and living infant, having all the members of an infant, which is born of a woman, but it will be far lesse. This wee call Homunculus.[3]

You may have thought of alchemy as a relic of the past. Well, in essence it is back, but today we call it genetic engineering. The twenty-first-century biotech scientist has the same elemental objective as the traditional alchemist: to transform matter and remake nature.[4] Paracelsus would have noticed further parallels. In vitro

In Goethe's play *Faust*, the character Wagner uses alchemical secrets to create a remarkably articulate and clever Homunculus.

fertilisation (IVF), first successfully undertaken for a baby in 1978, is an updated version of the Homunculus – an embryo produced by mixing sperm and eggs in a glass container ('in vitro' literally means 'in glass'). Over 12 million babies have been born worldwide using the process, with the advent of pre-implantation screening tests in the 1990s allowing parents to reject embryos showing signs of genetically inherited diseases such as cystic fibrosis.[5] The discovery of the gene-editing technology CRISPR-Cas9 in 2012 has brought us even closer to the alchemists' dream of perfecting nature, granting us a godlike power not just to refashion plants and animals, but to mould and enhance our own species.[6] Using a relatively simple cut-and-paste process, it makes it possible to remove, add or alter sections of the DNA sequence. Patients with the life-threatening genetic blood disorder sickle-cell anaemia – which is caused by a mutation of a single base in the DNA sequence – have been successfully treated using CRISPR-Cas9.

The alchemy of gene editing and embryo screening offer the prospect of creating our very own designer Homunculus. Soon parents may be choosing – if they can afford it – not just the features of a new phone but the traits of a new baby. They could be selecting the sex, hair colour and eye colour (options already offered by some fertility clinics in the US), or ensuring that their baby is born free from genetic diseases such as haemophilia or has a low susceptibility to Alzheimer's or breast cancer.[7]

As the technology advances over the coming years, there may be much more on offer at the genetics superstore. Want an enhanced child with upgraded musical or athletic capabilities? Perhaps a genetically modified pig heart to replace your own failing organ? Or maybe gene therapy to improve your memory or delay ageing? A company in Texas can clone your cat for a mere $50,000 – so why not some cloned humans to do the drudge work? Although gene-therapy techniques are still at an early stage of development, and there are strict legal limitations on genetically editing embryos and embryo screening in many countries, most of the science to create the fictions of Aldous Huxley's *Brave New World* (1932) and the film *Gattaca* (1997) already exists, waiting to be let loose on reality.[8]

The genetics revolution is one of those rare turning points in history – like the invention of fire or the rise of agriculture – that fundamentally changes the trajectory of the human journey. It signals a new stage in our relationship with nature, amounting to nothing less than a second Genesis. But now we are the master creators who can transform life on Earth and our evolutionary future. Darwinian 'natural' selection is being superseded by human-designed selection at breakneck speed.

How can we safely manage the risks of our new genetic super-powers? Biotechnology offers extraordinary opportunities to alleviate human suffering. Yet it also presents us with acute ethical dilemmas, social responsibilities and political perils. In Dante's *Divine Comedy* (*c.* 1321), the alchemists were cast deep into the eighth circle of Hell alongside the fraudsters and sorcerers for attempting to pervert God's divine laws. Might today's genetic scientists and biotech executives end up similarly judged by tomorrow's generations?

The inspiring story of the development of the first polio vaccine provides insights for using our newfound genetic knowledge for the common good. But we first turn to warnings from the past, tracing the unexpected pathways of an early and catastrophic attempt to genetically manipulate the human species: eugenics.

American Eugenics and the Path to Auschwitz

Roll up, roll up! The Better Babies Contest is about to begin!

It's the Indiana State Fair and the year is 1927. While farmers enter their best-bred cattle to be judged for excellence, parents enter their best-bred babies to compete for a coveted blue ribbon and cash prizes. The babies are put on display in a special Baby Contest Building, where they are judged first for physical attributes, with points deducted for uneven heads, misshapen ears and scaly skin, and then for mental aptitude, such as their ability to talk and recognise themselves in a mirror. It is the most popular event at the fair. There are media reporters and corporate sponsors, with thousands of people filing past to watch the babies being put through their paces. At the end, the winners – all white-skinned and dressed in matching white togas – are lined up to be admired by the crowds.[9]

The Better Babies Contests, which took place in Indiana (and several other states) each year between 1920 and 1932, were part of the

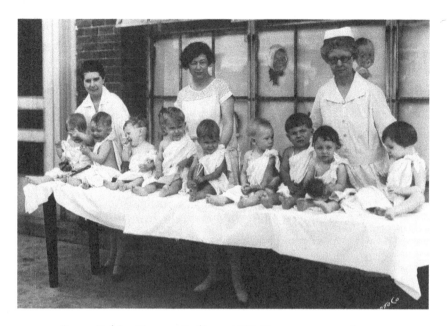

Better Babies Contest, Indiana, 1927. Togas were mandatory.
So was white skin. Image courtesy of Indiana State Archives.

wider eugenics movement that swept the United States in the early decades of the twentieth century. Eugenics – the belief that the human species could be improved through selective breeding like livestock – had been pioneered in the 1860s by the British statistician Francis Galton, who also coined the term. Picking up on his half-cousin Charles Darwin's idea of natural selection, Galton turned it into a full-fledged theory of scientific racism. His target was not just people with mental and physical disabilities. Galton was also a white supremacist who believed that dark-skinned peoples were intellectually inferior and should be bred out to prevent the degeneration of the human species. 'The average intellectual standard of the negro race is some two grades below our own', he claimed in 1869.[10] Little did he know how rapidly his ideas would permeate the Western mind.

Eugenics flourished in Galton's homeland of Britain but it spread even faster across the Atlantic. Indiana led the way in 1907 with a law permitting the forced sterilisation of 'confirmed criminals, idiots, imbeciles and rapists'. By 1931, 29 other US states had adopted similar laws.[11] Advocates of eugenics included public health bodies, university research institutes, Christian organisations and public figures, from the birth control campaigner Margaret Sanger to President Theodore Roosevelt. 'Society has no business to permit degenerates to reproduce their kind', wrote Roosevelt, 'I wish very much that the wrong people could be prevented entirely from breeding'.[12] Who were the wrong people? For the typical American eugenicist, it was not only the 'feeble-minded', physically disabled and criminals, but also African Americans and the rising tide of Jewish and Italian immigrants. Of the 60,000 people eventually sterilised against their will, a disproportionate number were African American women.[13]

The impact of US eugenics policies didn't stop there. In an unexpected historical twist, they became the primary model for the race-based state created in Nazi Germany. When Nazi lawyers were drawing up the antisemitic Nuremberg Laws, enacted in 1935, they turned to the US for inspiration, particularly California's forced sterilisation laws and legal restrictions on interracial marriage.[14] Hitler himself had long admired the country's eugenics policies and used them to help legitimise his plans to create an Aryan master race. His cause was helped by the US Rockefeller Foundation, which spent millions of dollars funding eugenics research in Germany throughout the 1920s and 1930s, including the institute that Josef Mengele worked at before conducting his grotesque genetics experiments on twins in Auschwitz.[15]

By the end of the Second World War, the Nazis had forcibly sterilised over 400,000 people and murdered more than 275,000 others who were considered genetically unfit, including children displaying mental or physical disabilities, individuals with bipolar disorder and homosexual people. Exterminating Europe's Jews – who Hitler considered the ultimate subhuman *Untermensch* – fitted seamlessly with the ideology of eugenics. As the science historian Adam Rutherford concludes, 'the pathway of eugenics led directly to the gates of Auschwitz.'[16]

While the eugenics movement gradually lost legitimacy in the post-war period due to its associations with the Holocaust, its history calls on us to reflect on the potential social and political impacts of our new genetic capabilities. It is easy to be dazzled by the biotech newspaper headlines that appear almost daily: the discovery of genes for everything from muscle strength to happiness, a genetic cure for leukaemia, gene therapy to enhance learning skills, the identification of 'hibernation genes' that may allow long-distance space travel. But behind all these scientific wonders is a lurking question: with our growing genetic powers, is there a new high-tech eugenics on the horizon?

You might think that the history of eugenics weighs like a nightmare on today's biotech community. Indeed, for some of them it does. Jennifer Doudna, co-inventor of the pathbreaking CRISPR-Cas9 gene-editing technique, recalls a dream where she encountered a silhouetted figure who wanted to know how it worked. 'As they turned around I realised with horror that it was Adolf Hitler ... I remember waking from that dream and I was shaking, and I thought, Oh my gosh – what have I done?'[17]

Yet for many biotech practitioners, such historical parallels are quickly dismissed. Take, for instance, scientist Stephen Hsu, founder of the US biotech firm Genomic Prediction, which offers embryo testing for genetic disorders such as Down's syndrome. He points out that the concept of eugenics just means 'good genes' and that to equate enabling parents to genetically test the health of an embryo with the Nazis' forced sterilisation policies is 'not just stupid but actually insane'. According to Hsu, it is equally important to recognise the wider public benefits of genetic testing: 'if you have a smaller fraction of your population with Down's syndrome, the average intelligence is a little bit higher, and society might run a little bit more efficiently.'[18]

Hsu frames genetic testing as a benign offering of personal choice for parents, in contrast to the coercive policies of the Nazis. But it is almost impossible to avoid hearing echoes of the dark history of eugenics in his views on disability and intelligence: in the name of social 'efficiency', some human lives are clearly deemed to be more valuable than others. In 2020, Hsu was forced to resign from his job at Michigan State University after being publicly accused of promoting 'eugenicist research' and 'scientific racism'.[19] Genetic engineering all too easily slips into social engineering.

This is precisely why so many disability rights campaigners and researchers are cautious about genetic testing and editing. Among them is Tom Shakespeare, a bioethics professor who has the genetic disorder of achondroplasia, whose primary feature is dwarfism. Shakespeare remembers when the gene for achondroplasia was discovered in 1989 and being shocked and outraged that 'a technology now exists which could have prevented you from being born'. He recalls how members of the Little People of America support network began wearing T-shirts with the slogan 'Endangered Species'. He also recognises that the rising popularity of genetic testing has made other disabled activists 'alarmed at the prospect of a new eugenics'. Among them are Deaf people, who typically regard themselves as a cultural minority united by sign language, not as people with an impairment that should be genetically engineered out of existence. As genetic technology advances, Shakespeare observes, 'the next generation of parents will have the responsibility of deciding which genetic conditions are worse than not living at all'.[20]

We are in the midst of a historic genetic transition: in the twenty-first century, eugenics is set to operate at the level of individual choice, not state policy, as it did in the past. Humanity is on a slippery slope towards a new kind of 'free-choice' eugenics, where well-meaning parents – driven by prevailing cultural norms – make decisions that mean someone like Tom Shakespeare, or the actress Sarah Gordy, who has Down's syndrome, or musician Woody Guthrie, who had Huntington's disease, may have never been born. Add together all these individual decisions, which could easily be based on deeply ableist, racist or sexist worldviews and unconscious bias, and the profile of a whole society might shift as much as if it were driven by government eugenics policies. This may take time to eventuate but it's still a frightening prospect, especially when so many countries remain riven by prejudice, xenophobia and social divides.[21]

As the science progresses and legal restrictions on gene editing are relaxed, more and more parents – especially those with the economic means – will also be opting not just to edit out diseases but to edit in enhancements for their children, giving them traits like superior memory or a high IQ. They might even ensure these traits are passed down the generations through 'germline' editing, where the genome of an individual is edited in such a way that the change is heritable. Enhancement science is still in its infancy, however: over 1,000 genes are associated with high IQ, which can also be influenced by environmental factors such as parental education, so it is not yet clear how to select or edit an embryo for this particular form of intelligence. Yet this has not stopped some fertility companies from already gearing up to provide enhancement services for their customers.[22] Their marketing campaigns are unlikely to be held back by scientific uncertainty.

What are the likely consequences? It is worth recalling two key aspects of the history of eugenics. First, it was not unique to Nazi Germany, as is commonly believed, but deeply embedded in Western culture on both sides of the Atlantic. Second, it spread with extraordinary rapidity: within just half a century it went from an obscure theory propounded by a Victorian gentleman-scientist to a mainstream social policy and a tool of mass murder. If history is anything to go by, the use of biotech to create 'better babies' will be upon us much faster than we think. And it will be wealthy parents in wealthy countries who will be the first to take advantage of it.[23]

The dangers are all too clear. Most human societies have developed forms of social stratification based on class, ethnicity, gender or religion, which have driven a wedge between a superior 'us' and an inferior 'them'. The biotech revolution now offers the prospect of a genetic caste system, which could easily reinforce existing economic and social inequalities. Society will increasingly be divided between what biologist Lee Silver calls the GenRich and the GenPoor – the modified and the unmodified.[24] Exactly what it will look like remains uncertain. Will the GenRich snap up the top jobs and the GenPoor be relegated to second-class citizens who can't get medical insurance – or who are even treated like the disposable colonial subjects of the nineteenth century? Might the GenRich eventually develop into a de facto superspecies with no desire – or even biological capacity – to crossbreed with their genetic underlings?

Biotech advocates tend to dismiss such fears and amplify the personal benefits of genetic testing: less suffering, better health, longer lives. These are, of course, very real: perhaps my mother, who died of cancer when I was ten, might have lived longer if genetic-based treatments had been available in the late 1970s. There could be wider public health benefits of the genetics revolution too. The AstraZeneca vaccine for COVID-19, for instance, was developed using gene-editing technology.[25] Eradicating major genetic diseases such as leukaemia may not only reduce individual human suffering but enable public spending on their treatment to be redirected towards alternative uses within government health systems. Genetic modification is also being used to develop drought-resistant crops that can survive increasing global temperatures and help feed a global population heading towards 10 billion people.

It is thus essential to explore how genetic technologies could be effectively deployed for the wider public good, not simply for the individual benefits of personalised medicine, such as allowing parents to choose their baby's eye colour or, some day (probably soon), enabling rich Californians to live to 130. And to consider how this can be done in such a way that avoids both the historic dangers of state-sponsored eugenics and the perils of newer 'free-choice' eugenics that could leave societies chronically divided between the genetically enhanced and the unmodified masses.

Here is where history can again come to our aid, this time not to provide a warning, as in the case of eugenics, but rather an inspiration for how medical innovation can be directed towards the common good.

The March of Dimes and the Crusade Against Polio

The ancient concept of the common good or *bonum commune* has fallen out of fashion in our age of individualism and personal choice. Its precise meaning has evolved over the centuries. For Aristotle, it was about nurturing virtues in society such as wisdom and moderation; for Thomas Hobbes, it required ensuring public safety; while for modern thinkers, it might include ideals of social welfare, political justice or preserving the ecological integrity of the planet. What unites all conceptions of the common good – one of the greatest social innovations of our species – is the idea of pursuing the well-being of the community as a whole rather than prioritising the interests of individuals. And that's what seems to be undervalued in current biotech debates, which overwhelmingly focus on me and my own choices, reflecting what the sociologist Amitai Etzioni calls a 'grand loss of commitment to the common good' in Western culture since the rise of individualism in the 1960s.[26] In our genetic era, every individual choice has collective consequences that could shape society for generations to come and potentially alter the evolutionary course of our species. Our responsibilities are not just to our individual genes but to the social genome.

So it is worth reflecting on what the common good might look like in the realm of public health and medical advancement, and how this could inform our thinking about the future of genetic technologies. An important example emerged in the United States not long after eugenics was at its height: the crusade against polio.

If you were an American parent in the first half of the twentieth century, one of your greatest fears would have been for your child to contract the dreaded disease of polio or 'infantile paralysis', a mysterious virus with unknown origins that could leave them permanently paralysed, requiring the use of awkward leg and body braces, and which might eventually kill them. Each summer, when the virus spread most rapidly, children were ushered indoors, public swimming pools and theatres were closed, and families prayed that their offspring would not end up in a wheelchair. The first recorded polio epidemic in the US occurred in 1894, with 123 cases and 18 deaths. The number of victims escalated year on year. During the most severe outbreak, in 1952, more than 51,000 people (mostly children) were infected, 21,000 paralysed and over 3,000 died.

For decades, polio induced a fatalistic terror that spread throughout American society. One of its most famous victims was President Franklin Delano Roosevelt. He had begun experiencing paralysis in his legs in the summer of 1921, early in his political career, and was to end up confined to a wheelchair. After receiving a diagnosis of polio, Roosevelt became intent on helping to find a cure for the disease.[27] In 1938, five years into his presidency, he established the National Foundation for Infantile Paralysis, a non-profit organisation that was to spearhead a national campaign to develop a polio vaccine through funding research in the nation's leading universities.

The campaign took off that year when the Hollywood celebrity Eddie Cantor – a close friend of the president – launched the National Foundation's March of Dimes, a fundraising effort named after a popular newsreel feature shown in movie theatres called *The March of Time*. Rather than the usual approach of seeking donations from wealthy philanthropists, the campaign pursued what we would now call a crowdfunding strategy, getting everyday members of the public to send their dimes (ten-cent coins) directly to the president at the White House. The response was overwhelming. The Oval Office was flooded with tens of thousands of letters each day, with coins and small notes piling up in the hallways. By the end of 1938,

Texas school children drop their dimes into the local March of Dimes post box in 1945, to be sent directly to President Roosevelt.

over 2.68 million dimes had been collected – enough to launch major programmes of medical research across the country.[28]

March of Dimes campaigns took place each year, raising tens of millions of dollars from citizens across the social spectrum for the 'war on polio.' Among the funding recipients was the virologist Jonas Salk, who led a team at the University of Pittsburgh that would eventually make history. In 1954, after years of dedicated research, largely funded by the March of Dimes, Salk was convinced they had developed a viable vaccine and embarked on what became the largest medical experiment in American history. The 'Salk Vaccine Field Trial' that year involved over 300,000 adult volunteers helping to inoculate more than 2 million children in 200 test centres around the nation. The trial was a success: the vaccine worked. Salk became a national hero.

In the fanfare following the discovery, Salk was interviewed by leading television journalist Ed Murrow, where they had the following exchange:

Murrow: Who owns the patent on this vaccine?
Salk: Well, the people, I would say. There is no patent. Could you patent the sun?[29]

Salk's legendary reply made absolutely clear that this was not a private product but a people's vaccine, which would be placed in the commons where it could be used in the public interest for the benefit of all.

Although commercial drug companies were uninvolved in the development of Salk's vaccine, the Dwight D. Eisenhower presidential administration of 1953–61 licensed six firms to mass produce it for a national inoculation drive. The result was a disaster: corner-cutting led to one manufacturer producing contaminated samples, which killed several children, while there was a huge shortfall in the required number of doses. Such turmoil was avoided in Canada, where the federal government took charge of producing the Salk vaccine and making it publicly available in sufficient quantities.[30]

Despite the initial setbacks, the incidence of polio plummeted in the US in the following years due to the new vaccine, and later thanks to a rival vaccine developed by Albert Sabin, also supported by the National Foundation for Infantile Paralysis. Both vaccines, especially Sabin's, were deployed by governments worldwide in the 1960s and 1970s. In 1987, the World Health Organization announced a global programme to wipe out the scourge of polio within 15 years, a goal that was largely achieved. It was a monumental accomplishment, which may never have happened without the mass citizen-powered public health initiative begun in the US in the 1930s.

What historical insights for managing genetic technology might we draw from the story of polio? First, the crusade to find a vaccine was firmly directed towards the common good, the *bonum commune*. This was not medical advancement to expand the realm of personal choice, like choosing a baby's eye colour or boosting them with enhancement genes. Polio was an epidemic disease that could affect almost any child, and the Salk vaccine was developed to help all children, independent of wealth or race or nationality. His emphatic statement that 'there is no patent' reflected a deep belief that it was a gift to humanity and the generations to come – it was about being what he called 'a good ancestor.'[31] Second, it is striking that Salk's vaccine (and also Sabin's) was developed largely without the involvement of the commercial pharmaceutical industry. This was a clear sign that innovation in the medical sphere did not necessarily require the financial incentives and upfront funding of the market. What really mattered was commitment to the ideal of public health.

Both these insights should be kept in mind as we contemplate the future of genetic medicine. How can we ensure that genetic advances such as CRISPR contribute to the common good rather than being geared towards individual and often cosmetic choices? And is it true – as today's biotech industry would have us believe – that the private sector should play the leading role in developing genetic technologies? We now turn to these questions, which revolve around the complex issue of who owns and manages the biology of life.

The Genetic Commons and the Entrepreneurial State

> The law locks up the man or woman
> Who steals the goose from off the common
> But leaves the greater villain loose
> Who steals the common off the goose.[32]

This anonymous eighteenth-century poem pithily condemns one of the most flagrant economic crimes in British history: the enclosure or fencing-off of common land by wealthy landowners and its conversion into private property. Between 1500 and 1800, an estimated 6.8 million acres of rural fields and woodlands (one-fifth of England's total area) that had previously been a shared resource for poor villagers, were expropriated from the public realm. Sometimes it was by force, sometimes with the help of laws drafted by the gentry who benefited from it.[33]

Their argument was that if common lands were placed in private hands, they could be used more efficiently to boost agricultural production. In a purely economic sense, they were right: crop yields went up and large-scale sheep farming delivered a bounty of wool and mutton. But at the same time, the enclosures brought impoverishment upon the rural population, who lost access to a precious source of subsistence. In England, millions of people were driven off the land, while in Scotland the forced evictions of the Highland

Clearances resulted in a series of devastating famines. 'Enclosures', wrote the economic historian Karl Polanyi, 'have appropriately been called a revolution of the rich against the poor.'[34]

Fast forward to the present day and we are witnessing a new enclosure movement happening before our very eyes – or rather inside our own bodies: the enclosure of the genetic commons.[35]

The human genome is the shared inheritance of our species, an ever-evolving commons of DNA dating back millions of years, which has long existed outside the realm of private ownership. But all that is changing. The field of biotechnology has become an immense commercial playground, particularly in the United States, fuelled by a neoliberal faith that almost anything can be privatised and subjected to market forces, even the DNA in our cells. Our genetic information is becoming the raw material of a new form of genomic capitalism, being bought and sold and spliced and diced for profit by biotech corporations. As the oil runs down and the metals become scarce, the human gene pool has emerged as untapped resource to generate wealth and keep the wheels of the capitalist economic system turning.[36]

The workings of the genetic economy provide ample evidence of this emerging enclosure movement. One area concerns *biopatents* – the use of patents and intellectual property law to give biotech firms ownership of genetic-related technologies. The US firm Bluebird Bio, for example, has patented gene therapy and editing techniques for the treatment of sickle-cell disease and various cancers. The adverse consequences emerged in a notorious case in 2021: the company wanted to charge $2 million per patient for its life-saving sickle-cell disease gene therapy, but when European governments refused to pay such a high fee, rather than take a price cut the company abandoned the market, leaving patients stranded.[37] Such is the reality of privatising the genetic commons. Patents are also being applied in the rapid growth areas of synthetic biology and recombinant DNA (splicing different organisms together), and for processes such as CRISPR-Cas9 gene editing, which is set to make the patent owners millions in lucrative licensing contracts once it starts being applied to human subjects on a large commercial scale.[38] Just as with the original enclosures, law remains at the service of capital, coding nature into a wealth-generating asset.[39]

A second marketised realm relates to *biodata*. There is now an ecosystem of biotech firms that will sequence your DNA for a price, with the ostensible aim of giving you information on your ancestry or health, but often with the larger commercial objective of selling on your personal data to third parties such as pharmaceutical companies, in the same way that Google or Facebook repackage your browsing data for sale to advertisers. In 2018, the genetic testing company 23andMe – founded by tech entrepreneur Anne Wojcicki, who was married to Google co-founder Sergey Brin – sold the data of more than 4 million of its customers to Big Pharma giant Glaxo-SmithKline in a contract worth $300 million.[40] Most people don't realise that by agreeing that their sample can be used for 'research', they are giving the firm legal ownership of their genetic data, which can then be sold on for lucrative contracts. Although it is possible to opt out of sharing your DNA to avoid its corporate capture, the company website doesn't make it easy to ensure that your personal data is exempted or destroyed.

That's the genetic enclosure movement in action. As legal historian Katharina Pistor writes, the US biotech industry resembles 'the landlords who banned the commoners from the land they had shared in the past'.[41] This creeping commercialism would have appalled someone like Jonas Salk, who considered life-saving medical knowledge to be the shared treasury of humanity, not a product geared to corporate profits. It is a view also common among today's academic biotech researchers, who often have a strong belief in the ideal of public health (although there remain many who have even stronger financial ties to the biotech industry). How, then, might we go about protecting the genetic commons, so that our developing understanding of genetic science is directed towards the *bonum commune*, while ensuring that the financial motives of the private sector are held in check?

Like the landed gentry of the past, the biotech industry typically argues that privatisation of the genetic landscape is necessary to deliver the public benefits of technologies such as CRISPR, as otherwise it would be impossible to attract sufficient investment for research or incentivise innovation. But is this really true? Is enclosure of the genetic commons the best way to reap and share the fruits of genetic knowledge?

The example of the polio vaccine already tells us that major medical advances need not depend on market incentives and commercial development. The broader history of tech innovation suggests this too. Silicon Valley sells us an image of the genius entrepreneur inventing revolutionary technologies in their garage. But as economist Mariana Mazzucato points out, most of the major tech breakthroughs of the past century emerged from the public rather than the private sector – from what she calls the 'entrepreneurial state'. The internet was pioneered by the US government's Defense Advanced Research Projects Agency (DARPA) in the late 1960s, while most of the tech that makes our phones 'smart' (microprocessors, touch screens, lithium batteries, voice activation) was also courtesy of government funding. Many more examples can be added to the list. GPS? The global positioning system technology that powers products such as Google Maps was first developed by the US Department of Defense in the 1970s to track and coordinate the deployment of military assets. How about the first breakthrough virtual assistant, Siri? That came out of a US government-funded research project involving 20 universities, whose technology was then snapped up by Apple in 2010.[42]

Governments have been equally big investors and entrepreneurial risk takers when it comes to genetics. The US government was the primary funder of the $2.7 billion Human Genome Project, which created the first ever genetic map in 2003 – no commercial firm would have ever embarked on such a colossal research project, although plenty have benefited from its groundbreaking discoveries. Similarly, 95 per cent of the funding for the research behind the AstraZeneca COVID-19 vaccine, developed at Oxford University, came from the public purse.[43] The idea that we need to rely on Silicon Valley venture capital for biotech investment and innovation is a myth. And that means there is the potential to keep far more genetic knowledge where it truly belongs: in the public domain, where it can best serve the common good.

How might this work in practice? An innovative 'entrepreneurial state' model has been developed by Genomics England, a company set up and owned by the UK's Department of Health and Social Care to provide gene-sequencing research to support the National Health Service. Its first major endeavour was the 100,000 Genomes Project, which sequenced whole genomes from NHS patients to be used – with their consent – on genetic research into rare diseases and some common cancers. The data gathered by Genomics England is made available for free to academic and clinical researchers, but is also accessible to private biotech companies through payment of a subscription fee (with discounts provided to some promising small start-ups). A monitoring system ensures that the data is only used for approved projects, while a 'Participant Panel' comprising individuals who have donated their genetic data provides a degree of citizen oversight. Most NHS patients, it turns out, are happy to contribute their genetic data (on an anonymous basis) if they know it is helping with essential medical research and not being used for profiteering.[44]

This hybrid public–private system might be preferable to the

Wild West commercialism of the US biotech sector, but it is far from watertight. On the one hand, in this kind of model the ownership of people's genetic data remains in the hands of a public body, unlike the case of 23andMe. So far so good: the state is effectively acting to safeguard the genetic commons. On the other hand, however, without effective oversight it could still create opportunities for private firms to develop patentable genetic treatments and technologies that put financial gain above public benefit, and which may only be accessible to a limited range of wealthy customers.

A standard solution would be to suggest that governments strengthen regulatory frameworks to ensure the biotech sector acts more clearly in the public interest. A bolder strategy might be for the entrepreneurial state to play a larger role in developing new genetic technologies, for instance by taking stakes in private biotech firms, as the German government did by investing in companies developing COVID-19 vaccines.[45] Beyond this, governments could support the development of alternative business models, such as steward ownership, where the company's financial goals are subordinated to broader social goals (see Chapter 9).[46]

As we confront the genetic future, it remains equally essential to stand back and maintain the bigger historical picture. The precedents of eugenics and land enclosure should make us extremely wary of the dangers posed by genetic technologies. We could easily slide towards what the futurist Jeremy Rifkin calls a 'commercially driven eugenics civilisation', where personal choices in the genetic marketplace gradually drive a wedge between the GenRich and the GenPoor.[47] We should trust neither the individualist values that dominate modern societies nor profit-driven corporations to steer us clear of the possible risks. At stake is the biology of life itself and the evolutionary pathway of the human species. It would be wholly irresponsible to just cross our fingers and hope everything will probably turn out fine if Big Biotech leads the way.

It can be hard to imagine an alternative to our current world, where private firms dominate and propel the biotech sector, most especially in the US, the heartland of global genetic research. But history reveals that it doesn't have to be this way. While we can look to instances of the entrepreneurial state in action, such as the development of smartphone technology or Genomics England, there is also the inspiring example of the people-powered campaign to eradicate polio, which produced breakthrough medical innovations without relying on the commercial pharmaceutical industry, and ensured that its discoveries remained an unpatented gift for humankind.

We could also cast our minds back to even earlier endeavours in the pursuit of knowledge, which similarly embodied the common good, such as the Great Library of Alexandria, founded by the Ptolemaic kings in Egypt in around the third century BCE. Their ambition was to create a universal library that contained and safeguarded all the world's essential knowledge – a treasure house of scientific, historical and philosophical learning that would be preserved for posterity. When visitors entered the city, their books – from medical texts to astronomical tables – were temporarily confiscated and copied by scribes for inclusion in the library. Its leading scholars, such as the mathematician Euclid, insisted that the library's contents should never be used for financial gain. Above its shelves there ran an inscription: 'The place of the cure of the soul.'[48]

The great genetic library of humanity, woven into our DNA, deserves to be treated with equal reverence and respect, as a common treasury to be shared by all.

8

Bridging the Inequality Gap

Struggles for Equality in Kerala and Finland

In order to continue the advance toward equality,
we must return to the lessons of history.
– Thomas Piketty[1]

It arrived in the Leicestershire village of Kibworth in the early weeks of 1349. Spreading along trade routes from Central Asia, across the Middle East, then ravaging the cities of Europe, the Black Death may have finally found its way into the settlement thanks to rat fleas in the saddlebags of young Robert Church, who had just returned from Oxford, where he had been pleading for a few acres of land from Kibworth's largest feudal landlord, Merton College. The plague swept through the village with nightmarish speed. Historian Michael Wood describes the scene:

> We have to imagine the dead rats in the streets and yards, sick villagers in agony with swellings and pustules; those suffering from pneumonic forms spewing blood; young children dying in their dozens; the desperate vicar, John Sibil, struggling to minister to his flock while knowing he himself was dying.[2]

The Black Death killed around one-third of England's population, but Kibworth suffered worse than almost any village in the land: within little more than a year over 500 people had died – around 70 per cent of its inhabitants.

Nobody could have predicted the economic impact of the plague over the following decades. Rapid population decline produced a sudden labour shortage, giving the surviving peasants of Kibworth unexpected bargaining power with landowners. The meticulous accounts kept by Merton College reveal that in addition to being able to negotiate lower rents, their tenant farmers effectively went on strike, refusing to pay rents due to the college.[3] Villeins – serfs who had been tied to the local manors in feudal bondage – increasingly turned against their masters and demanded to become wage labourers, free to work and travel where they pleased. Wages went up, just as they did across Europe, where they more than doubled in many regions. The growing confidence and clout of rural workers was evident in popular rebellions against large landowners attempting to maintain the old power structures, such as the Jacquerie uprising in France in 1358 and the Peasants' Revolt in England in 1381. The Black Death spelled the beginning of the end of feudalism itself, helping to erode the vast inequalities of medieval serfdom.[4]

According to economic historian Walter Scheidel, the plague that struck Europe in the fourteenth century is a perfect illustration of a general dynamic in history: that substantive reductions in wealth inequality are typically a result of 'massive and violent disruptions of the social order' caused by what he calls the Four Horsemen of Levelling. 'Across recorded history', he writes, 'the periodic compressions of inequality brought about by mass mobilization warfare, transformative revolution, state failure, and pandemics have dwarfed any known instances of equalization by entirely peaceful means.'[5] As a consequence of the Second World War, for example, Europe's upper classes faced unprecedented taxes on their wealth to finance enormous military expenditure, while the war itself destroyed the value of their assets. Combined with popular demands for better housing and healthcare that emerged from the experience of wartime deprivation, the result was several decades of declining inequality across the continent – *les Trente Glorieuses* (the Glorious Thirty) as they were known in France.[6]

No historical thesis could be more disempowering, for it suggests that all the well-intentioned peaceful efforts to tackle income and wealth inequality at the national level – from improving state education and more progressive taxes to microcredit schemes and universal basic income – are unlikely to have a fundamental impact on the status quo. There is similarly little chance that trade unions or other social movements can by themselves make much headway in dismantling deep structures of inequality within countries. As Scheidel argues, there is 'no compelling reason to regard [unions] as an independent agent of income compression'. What is really required, in his view, are extreme ruptures involving 'major violent shocks' such as the Black Death, World War Two, the collapse of the Western Roman Empire or a full-scale revolution that overthrows an existing regime like the Chinese Revolution of 1949.[7]

Inequality itself takes many forms. One of the recurring themes in this book has been racial inequality and injustice, whose long history has been evident everywhere from the slave uprisings of the nineteenth century and the racist ideology of eugenics, to the struggles of the US civil rights movement and the violence and intolerance experienced by migrant workers. This chapter turns our attention towards a different but related form of inequality: wealth inequality. Why exactly does it matter?

For some, it is simply about economic justice: vast gaps between rich and poor are inherently unfair, especially given the lottery of birth that places some people at the top of the scale and others at the bottom. Yet inequality also matters due to its damaging consequences. Richard Wilkinson and Kate Pickett's pathbreaking book *The Spirit Level* provides startling evidence that more equal countries – whether rich or poor – have better outcomes on multiple indicators such as social mobility, physical health, mental health, longevity, educational attainment, crime, drug abuse, community life and social trust.[8] The promise of equality of opportunity has few prospects of becoming a reality in societies that face stark divides in wealth distribution. When such divides are reinforced by racism and sexism, the promise is little more than a fairytale: in the US, for instance, the average wealth of white households is seven times higher than that of African American households.[9]

Highly unequal societies are also unstable societies. They are more prone to political turmoil and susceptible to the lures of far-right authoritarianism. They are less effective at dealing with shocks such as pandemics. They are more vulnerable to climate change and other ecological risks. Whole civilisations have spiralled into decline because of wealthy elites who suck up resources and shield themselves behind walls while the majority suffer economic destitution.[10] As Aristotle clearly understood, greater equality is a good recipe for civilisational health and longevity: 'When there is no middle class, and the poor are excessive in number, troubles arise, and the state soon comes to an end.'[11]

If the ancient Greek sage could look at today's inequality statistics, he would surely be sounding the alarm: the top 1 per cent has captured nearly 40 per cent of global wealth growth over the past 25 years, whereas the bottom 50 per cent – who mostly live in the Global South – has received just 2 per cent of it.[12] As many nations head towards a K-shaped future, with a rich elite at the top, the vast majority of people below, and fewer and fewer in between, it is essential to face up to Scheidel's levelling thesis. Is he right – that the greatest hope of tackling inequality is to wait for some catastrophe to befall us, like the plague that decimated Kibworth?

It all depends on where you start. There is no doubt that epidemics, wars and other crises in the past have often led to the erosion of inequality. But if we begin from the present, and trace back the histories of some of today's most egalitarian societies, an alternative and more empowering pathway towards equality begins to emerge.

Here I tell the remarkable stories of two places: the Nordic nation of Finland and the Indian state of Kerala. Neither are utopias but both have managed to forge relatively equal societies in defiance of the K-shaped global trend. Despite their obvious cultural, geographic and economic differences (one, for instance, is relatively rich and equal, the other relatively poor and equal), their shared histories harbour one of the vital ingredients of a more equal world: long-term social struggles. Equality is not simply a product of fortuitous circumstance or the gift of a benevolent state. Rather, it is the reward of committed citizen action that cracks open the social order from below. This is how we bridge the inequality gap. This is where radical hope lies. This is how the light gets in.

How Kerala's Women Defied Caste, Class and Colonialism

Imagine you are looking at a screen displaying a map of India, divided into its 36 states and territories. It starts by showing life expectancy across different parts of the country, then switches to infant mortality rates and access to vaccines and hospitals. This is followed by the number of years boys and girls spend in school, rates of literacy among women, nutrition levels and indicators of income and wealth inequality. You begin to notice a strange pattern: one state at the southwestern tip comes out top on almost every measure. You have found Kerala.[13]

For more than half a century, development economists such as the Nobel Prize winner Amartya Sen have puzzled over why this particular state, with a population of around 36 million people (roughly the size of Canada or Poland), has managed to achieve such high levels of equality and general human development relative to other

states in India.[14] The usual explanation is to point to Kerala's government, particularly the state's impressive statistics on health and
education spending. But this just raises more questions about why
these areas are given such priority in the first place. The real answer
lies much deeper and can be traced back to over two centuries of
dedicated social struggle.

When the British East India Company established rule over what
is now known as Kerala in the late eighteenth century, its officers discovered a land of lush, forested hills and huge cultural diversity, with
Hindus, Muslims and an ancient population of Syrian Christians
spread across the three main regions of Malabar, Cochin and Travancore. They also discovered one of the most rigid and inhumane caste
systems in India. Members of the lowest Hindu castes were restricted
to the most menial jobs and expected to stay at least 32 feet distant
from their Brahmin superiors. If required to speak to them, they
covered their mouths with their hands so as not to pollute the lis-
tener. They were not allowed to walk on major roads or into temples,
or even to carry umbrellas. Most humiliating of all, low-caste women
were not permitted to wear any clothing above the waist, being
forced to bare their breasts in public.[15]

In 1813 women from the low-caste Nadar community rose up
against these restrictions, protesting in defiance by wearing garments
over their breasts. This was the beginning of the Channar Revolt, a
series of rebellions led by women against the caste system. On
repeated occasions, when women began to wear cloth above the
waist in defiance of social and religious norms, they were attacked by
rival castes. During the so-called Breast Cloth Controversy of 1858,
when Nadar women once again began wearing cloth to cover their
upper bodies, men from the dominant Nayar caste responded with
violence, physically beating the women, tearing off their clothes,
burning their homes and poisoning their wells. Many of the women
followed the call of spiritual leader Ayya Vaikunda Swami: 'One

caste, one religion, one god, one language, one world, for humanity.' Their struggle was ultimately successful: in 1859 new regulations ensured that all lower-caste women could wear clothing of their choice.[16]

Alongside this courageous activism, Kerala was a global pioneer of mass education in the nineteenth century. The spread of schooling among both boys and girls is sometimes attributed to the championing of education by Christian missionaries and the maharajahs of Travancore, but significant pressure also came from grassroots activism. In the 1890s, for instance, members of the untouchable Ezhava caste campaigned for access to formal education and government jobs by presenting the ruling maharajah with a petition containing over 10,000 signatures, which contributed to an easing of restrictions. The large number of girls who gained schooling was also influenced by the prevalence of matrilineality, where property was passed down the female line, giving Kerala's women greater social standing and autonomy than elsewhere in India (the reasons for its development in Kerala, which dates back to the eleventh century, remain unclear). A census in 1891 revealed that at least 50 per cent of families were matrilineal. Although men remained powerful decision makers in Kerala's households, matrilineality helped diminish the social stigma attached to girls being sent to school.[17]

One result of the emergence of mass education was that Kerala developed a population with explosive political potential. People from across the social spectrum took citizen engagement to extraordinary levels, obsessively reading newspapers, attending political meetings and standing up for their rights. They fought against caste oppression. They turned on wealthy landlords, with scores of peasant revolts taking place in the pre-Independence decades, involving hundreds of thousands of farmers. They formed cooperatives, joined trade unions and went on strike (especially workers in the coir industry). They supported Gandhi's civil disobedience campaigns, taking to the streets in protest against British rule.[18]

Women were at the forefront of all these powerhouse movements.[19] On 23 October 1938, a 29-year-old schoolteacher, Akkamma Cheriyan, led more than 20,000 demonstrators to demand the release of prisoners arrested in Independence campaigns. When threatened by British troops who said they would shoot into the crowd, she shot back with her legendary reply, 'Now I am leading them, now shoot me first.'[20] They lowered their weapons. As she later wrote in her autobiography:

> Shakespeare has said that the world is a stage and that all the men and women merely players; but to me, this life is a long protest – protest against conservatism, meaningless rituals, societal injustice, gender discrimination, against anything that is dishonest, unjust ... when I see anything like this, I turn blind, I even forget who I am fighting.[21]

The importance of collective struggles in Kerala's path towards equality clearly challenges Scheidel's thesis about the decisive role of ruptures such as wars and disasters in 'levelling', and his downplaying of social movements. Where his perspective has some merit is that the Second World War served as a catalyst for change. Wartime scarcity of basic resources such as rice (the conflict disrupted imports from Burma) led government officials to introduce one of the farthest-reaching food-rationing programmes in India, supported by a network of 'fair price' shops. But this would likely never have happened if not for mass public protests against the shortages, organised by the Communist Party, which was also busy instigating pay strikes, setting up public libraries and promoting radical theatre that extolled the virtues of the workers. Following the end of the war and Independence in 1947, the Communists helped ensure that the wartime legacy of 'fair price' shops remained (they still exist today, distributing basic grains and other goods), while campaigning hard for education, health and land reform. They were rewarded by becoming one of the world's first democratically elected Communist governments in the newly formed state of Kerala in 1957.[22]

Since then Kerala has enjoyed the unusual distinction of government in effect alternating between a Communist Party that continues to engage in electoral rather than revolutionary politics, and a Congress Party that is generally supportive of social democracy. Spurred on by their demanding, highly politicised voters, the Communists introduced India's most radical land reform programme in 1970 – which dismantled entrenched feudal practices and inequalities – and together the two parties have managed to maintain the country's most extensive welfare and education systems through the traumas of neoliberal austerity. As Bill McKibben notes, 'the watchword of Keralite politics has been "redistribution".'[23]

Perhaps the Communists' greatest achievement took place in 1998, when they launched Kudumbashree – meaning 'prosperity of the family' – which is now widely recognised as one of the world's leading anti-poverty and gender justice programmes. And true to Kerala's past, women are at the heart of it. Kudumbashree invites one woman from every household to join a Neighbourhood Group of 10 to 20 women that establishes small collective enterprises in areas such as textiles, transport, construction and farming, which then get support from the government in the form of cheap loans and training. Based on a philosophy of radical decentralisation and women's empowerment, an astonishing 4.5 million women take part, covering 60 per cent of Kerala's households. More than a quarter of a million women have set up over 60,000 small collective farms – most of them low-impact and sustainable – to ensure food security for their families, while selling any surplus on the open market.

In effect, Kudumbashree is an exercise in the predistribution rather than the redistribution of wealth, giving women the economic means to make a decent living rather than relying on state benefits. Increasingly replicated around the world, it is an inspiring testament to the long history of the role of women in Kerala's struggle for equality and social justice. As one woman farmer stresses, 'Ours is a collective strength. We draw courage and willpower from our solidarity. Kudumbashree is all about solidarity.'[24]

It would be wrong to depict Kerala as some kind of social paradise. Despite the gender justice achievements of programmes like Kudumbashree, domestic violence against women remains highly prevalent in the state.[25] Critics also point out that while Kerala might be the highest ranked Indian state on the UN's Human Development Index – which includes indicators of health, education and standard of living – its GDP per capita is lower than the national

Women workers in a Kudumbashree cooperative cafe, Fort Kochi, Kerala, 2019. Image courtesy of Benny Kuruvilla.

average. The big picture, however, is that the so-called 'Kerala model' of development remains one of the world's most remarkable egalitarian success stories. What accounts for it? As we have seen, the crisis of the Second World War helped stimulate egalitarian reforms, but it was hardly as decisive as one might expect from Scheidel's theory about the critical role of such events. State initiatives, especially policies such as the land reform promoted by the Communist Party, have had significant impact in the post-war era. But taking the long view, underlying it all has been a deep culture of political activism dating back to the nineteenth century, much of it underpinned and galvanised by empowered and educated women.

Too often women's activism fails to find its place in the history books. Kerala offers a much-needed corrective. As historian Robin Jeffrey points out, 'A politically active, organising population, in which women were literate, moved freely and took salaried jobs, enabled people to demand – and forced elected governments to provide – basic services in health, housing, sanitation and education.' Or, as he more pithily puts the lesson from Kerala: 'Politics + Women = Wellbeing.'[26]

Finntopia: How Finland Went from Economic Backwater to Egalitarian Showcase

While Kerala is frequently singled out as one of the Global South's most equal regions, when it comes to the wealthy countries of the Global North, the spotlight typically falls on Scandinavia. The popular perception of the 'Nordic model' emphasises the strong role of the state in promoting egalitarian policies and providing comprehensive welfare systems. But like in Kerala, a historical perspective reveals the decisive part played by long-term social struggles – again prominently featuring women's activism – in bridging the inequality gap. The extraordinary economic transformation of Finland over the past century provides a case in point.

In December 2019, a post on Twitter showing an image of the five leaders of Finland's new ruling coalition government went viral on social media.[27] Why? Because all of them were women and most of them were young – including the prime minister, Sanna Marin, aged just 34.

Although the coalition lasted only a few years, it was emblematic of a country that is regularly rated among the most egalitarian and happy on the planet. It's not hard to understand why: Finland comes first, second or third on more than 100 global indicators of social, economic and political equality and wellbeing.[28] This success is evident in the nation's statistics on gender equality in the workplace, childcare support and parental leave, taxes on the wealthy, the share of income of the top 1 per cent, the quality of state education, living standards of the elderly, child poverty levels, proportion of GDP spent on public services, and progress towards the Sustainable Development Goals. Finland also happens to have the highest number of heavy metal bands per capita in the world. For the majority of Finns, life is pretty good – though the country still faces serious social problems such as suicide, alcoholism and racism, especially against people of African descent.[29]

Like Kerala, Finland's achievements have taken place within just a few generations. During the first half of the twentieth century, Finland was one of the poorest countries in Europe, with its mostly rural inhabitants eking out a living in farming and forestry. Its striking turnaround has taken place without huge oil and gas revenues like Norway or the economic benefits of colonial wealth like Sweden. So what explains the emergence of what has been called 'Finntopia'?[30]

Turn back the clock to 1907, when Finland was still part of the Russian Empire. Another age – and another all-women photograph.

This one shows 13 of the 19 women elected to Finland's new single-chamber parliament. It had not only just become the first country in Europe to give women the vote in national parliamentary elections (hot on the heels of New Zealand and Australia). It was also one of the first in the world to allow women to run as parliamentary electoral candidates – and the very first to have any of them succeed. Among the new female MPs were not just women from the middle-class intelligentsia, but also some from humbler backgrounds, including a seamstress, a weaver, a baker and a maid. Perhaps the best known was the Social Democratic Party's Miina Sillanpää, a former domestic servant and leader of the maids' union, who would later become minister of social affairs and – in the words of Tarja Halonen (Finnish president in 2000–12) – 'one of the mothers of the welfare state.'[31]

They hadn't got there without a struggle. Similar to Kerala, Finland had been at the forefront of women's education in the nineteenth

The first female MPs in the world, including Miina Sillanpää (top row, third from right), wearing a white blouse like her Social Democratic colleagues.

century. This was partly due to the influence of the Lutheran Church and the legacy of Russia's Catherine the Great, who had championed education for upper-class women in her dominions. It can also be traced back to Finnish nationalists, who were fighting for independence after hundreds of years of being a colonial plaything of Sweden to the west and Russia to the east, and who believed that educating the female population would help bring them into the patriotic fold. By the late 1800s, 40 per cent of high-school pupils were female, as were 14 per cent of university students.[32] This new generation of educated women was behind the foundation of the first Finnish Women's Association in 1884, which campaigned for female suffrage, but only for those from wealthy households.

Radical splinter groups soon formed calling for full voting rights for all women, no matter their background. Among those leading the way was the League of Working Women, established in 1900. Part of the growing Social Democratic movement, the League took to the streets with labour organisations in the general strike of October 1905, an uprising against Russian imperialism in Finland triggered by a wave of political unrest that had started in St Petersburg earlier that year. 'The strike week was a wake-up week for the rights of women,' noted the maid's journal *Palvelija-tarlehti*. In the following months, the League staged more than 200 public protests for the right of all women to vote and run for office. Its mass demonstrations, which mobilised tens of thousands, finally tipped the balance against those opposed to full female suffrage. In 1906, a Parliamentary Reform Committee gave in to their demands.[33]

This historic grassroots victory paved the way for the high level of women's participation in Finnish politics visible today: without it, that 2019 photo on the social media platform Twitter would never have been possible, and it is unlikely that 46 per cent of its MPs would be women (significantly above the European average of 33 per cent). It also laid the foundations of Finland's welfare state, as it was politically active women such as Miina Sillanpää who helped pioneer state healthcare and social support for women, children and the elderly. As historian Aura Korppi-Tommola argues, 'With Finnish women gaining the right to vote and stand for election so early, they have been able to play an important role in shaping the construction of democracy and the welfare society'.[34]

Finland's journey towards egalitarianism was hampered by a violent civil war erupting in 1918, causing the deaths of more than 20,000 Social Democratic sympathisers, known as Reds, many of them executed by the victorious rightist White forces.[35] The shared struggles of the Second World War, especially a long, icy conflict with the Soviet Union, helped reforge national unity. It also catalysed welfare reform in the immediate post-war period: similar to other European countries, war veterans called for pensions, housing and medical care.

In 1948, Finland was among the first countries in the world to provide universal child allowances, thanks to pressure from trade unions and mass women's associations, which had remained active since the granting of the vote.[36] The following year saw the introduction of a unique maternity pack for all pregnant women across the country. Still going strong and now known as the Baby Box, this starter kit contains clothes, blankets, a mattress, toys and books for newborns, while the box itself can be used as a cot. Receipt of the box has always been conditional on mothers visiting a prenatal health clinic before the fourth month of pregnancy, which has contributed to Finland's sharp decline in infant mortality rates since the 1950s. As a result of such policies, write demographers Danny Dorling and Annika Koljonen, if you are a Finnish baby, 'your start in life is one of the most equitable on the planet'.[37]

The post-war era also witnessed the birth of the tripartite system of wage agreements between unions, employers and the state, but

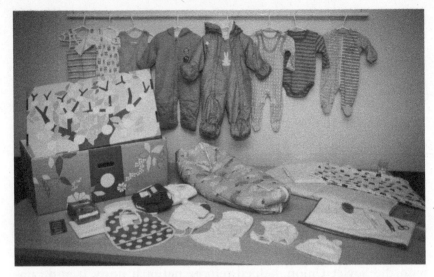

The contents of a Finnish Baby Box, still distributed free to
all expectant mothers.

this never really took off until an intense period of disruptive social
protest in the late 1960s and early 1970s.[38] Workers in the Central
Organisation of Finnish Trade Unions (*Suomen Ammattiliittojen Kes-
kusjärjestö*, SAK) confederation became the world's most militant
strikers when measured in terms of lost workdays. As more and more
women entered the workforce (partly due to labour shortages), they
were increasingly active in the union movement, with the number of
female SAK members more than doubling to over 400,000 between
1969 and 1977. This development contributed to a series of incomes
policy agreements, enabled by Social Democrat-led governments,
which increased the wages of the lowest-paid employees and women
workers, and secured improved state housing, pensions and unemployment benefits. 'In terms of income distribution', writes labour
historian Tapio Bergholm, 'Finland quickly became one of the most
egalitarian countries in the world.'[39] Spurred on by the expanding
feminist movement, the unions also managed to secure new child

daycare services so women could more easily work, as well as extending paid maternity leave.

Finland's history of egalitarianism, stretching in a long arc from women's suffrage in 1907 to innovations such as a 2020 law giving fathers and mothers equal parental leave, continues to provide visionary models for tackling deep inequalities. A few years ago, my partner was invited to give a talk in a secondary school in Finland and on arrival was struck by the small class sizes and quality of the facilities – science labs, music rooms, brightly painted high-tech classrooms. Was this a private school?, she asked her hosts, just to check. It took them several minutes to understand her question. What did she mean by 'private school'? It seemed to be an alien concept. No, it was a state-run school, they explained. Most private schools, she discovered, had been taken over by local government following the 1968 Basic School Act as part of the drive to create free, comprehensive education for all children. Now there was only a handful of independently run schools – mostly with religious affiliations and still state subsidised – and none of these was allowed to charge fees, make profits or have entrance tests. Most schoolteachers, she also found out, are required to hold a master's degree, while all children have – since 1948 – enjoyed a daily free lunch. And even though Finnish children don't start school until age seven, and take hardly any exams, they score among the highest in the world in educational attainment.[40]

'If you want the American Dream, go to Finland', quipped the former British Labour Party leader, Ed Miliband.[41] He is probably right. It is a dream whose egalitarian reality is often attributed to the country's provision of public services, generous welfare system and robust redistributive tax policies. Yet crediting the Finnish state – or indeed the impact of a rupture such as the Second World War – is far from enough. Like Kerala, the historical record reveals the crucial influence of social movements and trade unions in constructing one of the most equal societies on the planet, with women again playing a major role. It emerged from active citizenship that helped give rise to a progressive state.

Despite topping so many global indicators of equality and well-being, we should still be wary of celebrating Finland as a perfect ideal. Racism, particularly against the immigrant population, is among the most prevalent in Europe.[42] Moreover, as we hurtle towards the ecological uncertainties of the twenty-first century, Finns are still buying and burning too much stuff: their material environmental footprint is the worst in the OECD and four times higher per person than in Kerala.[43] The planet cannot support everyone living like the Finns. So we must pick and choose wisely from the *smörgåsbord* of Finnish egalitarianism. Luckily, equality does not have to cost the earth. Providing free education is not an environmental hazard. Public healthcare has a lower footprint than private healthcare. Taxing the wealthy – who have disproportionately high carbon emissions – reduces ecological impact.[44] And the Baby Box, I am pleased to report, is now made from sustainable cardboard, contains reusable nappies, and is well on its way to being carbon neutral.

Radical Hope and the Power of Solidarity

Wealth inequality remains one of the great scourges of humanity, both within and between countries. According to a recent Oxfam report, 'inequality contributes to the death of at least one person every four seconds', primarily due to hunger and lack of access to basic healthcare, with most of these deaths in the Global South.[45] In stark contrast, the digital revolution has created a new generation of tech billionaires who are capturing more and more wealth for themselves. The gig economy is replacing stable employment with the precarious temp jobs of Amazon couriers and Deliveroo riders. The climate crisis is hitting poor people hardest and threatens to deepen inequities in a new ecological apartheid, where only those with the economic means can protect themselves against rising temperatures, rising sea levels and rising food prices. So how can we close the growing inequality gap?

History is a source of radical hope. The odd couple of Kerala and Finland, seemingly so different from one another, reveals the power of social movements to help forge more egalitarian societies and compel governments to distribute resources more fairly. Their citizens have repeatedly risen up in defiance against colonialism, patriarchy, hierarchy, landlords, low wages and sheer poverty. They have organised ceaselessly and selflessly. They have taken opportunities and risks. They have confronted those in authority, challenging them with the cry, 'now shoot me first'. Their long struggles, sometimes lasting decades, reveal that equality has to be won, and is there for the taking when people stand together. This is all a direct counter to Scheidel's thesis that focuses on the impact of crises such as wars and disasters on creating equality: the Second World War undoubtedly helped catalyse egalitarian reforms in both Kerala and Finland, but it was only part of a much larger story in which citizen action that contested the status quo played a decisive and ongoing role.

The histories of Kerala and Finland are also emblematic of global processes of transformative change. Based on a series of data-driven international studies, the economist Thomas Piketty concludes that there was one overriding force that reduced wealth inequality in the twentieth century: 'it was social and political struggles that made institutional change possible', such as the introduction of progressive wealth taxes. In his words, this is the fundamental 'lesson from history' for creating a more equal world.[46] It is the disruptive power of collective solidarity – a force Scheidel vastly underestimates – that really makes the difference. The capacity of human beings to organise in movements that work together towards their shared goals, often against extreme adversity and with few immediate rewards, ranks as one of the most game-changing social innovations of the modern age (a topic to which I will return in Chapter 10).

As we have seen, women's movements have been crucial in this quest to create more egalitarian societies. They continue to fight on multiple fronts, from those campaigning against the gender pay gap and domestic violence, to the Black feminist movement and the women burning their headscarves in Iran as I write these words. Women similarly play a prominent part in the global ecological movement, among them youth activists such as Xiye Bastida, Vanessa Nakate, Greta Thunberg and Licypriya Kangujam.

While I have mainly focused here on the history of economic inequality and the role of women as agents of change, as we look towards the future, social activism will increasingly address multiple forms of inequality based around race, gender, sexuality, class, disability and other forms of discrimination, and the intersections between them. This will draw in a new generation of disruptive actors, who will take their place in the long and distinguished history of anti-oppressive movements stretching back to the peasant rebels who rose up against feudal serfdom in the fourteenth century. The efforts of such movements embody one of the central narratives of the human story: that social justice is forged in the red heat of collective struggles. In a world of seemingly insurmountable and entrenched inequities, let us remember the words of political activist Angela Davis: 'It is in collectivities that we find reservoirs of hope and optimism.'[47]

9

Keeping the Machines Under Control

Artificial Intelligence and the Rise of Capitalism

W e are living through a watershed moment in the development of artificial intelligence. Bill Gates has declared that AI
is one of humanity's greatest hopes, with the power to 'reduce some
of the world's worst inequities.'[1] It might help teach children essential literacy and numeracy skills where there are no schools, and
advise people how best to treat their illnesses if they have no access
to doctors. It could dramatically speed up medical breakthroughs to
cure certain cancers, enable progress towards nuclear fusion, and
develop drought-resistant crops – as well as compile the perfect Spot-
ify playlist just for you. What's not to like?

The extraordinary capabilities of AI have been just as successful
at instilling fear as hope. What happens when the bad guys get hold
of it – cybercriminals who use it to hack bank accounts, or terrorists
who send out AI-powered drones to assassinate politicians? And
what if it eventually becomes an electronic Frankenstein that gets
seriously out of control and decides we are an expendable species?
'AI Could Wipe Out Humanity', declared a recent front page of Britain's *Daily Mail*.[2]

As we seesaw between these two extremes, AI is insinuating its
way into almost every aspect of our lives: algorithms that determine
what fills our personalised social media news feeds, prompts for our
next purchase on Amazon, smart meters that finely calibrate our
heating systems, GPS that helps us avoid traffic jams, apps that can
draw anything in the style of Pablo Picasso, and large language
models such as ChatGPT and Bard that can perform multiple tasks

from writing complex computer code to creating recipes from the leftovers in your fridge (some authors even get them to write their books – though not this one).[3] These are all examples of what is known as 'narrow AI': digital machines that are programmed to achieve specific goals set by humans, which rely on crunching vast amounts of data and analysing it with far greater speed and efficiency than any human being. It stands in contrast to artificial general intelligence (AGI, sometimes called 'strong AI'), which is the type appearing in sci-fi dystopias like the *Terminator* and *Matrix* series: sentient machines that are self-aware and set their own goals, whether we like them or not.

This chapter focuses on the insights that history offers for confronting the dangers posed by the narrow version of AI, which is already spreading at breakneck speed, whereas AGI remains in the realm of speculation: it does not yet exist and requires technological leaps that may never happen. At first sight, history might seem scarcely relevant for helping us understand – and possibly mitigate – the risks created by something as hi-tech and unprecedented as AI. Yet there are surprising parallels to be found in the past.

Thinking historically, we can start with this overarching question: has humanity ever created a large-scale system that it has been unable to fully control, which bears a strong resemblance to AI? The answer is yes: an economic system we call financial capitalism.[4] Tracing its origins and development can help us better understand the dangers posed by AI.

It also turns out that AI has striking similarities with three other forms of capitalism that have emerged over the past 400 years: industrial, colonial and consumer capitalism. To fully grasp the deep connections between AI and capitalism, think of AI not simply in terms of its remarkable capabilities, but also the underlying foundations that enable its development and functioning. As tech scholar Kate Crawford argues, we need to understand AI as 'both embodied and material, made from natural resources, fuel, human labour, infrastructures, logistics, histories, and classifications.'[5]

Discovering the resemblances between AI and capitalism allows us to recognise that clues for averting critical risks of AI may be found hidden in alternatives to capitalism itself. But before getting to possible ways to limit these risks, let us begin with a deep dive into the origin story of financial capitalism and reveal what it illuminates about the operation – and potential perils – of AI.

How Financial Capitalism Became an Uncontrollable Supersystem

The roots of financial capitalism can be traced back to the clay tablets used by the Babylonians as instruments of credit and debt, and developments such as the invention of double-entry bookkeeping in Renaissance Italy. But its modern form as a complex integrated system began to emerge in Amsterdam in the early seventeenth century. Each day between noon and two o'clock, hundreds of eager traders would gather in the central square of the world's first stock exchange, the Amsterdam Bourse, and engage in frenzied share trading and commodity dealing. 'Handshakes are followed by shouting, insults, impudence, pushing and shoving,' reported one observer.[6] The stock exchange operated like an early form of computing machine, with jostling traders transmitting bits of information across the circuit board of its colonnaded courtyard. Many were holding shares in the Dutch East India Company, the first ever publicly traded joint-stock company and the forerunner of the modern corporation, which dealt in spices such as nutmeg, textiles and other colonial goods, and had made its first public share offering in 1602.

The circus of the Bourse was tempered by the steady hand of the Wisselbank, an early type of central bank, founded in 1609 to facilitate payments for Amsterdam's rapidly growing foreign trade. The

A human computing machine: traders making high-speed deals in the main courtyard of Amsterdam's stock exchange.

town hall housed the city chamber of marine insurance, while a few doors down – in case everything went wrong – was the bankruptcy chamber, with a carving of the Fall of Icarus over its doorway. Amsterdam had everything required to operate what historian Simon Schama called, 'the most formidable capitalism the world had yet seen'.[7] Yet few at the time foresaw just how easily it could all get out of hand.

Fast forward to the 1690s, when the flamboyant Scottish financier John Law arrived in Amsterdam. A 20-something gambling addict who had already squandered his family fortune, Law was on the run from the British authorities, having escaped prison after killing a man in a duel. He was entranced by the financial system he saw operating in Amsterdam, especially the pioneering Dutch invention of the joint-stock limited liability company, which protected investors from financial risks beyond the value of their original investment.

Soon Law was satisfying his gambling urges with speculative dealing on the stock market. He was also developing plans for a financial revolution that aimed 'to make gold out of paper' by establishing a public bank that went beyond the Amsterdam Wisselbank model and issued its own paper money.

He finally got his opportunity thanks to the spiralling debts of King Louis XIV of France. In 1716, Law was given approval to establish the Banque Générale in Paris, which quickly began issuing notes that helped pay off the government debt. Law made his next move in 1717, founding the Company of the West (Compagnie d'Occident), which was granted the monopoly of trade in the French colony of Louisiana, a territory covering nearly a quarter of what is now the United States.

That's where the trouble really began. Like one of today's swashbuckling tech entrepreneurs talking up their latest product, Law issued shares in the company on the promise that Louisiana was a bountiful Garden of Eden that would make the company and its shareholders (including himself) rich. The Banque Générale was renamed the Banque Royale and started granting loans so people could buy more shares, fuelling feverish speculation and a huge asset bubble. Some saw the writing on the wall. 'Have you all gone crazy in Paris?' wrote Voltaire. 'It is a chaos I cannot fathom.' Others made fortunes: this was when the word *millionaire* was first coined. By 1720, however, it was becoming painfully clear that Louisiana was a swampy, insect-infested backwater with little economic potential. Investors began dumping their shares.

Law began to realise he had unleashed a monster he could not control, just as many people today are beginning to recognise that AI could escape the original intentions of its makers. He desperately tried reassuring the financial markets, but was unable to restrain their herd mentality. He issued new kinds of shares to attract investors but to no avail. To prevent people shifting their savings into more secure metal coinage, he adjusted the official price of gold and silver dozens of times, but still couldn't slow the slump. He instructed the Banque Royale to buy up shares, but the consequent glut of paper money caused rocketing inflation. In response, he devalued the banknotes, but this led to public outcry and a complete loss of confidence in the financial system. Nothing could stem the tide.

The result was the world's first fully fledged financial crash, known as the Mississippi Bubble. Thousands had their livelihoods destroyed, the French economy was in ruins, and John Law was forced to flee the country. Icarus had fallen.[8]

Law is seen by some as a flawed genius; by others as a bad apple. But the Mississippi Bubble was not really about John Law at all. It was about what happens when a human-made system takes on a life of its own and gets out of control. Law may have catalysed the initial financial frenzy but in the end he couldn't prevent the meltdown, no matter how hard he tried. It was a pattern of speculative boom and bust that would be repeated over and over again, from the South Sea Bubble and the Panic of 1825 to the Wall Street Crash and the Global Financial Crisis of 2008, in which 4 million Americans lost their homes.

Since its origins in seventeenth-century Amsterdam, global financial capitalism has become a hyper-networked supersystem that is so big, powerful and interconnected, with millions of daily cross-border transactions happening at nanosecond speed, that governments find it effectively impossible to regulate and constrain. By the time of the 2008 crash, international financial flows had become so highly integrated that the collapse of a US bank such as Lehman Brothers had devastating contagion effects worldwide.[9] The historian Fernand Braudel had recognised this possibility half a century ago, noting that capitalism's preoccupation with financial gain, 'liberates forces that can never afterwards be adequately controlled'.[10] The genie inevitably escapes the bottle.

Let's take stock for a moment. What light does the story of financial capitalism shine on today's AI challenges? Where exactly are the parallels, and the key contrasts? They lie in three areas: system complexity, contagion risk and intentional design.

Firstly, AI clearly resembles financial capitalism in the sense that it is similarly developing into a vast, complex supersystem, which will make it just as hard to control or regulate as global finance.[11] The main difference is that its expansion is happening at a much faster rate. Within a few short years, AI has lured us, spider-like, into its intricate electronic web. Wherever you find digital information, you will now find AI, from search engines to surveillance systems, from smart assistants to chess bots. Just five days after being launched in 2022, ChatGPT had already acquired over 1 million users; within six months that figure had reached more than 100 million.

A special feature of AI that accelerates its widespread and rapid deployment is what social philosopher Daniel Schmachtenberger calls its 'omni-modal' nature, meaning that it can be effectively combined with many other technologies, for instance being used to enhance data analysis in gene-therapy research, or to improve weather satellite forecasts, or to help oil companies find new deposits, or to plan aeroplane flight routes. This transforms it into a kind of über-technology that permeates a world already hooked on tech. Capitalism has similar omni-modal elements that have enabled its growth, such as its use of markets, which can be applied to the buying and selling of almost any commodity or service, from apples in a supermarket to shares on a stock exchange.

Schmachtenberger also points out that AI tools spread so fast because they become 'obligate': if your competitor has them, then you will need them too if you're going to keep up.[12] So if one political party uses AI to target floating voters with online advertisements, other parties are likely to follow their lead. Or consider how, as soon as Microsoft-backed OpenAI released ChatGPT with such success,

Google had to fast-track its release of rival chatbot Bard. Nobody wants to be left stranded behind. This is what a supersystem with the potential to get out of control looks like – an echo of the herd mentality that has driven financial markets for over three centuries.

A second parallel with financial capitalism relates to contagion risk, or what is often known as systemic risk. In very large, interconnected systems, there is an increased probability that any problem that occurs in one area may spill over and infect the system as a whole. In a financial system, the key risk is that a downturn spirals out of control and ends up in a generalised collapse, just like the Mississippi Bubble or the Wall Street Crash. When it comes to AI, losing control looks different: AI is unlikely to 'crash' in the same way as a financial meltdown. But it nevertheless poses a range of system-wide threats.

One potential systemic risk concerns the exponential spread of fake information. There are now AIs that can listen to just three seconds of a human voice and then replicate it almost perfectly: so imagine you get a phone message from your partner saying they've just forgotten your joint bank account password – but you're really being scammed. Such ID theft is already spreading fast, and could raise serious threats to national security systems at a global scale. Tech ethicist Tristan Harris fears a world of 'fake everything', with AI technologies being used to create an avalanche of fake identities, fake political speeches, fake stock-market reports and even automated fake religions.[13] The societal impacts of such a seismic breakdown of truth and trust are difficult to discern but could be colossal. Can democracy really function effectively in a digitally fabricated world? Reality itself has become vulnerable to AI.

If that were not enough, a further contagion risk is runaway mass technological unemployment. It is clear that AI will threaten jobs in some sectors, such as IT, marketing, administration, law and finance. But as the technology develops and spreads from industry to industry, some studies suggest it could eventually result in unemploy-ment levels in the US and Europe escalating to 25 per cent.[14] We might end up with a situation resembling the 1930s Great Depres-sion, where unemployment similarly reached 25 per cent in the USA, and which then had multiple knock-on effects, such as creat-ing extreme political instability – including the rise of fascism in some countries.

Systemic risks also extend to AI's military applications. AI is set to transform war through the creation of lethal autonomous weap-ons systems, from killer robots that are programmed to achieve their military objectives with little concern for civilian casualties, to smart drones that act as delivery vehicles for deadly chemical and bio-logical weapons. Without anyone having necessarily intended or foreseen it, this could easily cause a system-wide arms race, with nations obligated to keep up with the AI capabilities of their rivals. This kind of risk is amplified by the ownership structure of the AI industry, which is dominated by a few giant corporations such as Google, IBM and Meta. These companies, driven primarily by finan-cial goals, are likely to consider such risks as acceptable collateral damage. Unsurprisingly, they are already starting to snap up lucrative military contracts: in 2022, Google, Microsoft, Amazon and Oracle shared in a $9 billion contract for the Joint Warfighter Cloud Cap-ability, which will provide the backbone data analysis for the military operations of the United States Armed Forces, such as analysis of drone imagery.[15]

A final similarity between AI and financial capitalism, which may seem almost too obvious to point out, relates to intentional design: both are non-sentient human creations. This is clearly the case for the financial system. But it is a point that frequently gets lost in public discussions about AI risk, which too often get hijacked by fears about AGI – that we might soon become the playthings of con-scious machines that make their own decisions. Despite the lack of evidence that the leap to self-aware superintelligence will ever happen (for instance, due to the difficulties of computer modelling human consciousness, which remains little understood), this hasn't stopped tech leaders from stoking fears about artificial intelligence going rogue and consigning *Homo sapiens* to history.[16] As OpenAI's CEO Sam Altman has said, 'a misaligned superintelligent AGI could cause grievous harm to the world' and become an 'existential risk' to humanity.[17]

Such statements in effect function to distract public attention from less extreme but still very real dangers of the narrow AI that the tech sector is so eagerly developing, including racial bias in AI algorithms, its use in state surveillance and military operations, the fact that ChatGPT can teach you how to brew up biological pathogens in your own home, and the monopolistic super-profits that tech companies are starting to generate from AI. According to Meredith Whittaker, AI scholar and president of the non-profit messaging service Signal, 'A fantastical, adrenalizing ghost story is being used to hijack attention around what is the problem that regulation needs to solve.'[18] Like a car that can spin out of control if its brakes fail, AI does not need to be sentient to get out of control and cause serious harm. So let's forget the ghost stories and remain grounded in the problems of reality.

Despite the immense risks posed by AI, a sliver of hope lies in the fact that, like the financial system that arose in Amsterdam in the seventeenth century, we humans designed it. So, perhaps we can redesign it too – or at least some aspects of it – before its growing supersystem qualities make it virtually impossible to rein back in. Doing so requires lifting the hood and looking more closely at the nuts and bolts of how existing AI really functions – its material and human underpinnings, and the structures of power behind them. It will gradually become clear that there is not simply an analogy between AI and the financial variant of capitalism. Rather, AI needs to be understood as an intrinsic part of the capitalist system itself, embodying three of its other historic forms: industrial, colonial and consumer capitalism. Once these connections are made, it will then be possible to envision a different and less perilous future for humanity's relationship with AI.

Capitalist Capture: AI as a Technology of Extraction

Capitalism can be broadly defined as a mode of economic organisation that seeks to maximise returns to the owners of wealth, with its core operating system based on private property, wage labour and the market mechanism.[19] To grasp the essence of its industrial form, which became increasingly prevalent in the eighteenth century, look closely at one of the recent designs of the English £20 banknote. Adam Smith gazes dispassionately at workers toiling in a pin factory, alongside the label, 'The division of labour in pin manufacturing (and the great increase in the quantity of work that results)'. In *The Wealth of Nations* (1776), Smith explained that there are 18 separate stages to making a pin, and that a worker attempting to do all of them himself 'could scarce, perhaps, with his utmost industry, make one pin in a day'. But through the economic miracle of the division of labour – one of the cornerstones of industrial capitalism – with each worker doing just one or two tasks, they could make, on average, around 5,000 pins a day each. Smith was the first to admit that the outcome was not just higher national income but boring, repetitive work that could give rise to 'torpor of the mind'.

AI promises no one need face the torpor of the pin factory. Smart machines will be doing all those tedious factory jobs, leaving workers free to fill their time with leisure. Rather than the smoke and filth of the industrial system, there will be a world of sleek handheld devices powered by AI with their data floating in a pristine cloud.

A British £20 note showing Adam Smith and the pin factory
based on division of labour.

But the reality of AI is much closer to Smith's pin factory than we
might imagine. Take a company like Amazon, a world leader in the
development and deployment of AI systems. The workers on the £20
banknote resemble tiny robots, integrated into the pin-making
machinery themselves: visit an Amazon warehouse today and you
will witness a similar scene. Amazon workers, known as 'associates',
are scanned and monitored just like the packages they handle, with
AI logistics software being used to track their movements and
improve their efficiency. Clocks are everywhere. As they deal with the
items that Amazon's AI-based recommendations system may have
nudged you towards buying, workers can only be off-task for 15 minutes per 10-hour shift, with a 30-minute unpaid meal break. They
perform the tasks that the orange Kiva robots can't easily do, such as
packaging oddly shaped items, constantly endeavouring to maintain
their 'pick rate' speed.[20] They are all part of the efficiency algorithm,
mere cogs in the machine just like Charlie Chaplin in *Modern Times*
(1936), working faster and faster as the assembly line speeds up.

There is also a vast labour force behind Amazon's Mechanical Turk, named after a turban-wearing mechanical chess player invented in 1770 that was secretly operated by a human being hidden inside it. Amazon's version is a crowdsourcing platform that connects businesses with tens of thousands of low-paid workers worldwide who bid against each other to do microtasks that AI cannot yet perform, such as detecting duplicate product pages on Amazon's website or labelling photos with emotion descriptions for facial recognition software. Standard pay for this digital piecework is $0.01 per task. In effect, humans are improving on and enabling AI systems and their algorithmic processes.[21]

AI is clearly not a lifeless 'artificial' technology. It is human, all too human. AI is a cyborg system, a hybrid of human labour and machine intelligence (much like the first 'computers' in the 1940s and 1950s were real people – typically women – who did complex mathematical calculations to support the tech in engineering, space travel and other fields).[22] Despite threatening technological unemployment, AI remains dependent on the capitalist staple of poorly paid workers in insecure jobs. In this sense, it is a modern update of the old factory system: workers are still 'an appendage of the machine', as Karl Marx described it in *The Communist Manifesto* (1848).

Marx also pointed out that the logic of capitalism reaches far beyond national borders: 'It must nestle everywhere, settle everywhere, establish connections everywhere.'[23] This expansionist drive gave rise to colonial capitalism, an accomplice of industrial capitalism that was premised on the extraction of cheap raw materials and labour exploitation in poor countries on the periphery of the world economy, to benefit the wealthy nations at its centre.[24] One of its earliest birthplaces was the Bolivian mining town of Potosí, which lay at the foot of a huge silver deposit known as the *cerro rico* or 'rich mountain'. This is where Spain's conquistadors opened the veins of

Latin America in the seventeenth century. By 1650 Potosí had a population of 160,000, with 22 dams powering 140 mills to grind the silver. While immense riches flowed back to Spain, the human cost was on a scale barely imaginable. The mines relied on forced local indigenous labour and enslaved Africans: as many as 8 million of them died. 'You could build a bridge of pure silver from Potosí to Madrid with extracted ore,' wrote Eduardo Galeano, 'and you could build a bridge back with the bones of those who died mining it.'[25]

There are distinct echoes of colonial capitalism in today's AI industry. Not far from Potosí, in southwest Bolivia, lies Salar de Uyuni, the richest site of lithium in the world. This 'grey gold' is the secret ingredient of rechargeable batteries and a vital resource on which the future expansion of AI depends. Think of a company like Tesla. Its electric cars are crammed with AI, for instance in their energy-efficiency systems, safety-monitoring devices and GPS. This AI dependency will escalate as more of its cars become self-driving. But each of its vehicles also requires more than 60kg of lithium for its battery packs. Without it, all of Tesla's high-tech AI becomes defunct. Currently much of the industry's lithium is sourced from China, Australia and Chile. But Big Tech now has its sights set on the fragile salt flats of Salar de Uyuni.[26] Unless the Bolivian government manages to maintain control of this precious resource, the situation may come to resemble that found in Democratic Republic of the Congo – home to 60 per cent of the planet's cobalt, which is also used to produce batteries – where mining is largely controlled by multinational corporations such as Glencore.

These colonialist economic relationships are likely to be replicated worldwide due to the dependence of AI-based products such as mobile phones and electric cars on raw materials that are mostly to be found in low-income countries. An iPhone contains two-thirds of the elements of the periodic table and has an average lifespan of just four years, with the vast majority being thrown on the scrapheap rather than recycled. The AI industry's (and more generally the tech sector's) hunger for lithium, cobalt and other metals is becoming as insatiable as the conquistador's greed for silver and gold.[27]

The nature of colonial capitalism is also transforming in the age of AI, which is ushering in a new era of what tech scholar Abeba Birhane calls 'algorithmic colonisation'.[28] Rather than just extracting raw materials to make its products, the tech industry has begun using AI itself to extract value from the Global South. Examples abound. Facebook has offered free internet access to low-income countries worldwide through its Free Basics service, a gateway drug that effectively locks tens of millions of users into its AI-driven advertising algorithms, with the revenues flowing back to Silicon Valley (India has been one of the few countries to ban it).[29] Micro-credit schemes, which are often celebrated for their anti-poverty credentials by granting small loans at low interest, are also part of this conquest dynamic, using AI to analyse personal browsing his-tory to determine creditworthiness. While the Kenyan government owns 35 per cent of Safaricom – which operates M-Pesa, Africa's leading microcredit lending platform – 40 per cent is owned by Vodafone and much of the remainder by wealthy investors from the Global North. Economist Milford Bateman puts it in historical context:

> Like the colonial era mining operations that exploited Africa's mineral wealth, the microcredit industry in Africa essentially exists today for no other reason than to extract value from the poorest communities.[30]

The classification schemes of facial recognition software reflect a similar colonialist mentality. UTKFace, one of the best-known data-sets for training AIs – containing tens of thousands of facial images – classifies people by skin colour into the reductive categories of White, Black, Asian, Indian or Other. The resonances with South Africa's apartheid Pass Laws of the 1950s are unmistakable, where people were classified as either White, Bantu (Black African), Asian or Coloured. In effect, AI builds the racial categories of colonialism into its algorithms. The impacts of such classification schemes are all too real. AI surveillance camera systems used in policing have been shown not just to be highly inaccurate but disproportionately to misidentify ethnic minorities as criminal suspects. A study by the American Civil Liberties Union using Amazon's Rekognition facial recognition software (which is used by US law enforcement agencies) showed that it falsely identified 28 members of Congress as criminals, 11 of whom were people of colour.[31] Women are also on the receiving end of these structures of domination: AI-powered social media algorithms show women lower-paid job advertisements than men.[32]

A final and more recent variant of capitalism – consumer capitalism – offers further insights into AI. A helpful thinking tool here is Marx's concept of 'surplus value'. This describes the value produced by the labour of workers over and above the wages they are paid, which is then retained by capital owners as profit. The AI equivalent is 'behavioural surplus', a term coined by social psychologist Shoshana Zuboff.[33] How does it work?

AI is constantly tracking our personal experiences: the products we buy, the movies we watch, the news we read, where we drive. Some of this data is used to help improve the quality of services or apps. But the remainder – the behavioural surplus – is syphoned off and repackaged for sale to advertisers, who use it to predict our consumer behaviour and target us with products. This digital theft of our personal information typically occurs without our knowledge or consent (with some exceptions, such as the permissions granted through the European Union's General Data Protection Regulation).

According to Zuboff, phones are really Trojan horse devices for extracting our valuable data: that's partly why they are so cheap. In a notorious case in 2012, a Minnesota father discovered ads for baby clothing being sent to his teenage daughter, who denied she was pregnant. It turned out that an AI algorithm had predicted she was pregnant before she knew it herself: it had targeted her because she had recently switched to buying unscented skin cream, a preference that is statistically associated with second trimester pregnancy.[34]

This focus on the consumer as the source of financial gain shows how AI represents a deep continuity in the history of capitalism. In the eighteenth and nineteenth centuries, industrial capitalism maximised its profits by keeping the wages of workers low. This became increasingly difficult with the growing power of trade unions, spurring the development of consumer capitalism in the early twentieth century. Profits would now be generated by creating new human desires through the use of advertising: getting people to buy things they didn't really need. The public relations and marketing industries that exploded into life after the First World War soon enticed them into a universe of consumer pleasures: taking up smoking, filling their wardrobes with clothes for every occasion, buying diamond rings and purchasing second cars. Behavioural surplus is a similar advertising-based model that targets the consumer, nudging them unconsciously towards products they didn't know they wanted. Google is not a search engine, it is an advertising company: around 90 per cent of its revenues come from ads. The click-through rate reigns supreme. Free will is the casualty.

'History doesn't repeat itself, but it often rhymes,' wrote Mark Twain. That is certainly the case with respect to AI. As digital scholar Kate Crawford observes, AI is 'a technology of extraction' and it embodies the fundamental traits of industrial, colonial and consumer capitalism.[35] It is time to put the sci-fi fantasies aside. Upon close scrutiny, AI is best understood not as a miraculous superintelligence but as something much more familiar: a component part of the giant supersystem of capitalism itself. And it is fast becoming the primary vehicle for a newly emerging form – 'information capitalism' – which is based on the accumulation of data rather than the accumulation of capital. Information has become the key resource at the heart of the global economy, and AI is being put to work to squeeze financial rewards out of it, bit by bit, byte by byte.

None of this would have surprised Karl Marx, who recognised that the key question to ask of any economic system is: who owns the means of production? When it comes to AI, the answer is clear. While some AI is being developed by governments, most is gestating in the womb of corporate America: fewer than ten companies in the world – among them Meta, Microsoft, Google and Palantir – have the immense resources required to develop and operate AI at scale. For all their technological innovation and vision, these Big Tech firms are ultimately guided by the long-standing algorithm of maximising return on investment and shareholder value that is rooted in the birth of capitalism in the seventeenth century.

Up to this point, the history of capitalism has served to reveal warnings about AI. So where can we find a measure of hope? Does the past contain any clues for mitigating the downsides of the emerging AI supersystem, while somehow preserving its enormous promise? If an underlying problem with the AI sector is having capitalism designed into its operating code, then the best place to discover remedies would likely be in alternatives to capitalism. That might sound like a challenge. As the philosopher Slavoj Žižek put it, 'it's easier to imagine the end of the world than the end of capitalism.'[36] Yet as we are about to find out, imagining a post-capitalist economy that can tame some of the dangers of AI may be easier than you think, as long as you look in the right places.

Distributed Ownership: From Silicon Valley to Co-op Valley

Should a technology as powerful and potentially dangerous as AI really be left in the hands of corporations whose primary drive is to pursue financial gain rather than the wellbeing of people and planet? The tech industry asks us to put our trust in it, arguing that it has the knowledge and good intentions to develop AI wisely, subject to a little light regulation from government. But you don't have to read Marx to realise this is a risky option. Just listen to someone like Elon Musk who, at the very same time as vowing that there would be direct democracy in his future colonies on Mars, was obstructing union organising in his Tesla factories. Who knows what he might get up to with his artificial intelligence company xAI? Then there's Google, which pulled out of a US military AI drone project in 2018 due to employee ethical concerns, but within a couple of years was back to winning contracts from the Department of Defense. Or consider OpenAI – developers of ChatGPT – which was launched in 2015 as open source and non-profit, but broke all its idealistic promises by becoming yet another closed-source, for-profit tech firm doing multibillion-dollar deals with Microsoft.[37]

So what is to be done? One option would be to bring the major AI companies into public ownership, so they are operated by an 'entrepreneurial state' that promotes their innovation while keeping them ethically in check (see Chapter 7). This is what many countries did when they nationalised essential industries such as coal and railways in the twentieth century. But state-based solutions bring their own dangers, evident in Vladimir Putin's use of Russia's AI capabilities to hack Western elections, or the Chinese government's deployment of AI facial recognition technology in mass surveillance of its own citizens.

History, however, offers another path, which for more than a century has provided a vibrant and viable alternative to both state control and corporate capitalism, and which may provide an inspiring model for companies developing AI as well as those putting it to use in their businesses. Today we call it 'distributed ownership', a form of economic democracy in which the owners of enterprises are not shareholders and investors but rather a broader range of community stakeholders.

Its origins go back to one of the great social innovations of the nineteenth century: the cooperative movement. Cooperatives, such as Dairy Farmers of America, Rabobank in the Netherlands and the Mondragon federation in Spain, are businesses owned and directed by the company's workers or customers, and whose statutes typically incorporate social goals alongside financial ones. In a related structure known as 'steward ownership', the company is put in the hands of a trust, which has a fiduciary duty to act on behalf of its employees, consumers or even the planet itself. Examples include big names like the British department store John Lewis, the German electronics manufacturer Bosch, the outdoor clothing company Patagonia and internet provider Mozilla.

In most countries these distributed ownership models are just a small segment of the economy, but in some they are one of the largest and most dynamic sectors. To see this in action, take a trip from Silicon Valley to Co-op Valley, also known as the Italian region of Emilia-Romagna, which has one of the densest cooperative economies in the world.

With a population close to 5 million people, centred on the ancient capital of Bologna, around one-third of the region's GDP is generated by cooperative businesses, which together employ nearly 30 per cent of the workforce.[38] A typical resident might work at a high-tech manufacturing firm owned by its workers, have lunch at a nearby cooperative café, visit their elderly father in a cooperatively run care home in the evening, then do some shopping on the way home at the COOP, one of the largest supermarket chains in the country, which is jointly owned by its customers. At some point, they may also drop into their neighbourhood bar for a glass of cooperatively produced wine. Walk around the cobbled streets of Bologna and you would hardly know that you are in a living co-op utopia: there are so many cooperative businesses that they don't even advertise the fact, apart from a few exceptions such as the supermarket.

How did it all happen? The origins of Emilia-Romagna's cooperative economy is often traced back to the communal institutions and civic spirit that emerged in the region in the Middle Ages. In the twelfth century its merchants, artisans and professional classes established a form of autonomous commune government that fought for independence from popes and princes (with varying degrees of success). Its workers were organised into tight-knit craft and trade guilds whose members swore oaths of mutual assistance. Neighbourhood and religious associations also flourished, while the University of Bologna, established in 1088, was run by its students for its first three centuries. Although local oligarchs remained powerful, Bologna was the undisputed 'capital of communal Italy'.[39]

These networks of civic community left a powerful legacy of collective solidarity that endured for hundreds of years. According to political scientist Robert Putnam, the workers' mutual-aid societies that sprang up in Emilia-Romagna in the nineteenth century, which were designed to support their members through illness and old age, were 'plainly traceable' historical descendants of the communal organisations of the Middle Ages. 'The medieval traditions of collaboration persisted, even among poor peasants,' he wrote.[41] The region's cooperative movement grew out of these mutual-aid associations (known in some countries as 'friendly societies') in the late 1800s. A typical example was the Cooperative Bank of Imola, a credit union that gave loans to farm labourers and factory workers. Following its first year of profitability in 1904, its members decided not to split the earnings among themselves but to put them aside as 'indivisible

Students at the University of Bologna – here listening attentively to a lecture from King Henry of Germany in the early thirteenth century – formed guilds to run the university themselves, and even fined teachers whose lectures were not up to standard.[40]

reserves' for future investment in the co-op. Here was an economic model premised on long-term stewardship rather than short-term financial gain, described by some as 'intergenerational mutuality'.[42]

The cooperative movement expanded rapidly over the following decades, promoted by both socialist organisations and the Catholic Church. Its members were subject to persecution during the period of interwar fascism, but the movement revived in the post-war era, partly due to being championed by the Communist Party, which soon came to dominate local electoral politics. It also flourished because of the Italian constitution of 1948, which gave cooperatives legal standing as an essential economic sector geared towards social benefit rather than profit maximisation.[43] This enabled co-ops to receive tax breaks and other forms of support that promoted their development. A legal requirement to set aside a portion of annual profits as indivisible reserves guaranteed that funds were available for future internal investment, as well as to help survive temporary economic downturns and to nurture the formation of new cooperatives.

The end result was that Emilia-Romagna's co-ops thrived like nowhere else in Europe, forming a diverse network which today comprises more than 4,000 businesses, whose distributed ownership structure ensures that it is one of the most equitable regions on the continent, while also enjoying low unemployment and high per capita incomes.[44] The benefits of a cooperative system based on the predistribution rather than the redistribution of wealth are plain to see. In our neoliberal age, in which it can seem almost impossible to imagine anything other than an economy dominated by large businesses owned by shareholders and private investors, Emilia-Romagna shows that another way may be possible.

In light of this historical excursion, let's return to artificial intelligence. The risks and challenges posed by AI are admittedly vast, ranging from its dangerous military capabilities to finding ways to stop driverless cars crashing into people. I do not pretend to offer any universal panaceas. However, it is worth considering whether a distributed ownership model, along the lines of that found in Emilia-Romagna, could help inject more ethics and accountability into the emerging AI economy.

This might at first sound fabulously utopian. One would think, for instance, that an individualistic nation such as the United States simply doesn't have comparable traditions of communal organisation on which to build cooperative-based AI companies. Yet there is compelling evidence that mutual aid has flowered in the US, just as in northern Italy, especially at times of economic crisis. During the 1930s Depression, when private investors were reluctant to set up rural electrification companies due to perceived lack of profitability, local farmers formed hundreds of electricity cooperatives to hook their isolated communities into the grid, with help from low-interest government loans under the New Deal. Remarkably they still exist today, totally under the radar, providing power to 42 million people.

'If we want a more inclusive tech economy, the New Deal legacy would be a good place to start,' writes cooperative researcher Nathan Schneider, who also believes we should be learning from the Emilia-Romagna model.[45] And it is beginning to happen. Co-op businesses are taking off in the tech sector, particularly what are known as 'platform cooperatives'. These are digital enterprises, increasingly reliant on AI data analytics tools, where ownership is primarily in the hands of their workers and users.

Among them is the Drivers Cooperative, a New York City taxi service founded in 2020, with nearly 10,000 drivers who can be booked through their Co-op Ride app, which uses AI to schedule and route driver trips with maximum efficiency. Designed to end exploitative conditions faced by for-hire drivers, many of whom are poor immigrants, it takes a smaller commission than its cut-throat commercial competitors such as Uber and Lyft. Moreover, its drivers, as co-owners, are able to vote on business decisions and receive a share of the profits. As with most platform cooperatives, the biggest difficulty was finding the financing to launch the business: tech-based companies typically experience early-stage losses due to their large start-up costs, making them reliant on venture capital that expects big returns further down the line. Thanks to financing from a community investor organisation called the Shared Capital Cooperative, the Drivers Cooperative was able to get off the ground. Now, as well as providing a better financial deal for its employees than private hire firms, it also earmarks 10 per cent of earnings for community development projects.[46]

The co-op model is spreading to social media too, one of the primary dominions of AI algorithms. When Elon Musk took over Twitter in 2022 and turned it into X, many of its users decided to seek out a more ethical alternative – and found it in Mastodon, a non-profit decentralised network based on free, open-source software. Within a month, its userbase jumped from 300,000 to around 3 million people. Among the servers on which it operates is the cooperatively run social.coop, which has been described as 'a vision of a user-owned Twitter'. Over time, such groups could develop into a federation of cooperative servers supported by decentralised AI-powered blockchain technologies (which can be used for tasks such as managing tamper-proof electronic voting).[47]

And don't think that Emilia-Romagna is being left out of the picture. The region is not only one of Europe's centres of AI innovation, with firms developing new AI technologies and applications; it also has a growing number of platform cooperatives, whose emergence is supported by municipal government.[48] If you are looking for an alternative to the extractive practices of Airbnb, which is increasingly critiqued for pushing up rents and emptying cities of local residents, then try Fairbnb instead, a co-op that puts 50 per cent of its platform fees back into local communities and is headquartered in the historical heartland of cooperative culture, Bologna.

The most obvious critique to make of the platform cooperative movement is that most people have never heard of it. It makes up only a fraction of digital enterprises, which, with a few exceptions, are generally so small they can barely compete with the behemoths of Big Tech. But this may be less of a problem than first appears.

One of the most effective ways to keep AI under control and in safer hands – and one of the only genuine options we have as it continues its rapid omni-modal spread – is to nurture a diverse ecosystem of cooperatives and steward-owned firms in the tech sector that can play the crucial role of decentralising and dispersing AI technologies among a larger number of actors. This will help erode one of the central dangers of the AI economy (and capitalism more generally): the concentration of ownership and power.

This strategy resembles what good chess players often do when they are losing or under pressure: they bring out all their pieces and make the board more complicated, which serves to prevent their opponents' powerful pieces from dominating, helps to prolong the game, and maybe – just maybe – can provide unexpected opportunities for victory if they can get their pieces to work effectively together. When it comes to keeping the AI industry in check, diversity is a virtue.

But this diverse ecosystem is unlikely to evolve without the presence of three supporting elements. First, governments need to step in and provide financing to get AI co-ops off the ground, which is currently their greatest hurdle. Second, governments also need to put on the regulatory screws. It is essential to help level the playing field: giants in the AI sector such as Google or Microsoft are unlikely ever to transition into co-ops or steward ownership, so it may be necessary to use anti-monopoly laws to break up the biggest tech firms (see Chapter 4). Advocates of such a strategy range from the tech scholar Douglas Rushkoff to former US secretary of labour Robert Reich.[49] The European Union's proposed Artificial Intelligence Act (2023), which may come into operation in 2025, includes regulatory strictures such as banning the scraping of facial images from the internet to create facial recognition databases.[50] Yet many analysts suggest that more substantive safeguards need to be put in place. According to Tristan Harris, the systemic risks associated with AI provide grounds for regulations that slow down and limit the public deployment of the most powerful new large language model AIs, until their safety can be guaranteed, similar to the way that nuclear-test-ban treaties successfully prevented the spread of nuclear weapons after the Second World War.[51]

A third element is a groundswell of public campaigning to

pressure governments to take this action. We need a new generation of social movements – the AI equivalents of Fridays for Future or Extinction Rebellion – to help hold the largest AI corporations to account and create space for innovative models like platform cooperatives. The good news is that this digital solidarity is beginning to emerge through organisations such as the Center for Humane Technology, the Algorithmic Justice League and the Stop Killer Robots global coalition, which campaigns to prevent the use of AI in autonomous weapons systems.

None of this will be easy, especially because the AI industry doesn't want to talk about anything as fundamental as ownership. While its leaders often discuss the dangers of AGI going rogue, it is the tech corporations themselves who are the real rogue actors, putting profit as their purpose. AI will never be truly safe until these companies are brought under control through strict regulation or eclipsed by more benign business models.

The history of Emilia-Romagna proves a vital point: that cooperatives can be the backbone of a dynamic, innovative and competitive economy, which is also based on principles of fairness, justice and equality. So why not apply this to the AI industry? Due to the social and environmental duties written into their statutes, cooperatives are less likely to exploit their workers through poor pay and conditions, less likely to sell out to the arms industry, less likely to commit ecological crimes, less likely to capture your personal data without consent. And they can provide the economic diversity that is essential for dispersing corporate power.

Distributing the ownership of AI among a larger number of players is not a cure-all for the multiple threats it poses. But AI will certainly present less of a threat if put in the hands of workers, customers and stewardship trusts, rather than the shareholders and investors who have been behind the long history of capitalism stretching back to John Law and the financial institutions of seventeenth-century Amsterdam. Think of it as markets without capitalism.

This is precisely what industrialist Leland Stanford had in mind when he founded Silicon Valley's iconic university in 1885. He was such a passionate advocate of worker cooperatives that his endowment grant stipulated that Stanford students should be taught 'the right and advantages of association and cooperation.'[52] His wishes were quickly forgotten. How ironic that its alumni should have given birth to so many digital corporate giants, from Google and Yahoo to PayPal and Instagram, which represent the antithesis of his vision. Just imagine if Leland Stanford had founded his university in Italy's Co-op Valley instead.

10

Averting Civilisational Breakdown

How Nations and Empires Have Survived Crises and Change

Without energy from the Sun, there would be no life on Earth. Without the energy provided by human labour, draught animals, water wheels and wood-fired forges, no cities or civilisations would have emerged. The capacity to harness energy has been the central driver of the human story for the past 10,000 years.[1] But there is a dirty secret: our species's extraordinary economic and social development since the nineteenth century has been based on a once-in-a-lifetime fossil energy bonanza, where we have been burning through a limited stock of oil, gas and coal at a rate millions of times faster than it took nature to create. And it can't go on forever. As the ecological economist and former Wall Street trader, Nate Hagens, puts it:

> A bunch of mildly clever, highly social apes broke into a cookie jar of fossil energy and have been throwing a party for the past 150 years. The conditions at the party are incompatible with the biophysical realities of the planet. The party is about over and when morning comes, radical changes to our way of living will be imposed.[2]

We face the prospect of what Hagens calls the Great Simplification. The build-up to the party began in the preindustrial era, when the energy inputs for our agricultural societies, such as running water and horse power, were relatively limited and sustainable. The party started ramping up with the Industrial Revolution, when we began using condensed hydrocarbons to fuel the new machine age, from steam engines to automobiles. Gradually we became ever more reliant on credit from financial markets to allow us to keep extracting energy resources and to finance mass consumerism, and so the party has continued while experiencing occasional readjustments such as the Wall Street Crash and the 2008 economic meltdown.

But according to Hagens, we are fast approaching a critical turning point where this system becomes untenable. The one-off carbon pulse on which we have built our societies will have pushed us over too many ecological limits, among them CO_2 emissions and biodiversity loss. The gap between the money accumulating in the financial system and the physical resources the planet can sustainably offer will have become too large. This will produce a moment of rupture when the party is over and we will have to seriously sober up. This is the Great Simplification, an anticipated phase of massive adjustment where we are forced to operate our societies at far lower and more sustainable energy levels provided by renewable resources, and where global GDP – no longer bolstered by the cheap and dirty energy of the industrial era – will significantly contract.[3]

The question Hagens leaves us with is this: will we 'bend or break' during the Great Simplification?[4] In other words, will it be a traumatic societal breakdown or a more gradual transformation where we bend with the winds of change and forge a new ecological civilisation?

We are currently most likely to face the break scenario. The world's wealthy countries keep postponing the day of reckoning, kicking the can down the road by continuing to extract fossil fuels, degrade the land and pollute the oceans, all in pursuit of endless growth and with fingers crossed that technology will clean up the mess they have made. This is magical thinking that denies the fact that GDP growth and environmental damage remain inextricably coupled across most of the globe.[5] An emerging polycrisis is all too visible: rampant wildfires, swirling super-tornadoes, rapid pollinator decline, far-right extremism, geopolitical instability, escalating cost of living, threats of pandemics, risks from AI and cyberterrorism. This is what a civilisation teetering on the brink looks like.[6]

Can history help us learn to bend rather than break? This question takes us into the field of 'collapsology', which searches the past for clues about what makes civilisations rise and fall, die or survive. The value of applied history is obvious to collapse scholars. 'We will only march into collapse if we advance blindly, we are only doomed if we are unwilling to listen to the past', writes global risk researcher Luke Kemp.[7] So we had better start listening.

No civilisation lasts forever: empires and dynasties are born, they flower and then die, sometimes abruptly but usually over decades or centuries (making 'breakdown' a more appropriate term than 'collapse'). Some collapsologists seek to discover singular tipping-point explanations, such as the theory that Easter Island society died out due to chopping down all the trees in a tragic case of ecological overshoot. Others develop complex frameworks highlighting dozens of factors responsible for collapse: one study identified 210 causes for the decline of the Roman Empire, from barbarian invasion to lead poisoning the water.[8]

If we hope to bend rather than break as we traverse the Great Simplification, however, then we need to focus less on cataloguing these specific causes of historic breakdown than on understanding what makes civilisations resilient and able to survive over long periods. That is, what gives them the capacity to cope with crises and change? Think of it as preventative healthcare, or preparing for a major mountaineering expedition where there is the possibility of dangerous and unpredictable weather, but at the scale of a whole society. Taking this perspective reveals three broad features that are likely to give a civilisation an ability to adapt and transform over time: *asabiya*, *biophilia* and *crisis response*. While some of these terms may be unfamiliar, they are all essential vocabulary for our turbulent century.

Asabiya and the Power of Collective Solidarity

In 1375, the Arab scholar Ibn Khaldun retreated to a remote castle in western Algeria to write his masterpiece, *The Muqaddimah*, a treatise on history described by world historian Arnold Toynbee as 'undoubtedly the greatest work of its kind that has ever been created by any mind in any time or place'.[9] Just as Edward Gibbon was inspired to write *The Decline and Fall of the Roman Empire* after visiting the crumbling columns of ancient Rome in 1764, Khaldun was stirred by the surrounding ruins of once glorious North African cities that had been devastated by warfare, internal strife and the Black Death (in which both his parents had died). What was it, he wondered, that explained their growth and then decay? And what lessons might be learned for the future?[10]

Khaldun emerged four years later with his book complete and returned to his stormy political career. Although a celebrated scholar, he had also been a judge and advisor to a succession of dynastic rulers in Muslim Spain and the Islamic kingdoms of North Africa, yet had been repeatedly dismissed and even thrown in prison for his shifting allegiances. In 1384 he managed to secure a new position as chief justice in Cairo. Then in 1401 he got caught in the siege of Damascus by the Turco-Mongol conqueror Timur (or Tamerlane). Hearing that the renowned historian was captive in the city, Timur had him lowered by rope in a basket over the city walls to spend a month in his encampment, explaining to the infamous tyrant what he had discovered about the rise and fall of states and empires.[11]

Khaldun eagerly described his central thesis to Timur, which revolved around the concept of *asabiya*, an Arabic term meaning 'collective solidarity' or 'group feeling', which appeared over 500 times in *The Muqaddimah*. Khaldun believed that the most successful, long-lived states were those that possessed strong *asabiya*. The Berber tribes of the Maghreb region were able to establish powerful kingdoms in North Africa due to their highly developed *asabiya* – the harshness of desert life required cooperation and group loyalty for survival. The Muslim armies of the seventh century were able to defeat their foes despite having fewer troops because their fervent religious belief generated *asabiya* and a willingness to sacrifice their lives for God. Khaldun also stressed that wealth inequalities could weaken *asabiya*: most dynasties eventually declined because their rulers succumbed to the desire for riches and luxury, which sapped their finances, caused internal dissent and left them prey to outside enemies, such as nomadic tribes on the periphery. This had been the fate of the Umayyad dynasty in Islamic Spain in the eleventh century. Like Aristotle and Polybius before him, Khaldun wrapped his ideas in a cyclical theory of history: a typical dynasty, he argued, lasted three to four generations or about 120 years, with *asabiya* diminishing with each successive generation.[12]

Khaldun declared that his book offered 'an entirely original science' that was 'new, extraordinary, and highly useful'.[13] His brilliance was to move beyond mere factual chronicles of the past, or entertaining histories of heroic figures, by providing perhaps the world's first sociological theory of historical change. Khaldun's cyclical model is widely critiqued today as empirically flawed – the Habsburg and Ottoman empires, as well as many Chinese dynasties, lasted far longer than 120 years – and his theory lacks analysis of the environmental causes of civilisational decline, a core focus of today's collapse research. Yet his ideas around the importance of social cohesion and group solidarity still resonate.

How so? Based on a study of the demise of 87 ancient civilisations, Luke Kemp concludes that 'wealth and political inequality can be the central drivers of social disintegration' as 'inequality under-mines collective solidarity and political turbulence follows.'[14] Jared Diamond similarly cites the examples of the Mayan kings and Green-land Norse chiefs to suggest that civilisations commonly collapse due to inequalities, as ruling elites use their wealth and privilege to insulate themselves from the acute social and ecological problems they are creating. In her pioneering book *A Paradise Built in Hell*, Rebecca Solnit shows how, throughout history, collective solidarity and cooperation tend to emerge at times of mass disaster, giving societies the resilience they need to cope with crisis. In the aftermath of the San Francisco earthquake of 1906, for instance, local residents set up improvised soup kitchens that fed thousands of homeless fam-ilies. As she writes, 'In the wake of an earthquake, a bombing, a major storm, most people are altruistic, urgently engaged in caring for themselves and those around them, strangers and neighbours as well as friends and loved ones.'[15] Such examples would have made com-plete sense to Khaldun: *asabiya* bonds societies together, enabling them to survive trauma and turbulence, and they are unlikely to endure long without it.

Among Khaldun's greatest contemporary admirers is the histor-ian Peter Turchin, founder of the field of cliodynamics, which uses quantitative data to study long-term historical processes. Turchin argues that Khaldun was right to stress the importance of *asabiya* in determining the rise and fall of empires, but puts far more emphasis than him on a specific factor that generates it: the threat of an exter-nal enemy.

It is remarkable, notes Turchin, that humans have evolved from living in small communities of hundreds of people to huge empires and nation-states encompassing tens of millions of citizens, who have a sense of communal solidarity that extends beyond their immediate neighbours to include total strangers within the bound-aries of their polity. The most crucial factor that has made this

The collective solidarity of *asabiya*: an improvised community kitchen set up on the street in the aftermath of the San Francisco earthquake, 1906.

possible is the threat of invasion from outside forces, which gets people to put aside their differences, bond together and make sacrifices for the common good. It is what made ancient Sparta such a formidable fighting force, with its soldiers ready and willing to lay down their lives to keep its many enemies at bay. It compelled a whole generation of patriotic British youths to volunteer in the First World War, and likewise motivated rural families to take in over a million child evacuees from the cities during the Second World War. Today, it drives Ukrainians to unite in defence of their nation against Russian invasion. We have built our societies on the foundation of this group solidarity, which has generated the collective vision to establish everything from public health systems to national education institutions. *Asabiya* thrives on competition between states. The threat of violence, paradoxically, has been essential for the evolution of large-scale sociality. Or as Turchin puts it, '10,000 years of war made humans the greatest co-operators on Earth.'[16]

If Turchin is right, then we are in big trouble. The climate and ecological emergency requires humanity to cooperate on a global scale. It is an intrinsically cross-border issue: positive environmental policies by one nation can easily be negated by the harmful actions of another, and the carbon emissions of rich countries have their most devastating impacts on poor ones. If we are to bend rather than break during the Great Simplification, we need legally binding international agreements to reduce CO_2 and other dangerous greenhouse gases. We need oil-rich countries to forgo their immediate national interest and keep their black gold in the ground. We need chemical pollutants and deforestation to be banned or severely restricted not just in one country but in many. And the inconvenient truth is that this kind of global cooperation has been almost entirely absent (with rare exceptions such as the 1987 Montreal Protocol, which banned chlorofluorocarbons that depleted the ozone layer).

Turchin's theory, building on Ibn Khaldun, explains why this is all such an immense challenge: there is no external enemy creating the planetary-level *asabiya* we need to act in solidarity together. Climate change simply doesn't feel like a military invasion force – the kind of threat that got the Allies to unite against Nazi Germany despite their extreme political and ideological differences. Its impacts are slower and less immediately noticeable or violent. There is no singular actor behind it all, and its effects – like floods or droughts – are sometimes difficult directly to attribute to specific causes. No wonder most nations do not want to band together and sacrifice short-term economic gains or relinquish their sovereignty, just as most individuals don't want to make sacrifices such as limiting how often they take plane flights or to give up eating meat.

Yet, as Turchin argues, sacrifice is precisely what we need: 'The capacity to sacrifice self-interest for the sake of the common good is the necessary condition for cooperation. Without it, concerted collective action is impossible.'[17] Sacrifice has, in fact, become a dirty word, with most governments searching for 'win–win' solutions to the ecological crisis, such as the economic benefits of developing their renewable-energy sectors. Ultimately, however, we will have to give some things up for the common good, especially the conveniences and luxuries of high-carbon and materially intensive consumer culture. That is the harsh reality of the Great Simplification.

Perhaps only an alien invasion would be enough to prompt global level cooperation (and even this is unlikely if the 2016 film *Arrival* is anything to go by). So what to do? If there is no external enemy, then we may need to generate internal villains instead to unite us. The most obvious candidates are fossil fuel companies that have spent decades obfuscating the seriousness of the climate crisis while accumulating megaprofits as the global energy crisis deepens. Indeed, they are increasingly vilified in the press, targeted by activists and demonised in movies such as *How to Blow Up a Pipeline* (2022). Other potential climate criminals to focus our attention on include the growing number of millionaires and billionaires jetting around in private planes and tanning themselves on superyachts, who alone are on track to burn through 72 per cent of our remaining carbon budget to stay below 1.5°C.[18] Or how about the big fossil fuel-producing countries such as Saudi Arabia, Russia and even Norway, which is one of the world's largest gas and oil exporters despite its climate-friendly image?

Some might argue that it is possible to forge the planetary-level consciousness and cooperation we need without targeting such specific groups, and just promoting a general and inclusive sense of human solidarity. I wish it were so. The European Union, for example, has managed to set aside national differences to pursue its Green Deal agenda of carbon reduction policies. Yet the EU's long history of collaborative efforts in this and other policy areas has itself been born out of the ashes of the Second World War and a recognition that cross-border cooperation is vital to prevent the emergence of another pan-European conflict. Moreover, having a belligerent Russia on the doorstep also helps drive collective policies among member states, from energy independence to defence. In the end, as Turchin's research demonstrates, mass-scale cooperation is typically associated with a mentality of having an enemy at the gate. If global *asabiya* is the goal, then we may have to accept that one of our surest strategies is to seek out adversaries within, in defence of a liveable future.

Biophilia and Reconciliation with the Living World

As a child growing up in suburban Sydney in the 1970s, I had little understanding about the history and culture of Indigenous Australians (who were then generally referred to as 'Aborigines'). The school I went to, the parks I played in, the streets where I rode my bike were – unbeknownst to me – all on land stolen from the Darug and Guringai peoples. My mind began to open when I was eight years old, when my grandfather brought a friend to our home, the Indigenous Australian artist Goobalathaldin (also known as Dick Roughsey), who gave me a copy of his 1975 children's book *The Rainbow Serpent*. It tells the Dreamtime creation story of Goorialla, a giant snake who carves the shape of the land from its twisting body, teaches the people to dance and then turns many of them into plants, birds, insects and animals. 'Now the remaining people have to look after all the animals, all the living things which were men and women in the beginning,' the story ends.

The Rainbow Serpent speaks to an intimacy and interdependence between humankind, the land and the living world, which is present in many Indigenous cultures but largely absent from Western societies, where what we call 'nature' is primarily viewed as a resource rather than a relative. A worldview based on such deep interconnections is a crucial foundation for long-term civilisational survival and renewal. Multiple studies show that a primary cause of civilisational breakdown is overexploitation of the environmental resources on which the society's very progress was based, as occurred with the Akkadian Empire (*c.* 2350–2150 BCE) degrading its rich agricultural lands.[19] Conversely, numerous studies reveal how traditional Indigenous land, sea and forestry management practices have enabled people to live sustainably for hundreds or thousands of years without degrading the fragile ecologies on which they depend, from the Greenland Inuit to Indigenous Australian hunter-gatherers.[20] As environmental biologist Robin Wall Kimmerer observes, 'biodiversity is declining perilously all over the planet, but the rates of loss are dramatically lower in areas under Indigenous control'. As we continue to ravage our ecosystems, there is an urgent need, she suggests, to draw on Indigenous wisdom, asking not 'What more can we take from the Earth?' but rather 'What does the Earth ask of us?' We must leave a world that is 'as rich for the seventh generation as it is for us', she writes.[21]

Embracing this philosophy of ecological stewardship, which treats the Earth as a gift to be handed on through the generations, takes us beyond the theories of Ibn Khaldun. If we hope to navigate the trials of the Great Simplification and forge civilisational resilience, it is not enough to nurture *asabiya* among humankind: we must also extend its scope to include solidarity with the whole web of life. Call this idea biophilia, a term popularised by the evolutionary biologist Edward Wilson, which describes a feeling of innate connection with the living world and a profound recognition that human beings are an inseparable part of it – that the trees are our external lungs providing the oxygen we breathe, that listening to birdsong can repair our mental health, that our flourishing depends on maintaining the integrity and balance of the wafer-thin biosphere that contains all life on Earth.[22] Biophilia is the mental scaffolding we need for creating regenerative economies and societies that operate within the ecological limits of the planet, and that have a greater chance of bending rather than breaking.

Indigenous philosophy and science are essential guides for the development of biophilia consciousness. But we can also learn far more than what one might expect from the remnants of nature connection that remain hidden in the Western mind. It is a history that lies deep within us, if only we cared to unearth it.

This might seem an unlikely prospect. For more than half a millennium, we – the peoples of the wealthy Western world – have been subjecting nature to an ecological blitzkrieg. We have razed forests for agriculture and shipbuilding, dug out minerals and hydrocarbons to fuel industrial capitalism, hunted whales to extinction and treated rivers as sewage dumps – all justified in the name of 'progress'. Technology and commerce, backed up by the Christian doctrine of dominion, in which the fruits of the earth exist to serve humankind, have together wreaked unaccountable havoc for hundreds of years. There may be no more telling symbol of this unholy trinity than the 30 copies of the Bible that Johannes Gutenberg had specially printed on vellum paper in 1456, whose production required the skins of around 5,000 calves. In the nineteenth century, British Prime Minister William Gladstone was famous for his favourite hobby of chopping down oak trees and was sent dozens of axes from well-wishers around the world.[23] Since then we have been swinging our axes faster and faster, committing untold ecological crimes. As we head towards a human-made sixth extinction, Goorialla must be writhing in agony.

Yet it is curious just how much of our biophilic instinct remains, despite this sordid history. Why is it that even in Britain, the home of the Industrial Revolution, the Royal Society for the Protection of

Birds has over 1.2 million members – far more than any political party? Why are there more than 20 million active gardeners from across the social spectrum, who love nothing better than sticking their hands in the soil and watching things grow?[24] Why was David Attenborough's *Blue Planet II* documentary series of 2017 watched by over 14 million people? Why do tens of thousands go rambling in the countryside on the weekends, seeking out bluebells, beech woods and the thrill of spotting a wild deer? Perhaps we are not quite as alienated from nature as we are often told. And it all needs explaining.

According to historian Keith Thomas, a 'profound shift in sensibilities' took place in Britain between the sixteenth and eighteenth centuries, which still resonates today.[25] This was, on the one hand, the period when the idea that civilisational progress required subduing and exploiting nature was firmly taking hold. At the very same time, however, a counter doctrine was developing that challenged the right of humans to exploit plants and animals for their own advantage.

A key turning point was the publication of John Evelyn's book *Sylva* in 1664, which advocated reforestation of the increasingly denuded British landscape and kickstarted a tree-planting craze across the country. Aristocrats started planting hundreds of thousands of saplings on their estates, not simply to reap the valuable timber but just as much for aesthetic pleasure. After centuries of woodland decimation, mass planting took place in the Royal Forests, while Oxford and Cambridge colleges embarked on creating ornamental tree walks. Among the more vociferous supporters of this new veneration of trees was the merchant and vegetarian Thomas Tryon, who in 1691 declared that 'trees suffer pains when cut down, even as the beasts and animals do when they are killed'.[26] Gardening concurrently began to emerge as a recreational activity. An explosion of gardening manuals encouraged planting rose beds and gillyflowers, with the number of plant varieties rapidly expanding due to colonial imports. The Romantic movement took such sensibilities a stage further in the eighteenth and nineteenth centuries, turning nature into an object of awe and wonder and prompting the Lakeland Poets to write lyrical verses in honour of mountains, streams and ancient trees.[27]

A similar shift in attitudes took place with respect to animal life. Whereas animals had previously been considered mainly in utilitarian terms as sources of food and for farmwork, the seventeenth century saw the exponential growth of a very different category of animals: pets. The Stuart kings were obsessed with dogs – hounds, spaniels, poodles – with Charles II being notorious for playing with his dog during Privy Council meetings. Aristocrats particularly loved their hounds, which were often better fed than their servants and appeared in portraits by their sides. Over time, the keeping of pet dogs spread across social classes and the British bulldog, originally used in the blood sport of bull baiting, became a national emblem of courage and tenacity. It took longer for cats to acquire the status of pets – it was not until the eighteenth century that they were commonly considered objects of affection rather than just useful for catching rats and mice. By then, it was clear what distinguished a pet from other animals: they were allowed in the house, they were given individual names, and they were never eaten.[28]

This gradual reconnection with the natural world was in part a reaction to urbanisation and industrialisation. There was a growing desire to rediscover older traditions of country living that were fast disappearing as the factories and mills spewed their billowing smoke, evident in the popularity of Gilbert White's *Natural History of Selborne* (1789), whose pages celebrated everything from wildflowers and mosses to humble creatures such as earthworms and spiders. But it was also a response to scientific advances in botany and evolutionary theory, which increasingly questioned the assumed superiority and separateness of human beings from other forms of life, and eroded the idea that nature was simply a resource for our benefit. When Carl Linnaeus published his new system of botanical classification in the 1730s, plants were no longer categorised in terms of their usefulness to humans (for instance, as medicines) but with reference to their innate physical structures. Charles Darwin then revealed that we were just one branch of a great evolutionary story and, shockingly, that chimpanzees were among our closest relatives.[29]

These scientific developments combined with the remnants of pagan traditions of nature worship that had survived from the Middle Ages. From Britain to Bulgaria, rural communities continued to perform rituals to honour the corn-mother spirit, making corn dolls and puppets at harvest time, much like Indigenous Mayan peoples in Central America have been worshipping corn for thousands of years. Towns and cities across Europe, such as Munich and Uppsala, also celebrated ancient folk festivals, including May Day, when people wrapped themselves in leaves to become Green Men and danced in celebration of the spring.[30] The first eyewitness account of May Day in Oxford, which dates back to 1598, describes how 'men attired in women's apparel, brought into town a woman bedecked with flowers and garlands named by them the Queen of the May', and that there were also 'Morris dancers, and other disordered and unseemly sports'.[31] Such practices are still going strong: on May Morning each year, I dress in green with a leafy hat and join thousands of other revellers at dawn on the streets of Oxford alongside the Morris dancers.

I am certainly not claiming that Western society retains a connection with the living world that can be compared to that of today's Indigenous peoples: I may have read my old copy of *The Rainbow Serpent* to my twins, but Goorialla is not part of their culture. Rather, I wish to challenge the simplistic and widespread idea that we have

May Morning is still celebrated in Oxford after more than 400 years, complete with Morris dancers and Green Men. Photo courtesy of Oxford University Morris.

been completely severed from nature by the pursuit of progress and modernity. As Keith Thomas writes, 'The explicit acceptance of the view that the world does not exist for man alone can be fairly regarded as one of the great revolutions in modern Western thought, though it is one to which historians have scarcely done justice.'[32] Over many centuries, we gradually reconnected ourselves with plants and animals. This was, admittedly, typically in a limited, tamed and highly controlled way – we desired neat gardens for their aesthetic delights and obedient pets for the pleasures of companionship. But by doing so, we managed to maintain and nurture at least a thread of our biophilic selves.

This history has profound implications for the way we confront the systemic ecological threats of the twenty-first century. It tells us that we have surprisingly strong foundations for making the leap to the biophilia consciousness required to steward the Earth for the citizens of tomorrow. While Britons might spend much of their leisure time shopping and watching television, there are millions of gardeners and other nature lovers who comprise an untapped revolutionary eco-force. Some of them are already taking to the streets, urged on by public figures such as radical naturalist Chris Packham. Others are shifting from support for traditional conservation organisations to more transformative approaches like rewilding, which seeks a return to the wild landscapes of the past by allowing nature to find its own way in damaged ecosystems. Many are pushing schools to educate their children in the woods, drawing inspiration from the forest schools that are so popular in countries such as Denmark and Germany.[33] This is just the beginning of a nature reconciliation movement with the power to switch on and unleash the biophilic instinct that lies within us all.

Crisis Response: How Crises can Kickstart Transformative Change

Asabiya and biophilia are two fundamental pillars on which we can build the resilience that can help us bend rather than break during the Great Simplification. They ground humanity in both intra- and inter-species solidarity, enabling us to create stable and unified societies that respect the non-negotiable biophysical limits of the planet. But forging them at scale is a slow process, one of inculcating new values and worldviews over years, even generations. So we also need, just as much, to develop a capacity to respond at speed to an unprecedented environmental crisis that has already begun to cause global convulsions. David Attenborough has spelled out the urgency of our predicament in the starkest terms: 'It may sound frightening, but the scientific evidence is that if we have not taken dramatic action within the next decade, we could face irreversible damage to the natural world and the collapse of our societies.'[34]

How can we act with the necessary agility to counter this crisis and – ideally – use it as an opportunity to embark on a radically new pathway towards an ecological civilisation? An answer lies in thinking historically about the meaning of 'crisis' itself and understanding the conditions under which societies manage to undergo supercharged transformations.

There is a popular myth – often traced back to a speech by John F. Kennedy – that the Chinese word for 'crisis' (*wēijī*, 危机) is composed of two characters meaning 'danger' and 'opportunity'. Not so. In fact, the second character, *jī* (机), is closer to meaning 'change point' or 'critical juncture'.[35] This makes it more like the English word 'crisis', which derives from the ancient Greek *krisis*, whose verb form, *krino*, meant to 'choose' or 'decide' at a critical moment. In a legal context, a *krisis* described a crucial decision point at which someone might be judged innocent or guilty. In the medical sphere, it was the turning point in an acute disease when a patient might live or die. New layers of meaning were added over time. For Thomas Paine in the eighteenth century, a crisis was not just a threshold moment when a whole political order could be overturned but also involved a fundamental moral decision, such as whether to support the war for American independence. In the nineteenth century, Karl Marx argued that capitalism experienced inevitable crises, which could lead to economic and political rupture.[36] More recently, Malcolm Gladwell popularised the idea of a 'tipping point', which represents a similar moment of rapid transformation or contagion in which a system undergoes change. In everyday language, we use crisis to name a time of intense danger or difficulty that implies an imperative to act – a crisis in a marriage or the climate crisis itself.

Drawing on this legacy of meanings, we can think of a crisis as an emergency situation that requires a bold decision to go in one direction rather than another. Alongside *asabiya* and biophilia, a capacity to react effectively to a crisis – what I term 'crisis response' – constitutes a third pillar of what makes a civilisation resilient and able to avert cataclysmic breakdown. But what exactly are the conditions in which governments tend to carry out an effective crisis response that yields rapid and transformative policy change? Historically, such agile responses have usually occurred in four contexts: war, disaster, revolution and disruption.

The most common context is war. Just recall the seismic restructuring of the US economy that occurred after the Japanese bombing of Pearl Harbor in December 1941, when the country entered the Second World War. Despite fierce opposition from industry, the US government imposed a ban on manufacturing private cars and rationed petrol to 3 gallons per week. Car factories were instructed to produce tanks and planes instead, and citizens were encouraged to 'Join a car-sharing club TODAY' to help defeat Hitler. To support the war effort, Roosevelt introduced the first ever federal income tax, with the top rate rising to 94 per cent by 1944. The government also borrowed heavily, spending more between 1942 and 1945 than in the previous 150 years.[37] And all this was happening in one of the most hyper-capitalist, free-market economies in human history. At the same time, the US took the decision to enter a military alliance with its ideological arch enemy, the USSR. In the face of crisis, the political rule book was thrown out the window.

Governments also take radical crisis action in the wake of disasters. Following devastating floods in 1953, which killed over 2,000 people, the Dutch government embarked on its Delta Works project to build new flood defences to protect the country from future flood risks. It was one of the most ambitious infrastructure projects of the twentieth century and the cost was gargantuan, amounting to over 20 per cent of GDP at the time. No government today is committing anything close to this to deal with the climate crisis – not even in the

Netherlands, which faces sea-level rises over the next century that the Delta Works may be unable to contain.[38] The COVID-19 pandemic provides a more recent example. In the face of a public health emergency, a centre-right British government managed to close the borders, shut schools and businesses, ban sports events and air travel, pour billions into vaccination programmes and pay the salaries of millions of people for more than a year. It was extraordinary, given that this was a government that had criticised state intervention in the economy for years. And the sky did not fall in.

A third category of rapid, transformative change is in the context of revolutions, which produce upheavals that can create dramatic openings in the political system. During the Chinese civil war in the late 1940s, and immediately following the revolution of 1949, the Chinese Communist Party introduced radical land reform programmes that redistributed agricultural property from wealthy landlords to poor peasant farmers.

Another example is the Cuban National Literacy Campaign, one of Fidel Castro's first major policy initiatives after his revolutionary forces took power in 1959, which aimed to tackle mass illiteracy. In early 1961, the government embarked on one of the most far-reaching and effective education programmes the world has ever seen: more than 250,000 volunteers were recruited – 100,000 of them under 18 and over half of them women – to teach 700,000 Cubans to read and write. Schools were closed for nine months so teenage *brigadistas* from the towns could go and live with poor rural families, working side by side with them in the fields during the day and teaching them literacy skills at night under lamplight. It was arduous and sometimes dangerous work: the CIA-backed Bay of Pigs invasion took place not long after the scheme was launched, with anti-Castro insurgents targeting the student teachers and killing several of them. Yet by the end of the year, the campaign had reduced national illiteracy from 24 per cent to just 4 per cent. Although the teaching materials have been criticised for spreading revolutionary propaganda, the campaign was supported by the mass of the Cuban population, many of whom still remember their teaching duties as a transformative moment in their lives. Whatever you think of Castro's Cuba, there is no doubt that revolutions can drive radical change.[39]

The challenge of today's ecological emergency is that it is the wrong kind of crisis, failing to fit neatly into any of these three categories. It doesn't resemble a war with a clear enemy. It is not taking place in the wake of a revolutionary moment that could inspire transformative action. And it is not even clear that disasters, such as the Dutch floods of 1953, provide an appropriate model either. The Dutch government only acted *after* the floods took place, having ignored years of warnings from water engineers that they might occur, whereas today we ideally need nations to act *before* more ecological disasters hit and we cross irreversible tipping points of change. Governments generally have a good record of responding to disasters or public emergencies once they have happened, yet a far weaker record of taking preventative action, as was similarly revealed by the lack of pandemic planning in place in most countries when COVID-19 erupted. But when it comes to planetary health, prevention rather than cure is the only safe option.

This leaves us in a quandary: what would it actually take for governments to treat the ecological crisis with the urgency and seriousness it deserves, enabling us to bend not break in the decades ahead? Fortunately, there is a fourth crisis context that can jumpstart radical policy change: disruption. By this I mean a moment of system instability that provides opportunities for rapid transformation, which is created by a combination or nexus of three interlinked factors: first, some kind of crisis (though not usually as extreme as a war, revolution or cataclysmic disaster), combined with disruptive social movements and visionary new ideas.[40] These are brought together in

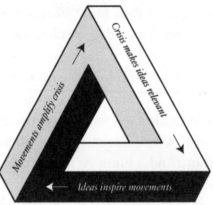

Crisis
Political, economic, tech or
ecological rupture that
destabilises the system

Crisis makes ideas relevant

Movements amplify crisis

← *Ideas inspire movements*

Movements
Disruptive movements and
activism that challenge
power holders

Ideas
New ideas, worldviews
and policies that reshape
society

Disruption Nexus

Rapid, transformative change is most likely to happen when a Crisis occurs in
conjunction with disruptive Movements and visionary new Ideas permeating
society. None of them alone is sufficient.

a model I have developed called the Disruption Nexus. Here is how
it works.

Let's start in the top corner of the triangular diagram with Crisis.
The model is based on a recognition that most crises – whether a
financial crash like in 2008 or an ecological calamity like the spate of
wildfires in California in 2022 – are rarely in and of themselves sufficient to induce a swift and substantive policy change (unlike a war).
I used to think that if we just had enough climate disasters, such as a
single week in which hurricanes hit Shanghai and New York, and
London experienced massive flooding, then the world might wake
up to the ecological emergency. I now believe I was wrong: there are
too many reasons for governments not to act, from the lobbying

power of the fossil fuel industry to the ever-dominant imperative to pursue economic growth. Rather, a crisis is only likely to create rapid, transformative change if two other key elements are present at the same time: movements and ideas.

One of the recurring themes in this book is the power of social movements to bring about change. They typically do this through amplifying crises that may be quietly simmering under the surface or are ignored by dominant actors in society. As Naomi Klein points out:

> Slavery wasn't a crisis for British and American elites until abolitionism turned it into one. Racial discrimination wasn't a crisis until the civil rights movement turned it into one. Sex discrimination wasn't a crisis until feminism turned it into one. Apartheid wasn't a crisis until the anti-apartheid movement turned it into one.

In her view, today's global ecological movement needs to do exactly the same thing, so the political class recognises that 'climate change is a crisis worthy of Marshall Plan levels of response.'[41]

The historical record bears out this close relationship between disruptive movements and crisis. We have seen how 'radical flank' movements, such as the Jamaica slave rebellion of 1831, helped generate a major political crisis that threw the government into a state of panic, leading to the Slavery Abolition Act of 1833 (Chapter 1). Similarly, the Finnish women's movement took to the streets during the general strike of 1905, exacerbating the crisis and using it to push forward their cause of votes for women (Chapter 8). More recently, the mass popular uprisings in Berlin in November 1989 amplified a political crisis that had been building up over previous months, with turmoil in the East German government and destabilising pro-democracy protests that had been taking place across the Eastern Bloc, partly fuelled by Soviet leader Mikhail Gorbachev's reforms. Their actions made history: on 9 November the wall was finally breached and the system visibly came tumbling down.[42]

But in all these cases, a third element was required to bring about change: the presence of new ideas. The economist Milton Friedman famously said that while a crisis is an opportunity for change, 'when that crisis occurs, the actions that are taken depend on the ideas that are lying around'.[43] In the cases above, new ideas around racial equality, women's rights and democratic freedoms were vital inspiration for the success of transformational movements. The aftermath of the 2008 financial crash reveals what happens in the absence of unifying new ideas. Two corners of the triangle were in place: the crash itself and the Occupy Movement calling for change. But missing were the new economic ideas and models to challenge the failing system (best summed up by the Occupy slogan, 'Occupy Everything, Demand Nothing'). As a result, the traditional power brokers in the investment banks got themselves bailed out and the old financial system remained in place. This would be less likely to happen today, when new models such as post-growth economics and modern monetary theory (MMT) have gained far more public prominence.

Much like Friedman, the German-born philosopher Hannah Arendt, in a series of post-war writings on the nature of political crisis, argued that a crisis was a fruitful moment for questioning orthodoxies and established ideas. It brings about 'the ruin of our categories of thought and standards of judgement', such that 'traditional verities seem no longer to apply'.[44] Dominant old ideas are in a state of flux and uncertainty, and new ones are potentially ready to take their place. While a crisis could lead to dark forces such as totalitarianism taking over (as occurred in Germany in the 1930s, when the mass unemployment of the Depression enabled the rise of Hitler), it equally offers a chance to pursue ideas that disrupt traditional models of political rule and social organisation.

This three-cornered dynamic model of system change – in which movements amplify crisis, crisis makes ideas relevant, and ideas inspire movements – has the virtue of providing a substantive role for collective human agency. In a wartime crisis, political and military leaders typically take charge. By contrast, a disruption nexus offers opportunities for everyday citizens to organise and take action that can potentially shift governments to a critical decision point – a *krisis* in the ancient Greek sense – where they feel forced to respond to an increasingly turbulent situation with radical policy measures. The interplay of the three elements creates a surge of political will, that elusive ingredient of change.

Therein lies our greatest hope for the kind of green Marshall Plan that the planetary emergency calls for. This is not the time for lukewarm reform, for 'proportionate' responses, for the low flame of gradualism. If we are to bend rather than break in the Great Simplification, we will need rebellious movements and system-changing ideas to coalesce with the ongoing environmental crisis into a Great Disruption that redirects humanity towards an ecological civilisation.

Will we rise to the challenge? Humans are a highly adaptable species: we have managed to occupy almost every environmental niche on the planet and expand our numbers to extraordinary levels. But as historian Peter Frankopan makes clear, 'much of human history has been about the failure to understand or adapt to changing circumstances in the physical and natural world around us'.[45] That is why the great ancient civilisations of Mesopotamia and the Yucatán Peninsula have gone. Moreover, since the dawn of agriculture we have never encountered environmental change occurring at anything like the rapid pace of today, nor with such catastrophic consequences or on such a global scale. Whether we can mount a successful crisis response is the fundamental uncertainty of our age.

The insights of history suggest a place to start the enormous task of planetary renewal. *Asabiya* offers the collective solidarity we need to navigate a tumultuous future: we must endeavour to nurture empathy and social cooperation both within our communities and across national borders, as well as tackle the extreme inequalities that cause societies to fragment. Biophilia provides a deep mindset of ecological connection, stewardship and resilience through which we can create regenerative economies that no longer overshoot the biophysical limits of the planet.[46] Finally, history tells us that a crisis, when amplified by social movements that are inspired by powerful new ideas, can ignite the rapid, transformative policy change we so urgently need. We know what it will take to bend rather than break. And that is a beginning.

Conclusion

Five Reasons for Radical Hope

If the present seems an irrevocable fact of nature, the past is most usable
as a way of suggesting possibilities we would never otherwise consider;
it can both warn and inspire.

– *Howard Zinn, 'Historian as Citizen', 1966*[1]

How far back in history are our imaginations able to reach? It is
a crucial skill if we are to escape from present realities. But we
seem to be suffering from something akin to what ecologists call
'shifting baseline syndrome'. This is a phenomenon where the current state of the living world – be it fish stocks or forest cover – is
measured with reference to a baseline that typically corresponds
with what was considered 'normal' during the researcher's early
career or childhood. Over time, each succeeding generation re-
defines the state of normality, and the earlier – and usually more
abundant – conditions get forgotten. When such recent baselines are
used, the result can be a serious underestimation of long-term
decline: nobody alive today remembers the teeming shoals of mack-
erel or vast size of cod off the British coastline in the eighteenth
century, before the onset of large-scale ocean trawling. In effect, the
extent of depletion gets masked. Shifting baseline syndrome is a
kind of creeping memory loss that can ultimately lead to ecological
devastation.

I believe that shifting baseline syndrome is also at work in the
realm of human affairs: what we consider normal, or even just

possible, is typically limited to what we have encountered within our own lifetimes. Most people find it difficult to imagine any form of democracy other than the representative system they have grown up knowing, or any means of running our economies other than through neoliberal markets. With each generation we move further and further away from the cornucopia of ways that our forebears organised their societies. The consequence: humankind is suffering from a collective failure of historical imagination (especially those of us living in the Global North).

This book is intended as a remedy. The array of historical cases it has presented – summarised in the table below – is an attempt to break through the false baseline of our own memories. It reconnects us with the vast richness and variety of possibilities that have appeared over the course of the last millennium, and reveals how they shed light on the most urgent challenges facing humanity in the twenty-first century.

What kind of message does this journey through history convey? It certainly does not provide definitive 'lessons' or formulas for the future. There are no iron laws of history, there are no fixed patterns that cross boundaries of geography and time. Searching for them is an exercise in futility. Ultimately, nothing in history is inevitable until it happens.

But once we open our minds to the landscape of the past, there is so much to rediscover that still resonates today. On the one hand are the warnings, those episodes such as European colonialism or inter-war fascism, which we must be wary of repeating. Yet history is also replete with inspiration we can draw on to face the multiple crises of our times. It is essential to remember what went right as much as what went wrong.

That is not to say that human history is a cause for rosy optimism about the future: there have been too many wars and genocides, too

Challenges

Selected cases from the last 1000 years

Challenges	1000 CE	1500	1700	1900	2000 CE
Fossil fuels			Caribbean slave revolts	Captain Swing rebellion, UK	Civil Rights Movement
Tolerance	Islamic kingdom of Al-Andalus			Chinese immigration, USA	Ghana nation-building
Consumerism		Quaker simple living	Circular economy in Edo, Japan		Rationing in World War Two
Social media		Printing revolution	Georgian coffee house culture	Development of mass media	
Water	Chinese water governance		Valencia Tribunal of Waters		Six Day War, Middle East
Democracy	Djenné-Djeno Mali	Italian city-states	Rhaetian Free State, Switzerland	Igbo governance, Nigeria	
Genetic engineering		Medieval alchemy	Land enclosures in Britain	Eugenics movement	Polio vaccine campaign
Inequality		Black Death in Europe		Kerala women's movements, India	Finnish welfare state
Artificial intelligence		Spanish colonialism	Dutch financial capitalism	Industrial revolution	Emilia-Romagna cooperatives
Civilisational breakdown	North African dynastic collapse		Pre-industrial nature relations	Carbon energy escalation	Cuban literacy campaign

much oppression and greed, too much infighting and myopic short-termism, to believe that we will easily rise to challenges such as the climate emergency or wisely manage the risks of artificial intelligence. Yet there is good cause for what I have described in this book as 'radical hope'. Unlike the glass-half-fulness of optimism that says everything will turn out fine, radical hope is about recognising that the chances may be slim and the odds against you, but still being driven to act by the values and vision you are rooted in. As the historian Howard Zinn wrote, we should aspire to a collective credo of 'as if': to always act as if change were possible.[2] Because it just might well be. And do we really want to live with the regret of not having tried?

So let me offer five reasons for radical hope, drawn from the history explored in this book, which can inspire the transformative action we need to navigate an age of turbulence.

1. Disruptive Movements Can Change the System

Disruption works. Time and again, human beings have risen up together in solidarity to demand change – from the rebellions of enslaved people in the Caribbean in the nineteenth century to movements against caste oppression in India and the women's organisations that fought for equal rights in Britain and Finland. One of the secrets of success has been the role played by 'radical flank' movements, whose militant and sometimes illegal tactics have helped shift the terms of public debate and amplified existing crises to a point where those in power have felt compelled to respond. As humanity pursues a course of ecological self-termination, where the window for changing course becomes ever smaller, it would be reckless to rely on the low flame of gradualism. Instead, we need the fiery spark of collective disruption.

2. 'We' Can Prevail over 'Me'

History bears out the deep evolutionary story that *Homo sapiens* are not simply driven by individualistic goals but are social animals with an extraordinary capacity for cooperation, empathy and mutual aid. In the right conditions, 'we' prevails over 'me'. Just think of Valencia's ancient Tribunal of Waters, whose commons principles still enable sharing of their most precious resource. Or the cities that nurtured cultural tolerance in the medieval kingdom of al-Andalus. Or the conversations between strangers that flourished in the coffeehouses of Georgian London. Or the soup kitchens that sprang up following the San Francisco earthquake. Ibn Khaldun's ideal of *asabiya* – 'group feeling' – is an invisible thread that runs through human history, binding us to one another. The question that remains is not just whether we can maintain it in the face of pressures such as economic insecurity and increasing migration, but whether we can extend such solidarity to both future generations and the rest of the living world.

3. There Are Alternatives to Capitalism

Capitalism lies at the root of so many contemporary crises, from the fossil-fuelled industrialisation and consumerism that is pushing our planet over the brink, to the finance-focused corporations propelling the AI and biotech revolutions with scant regard for the extreme risks. Yet we retain a disturbing failure to imagine any feasible alternative and instead retreat into a capitalism modified by adjectives, seeking to make it 'conscious', 'sustainable', 'inclusive' or 'green'. History encourages us to consider the viable and vibrant alternatives. The economy of eighteenth-century Japan was driven not by the capitalist imperative of endless growth but was a regenerative economy founded on principles of radical circularity and sustainable resource use. The deep-rooted cooperative economy of Emilia-Romagna provides a model of distributed ownership that stands in contrast to shareholder capitalism, promoting social justice and intergenerational stewardship. The 'entrepreneurial state' demonstrates the capacity of governments not just to provide essential public services, but to innovate in areas such as medical research and digital technology without dependence on commercial incentives. There are economic possibilities beyond capitalism.

4. Humans Are Social Innovators

Civilisations are not simply driven by technological innovation: some of humanity's greatest advances have been just as much in the realm of social innovation. Our forebears pioneered multiple ways of organising to survive crises, tackle injustices and live peacefully together. They invented social movements. They discovered how communally to manage common-pool resources such as woodlands and fisheries. They built cities in which to live and work and play. Their innovations included the public sphere – a space for open political discussion and fostering citizenship – as well as ideals such as the common good, which inspired actions like the campaign to eradicate polio. So let's not simply look to technologies to save us, or to great leaders or powerful gods. Let us look to each other, to people's ingenious ability to work together to solve problems, inspired by our collective values.

5. Other Futures Are Possible

In an age that feels increasingly apocalyptic, when our political institutions and economic systems are flailing in the face of a cluster of crises, history can help widen our horizons. It tells us that it doesn't have to be this way. If our ancestors learned to do things differently in the past, then maybe we can too. That is reason enough for radical hope. A prime example is representative democracy, which is systematically failing to deal not just with the ecological crisis, but with a multitude of other issues from growing inequality to far-right populism. While it may seem hard to envision a better alternative, history is rich with possibilities. We might turn for inspiration to the great communal democracies of the past – classical Athens, the city of Djenné-Djeno and the Rhaetian Free State in Switzerland – which offered their citizens a far more participatory form of politics than our occasional visits to the ballot box. History enables us to break out of the straitjacket of the present, so we can envision a plurality of futures.

So where to go from here? The renowned Canadian environmentalist David Suzuki warns against the danger of what he calls 'hopium' – mere hope without action.[3] He is right to do so. At a personal level, history can do much more than help us realise that there is hope for transformative change: it can also spur us to become one of the changemakers ourselves. Whether in our communities, or workplaces, or anywhere else where we may want to make a difference, we can look to the past as an array of possibilities. From joining a protest movement or setting up a cooperative enterprise to taking part in a citizens' assembly, history reminds us that we are part of great traditions of active citizenship that stretch back far into the past.

My hope is that we can also educate ourselves in the value of applied history. There are already some university courses dedicated to it, but imagine if school students too had history classes exploring how the topics they covered might offer insights into the challenges of the present.[4] Imagine if you could visit a Museum of Applied History, with exhibits that looked at contemporary issues through the lens of the past, revealing both warnings and inspiration, and without succumbing to rose-tinted nostalgia. And imagine if politicians, activists and changemakers of all kinds gave a seat in their discussions to the voice of our ancestors from different epochs and countries and cultures – perhaps an actual chair, as they do for future generations in many municipal authorities across Quebec.[5] What advice might they offer? What wisdom might they share?

Humanity needs to look backwards in order to move forwards. History has the power to crack through the baseline of our imaginations, opening our minds to the inspiring possibilities of the past that lie buried like some lost treasure. There is good reason to fear that we will not meet the challenges of our age: we may respond to crises far too late, or succumb to the risks of runaway technologies. But with history as a guide, there are just as strong grounds for believing that we can create a civilisation that bends rather than breaks as we confront the turbulence of the twenty-first century. It is time to draw on history for tomorrow, and turn radical hope into action.

Thanks

In a book about the power of human solidarity throughout history, it seems only right to stress the extent to which its creation has been a collective endeavour.

My foremost debt is to the hundreds of historians and other experts whose research I have relied upon, from specialists in witchcraft in sixteenth-century Germany to water management in Qing dynasty China. Without their scholarship, writing this book would have been impossible.

I am also hugely grateful to the array of academics, policymakers, friends and colleagues who gave comments on the manuscript, including those who attended a series of 'Kitchen Seminars' in my home, where we discussed and debated early chapter drafts. None of them is responsible for the final content but all of them made valuable contributions. They include: Judith Herrin, Michael Wood, Anthony Barnett, Sarah Knott, Hélène Neveu Kringelbach, Emily Jones, Kevin Watkins, Rebecca Fox, Al-hassan Adam, Kate Sahan, Erinch Sahan, Sophia Swithern, Dianali Rodríguez Fernández, George Marshall, Liz Goold, Caspar Henderson, Annalise Moser, Phil Mann, Rebecca Abrams, Mariana Zahar Ribeiro, Peter David Pedersen, Geoff Baker, Xander Cansell, Luciano de Castro Silva and Sasha Abramsky. I also received help and advice from: George Monbiot, Morten Kringelbach, Tom Chatfield, Gijs van Hensbergen, Jerrilynn Dodds, Shoukei Matsumoto, David Kelly, Lucy Forman, Daan Roovers, Jan Rosenow, Dirk Holemans, Tim Davies and Graham Smith. My regular morning coffee sessions with Ken Palmer were an especially important part of the writing and thinking process.

I feel incredibly lucky to have such a wonderful editor at Ebury (Penguin Random House UK), Suzanne Connelly, who (once again) has provided the perfect combination of superb structural advice, intellectual insight and personal support during my three years of working on this book. My big thanks to the whole team at Ebury who have helped launch the book into the world, including Jamie Joseph and Jessica Patel (editorial), Laura Nicol (publicity), Howard Watson (copyediting), Ben Murphy (index), Ross Jamieson (proofreading) and everyone in the international rights team. Sophia Blackwell sharpened the text with her excellent editorial suggestions. Dan Mogford created the brilliant cover design and Ruurd Priester designed the elegant graphics.

My agent Maggie Hanbury has been there as always, offering wise guidance from beginning to end. Special thanks to Alicia Carey and Hawkwood Centre for Future Thinking for offering me a much-needed writing residency in beautiful surroundings.

My partner Kate Raworth has been a constant companion throughout the journey of writing this book, helping me hone the ideas, sculpt the words and find direction when I wavered. Our children Siri and Cas have been there too, having now come of age as sharp-eyed and sharp-minded editorial advisors.

Finally, a dedication to my stepmother Anna Maria Njiradi Krznaric, who died when this book was just a kernel of an idea. I hope that *History for Tomorrow* honours her belief that history is not simply a means of understanding the past but a way of reimagining our relationship with the future.

History is the witness of time, the light of truth, the essence of remembrance,
the teacher of life, the messenger from times past.

– *Marcus Tullius Cicero*

Endnotes

Introduction: Looking Backwards to Find a Way Forwards

1 For overviews of the field, see Harm Kaal and Jelle van Lottum, 'Applied History: Past, Present, and Future', *Journal of Applied History* 3/1–2 (December 2021), https://doi.org/10.1163/25895893-bja10018; Pamela Cox, 'The Future Uses of History', *History Workshop Journal* 75/1 (2013), https://doi.org/10.1093/hwj/dbs007; John Tosh, 'In Defence of Applied History', *History and Policy* (February 2006). Prominent contemporary scholars who draw lessons from the past for today's world include Timothy Snyder, Angela Davis, Ha-Joon Chang, Ibram X. Kendi and Jared Diamond. A particular champion of applied history is Niall Ferguson, who has written an Applied History Manifesto, co-authored with Graham Allison: https://www.belfercenter.org/publication/applied-history-manifesto.

2 This quote originally appears in Goethe's *West-Eastern Diwan* (1819), Book 5, Section XV. The English translation quoted here can be found in Charles Needham, 'Finding the Ethical Standard of Medical Science in the Age of Sciences', *Journal of Evaluation in Clinical Practice* 5/1 (1999), https://doi.org/10.1046/j.1365-2753.1999.00166.x.

3 Robert Kennedy, *Thirteen Days: A Memoir of the Cuban Missile Crisis* (Signet, 1969), p. 127.

4 Margaret MacMillan, *The Uses and Abuses of History* (Profile, 2010), p. 161; Richard Neustadt and Ernest May, *Thinking in Time: The Uses of History for Decision Makers* (The Free Press, 1986), pp. 7–16, 44; Serhii Plokhy, *Nuclear Folly: A New History of the Cuban Missile Crisis* (Penguin, 2021), pp. 103, 147–8, 178, 185; Andre Pagliarini, 'The Book That Stopped the Outbreak of War', *The New Republic*, 16 April 2021, https://newrepublic.com/article/162058/book-stopped-outbreak-nuclear-war. It is worth noting that Tuchman's explanations for the outbreak of the First World War are now contested. Nevertheless, her interpretation had a major impact on President Kennedy.

5 https://www.gutenberg.org/files/15000/15000-h/15000-h.htm.

6 Howard Zinn, *A People's History of the United States* (Harper Perennial, 1995), p. 622. See also the essays in Howard Zinn, *On History* (Seven Stories Press, 2011).

7 I have explored conceptual models of historical change in Roman Krznaric, 'How Change Happens: Interdisciplinary Perspectives for Human Development', Oxfam GB, 2007.

8 Important sources on civilisational collapse and global risk include: Joseph Tainter, *The Collapse of Complex Societies* (Cambridge University Press, 1988); Jared Diamond, *Collapse: How Societies Choose or Fail to Survive* (Penguin, 2011); Hugo Bardi, *The Seneca Effect: Why Growth is Slow but Collapse is Rapid* (Springer, 2017); Sandrine Dixson-Declève et al., *Earth for All: A Survival Guide for Humanity* (New Society Publishers, 2022); Graeme Cumming and Gary Peterson, 'Unifying Research on Social-Ecological Resilience and Collapse', *Trends in Ecology and Evolution* 32/9 (2017); Tim Lenton et al., 'Operationalising positive tipping points towards global sustainability', *Global Sustainability* 5 (2022), https://doi.org/10.1017/sus.2021.30; Brian Fagan and Nadia Durrani, *Climate Chaos: Lessons on Survival from Our Ancestors* (Public Affairs, 2021); Toby Ord, *The Precipice: Existential Risk and the Future of Humanity* (Bloomsbury, 2020). This research has been cross-checked with survey data, such as the *Global Risks Report* published annually by the World Economic Forum, which surveys hundreds of experts on future risks and global trends.

9 My most directly historical book, *The Wonderbox: Curious Histories of How to Live* (Profile, 2011), explores the inspiration we can find in the past for the struggles of everyday life, from work and time to love and death. Much of my perspective on history has been influenced by the cultural historian Theodore Zeldin, with whom I worked for several years, who helped me understand just how much of who we are today – our ambitions, passions and fears – has been shaped by the past.

10 MacMillan, *Uses and Abuses of History*, pp. 86–8.

11 Methodologically, I draw on three approaches common among applied historians for learning from the past. First, *genealogy*, which asks of the contemporary phenomenon in question (such as our fossil fuel-intensive lifestyles or the risks of artificial intelligence): what's the deep story of how this happened, going back decades or centuries? Second, *analogy*, which explores: how is it similar or different to other moments in the past? Third, *pattern*, which draws on the insights of systems thinking and asks: does it display system-level patterns such as feedback loops, cycles or tipping points? For discussions, see Neustadt and May, *Thinking in Time*, pp. 196–211, 232–46; John Tosh, *Why History Matters* (Palgrave, 2008), pp. 46–8, 61–77; MacMillan, *Uses and Abuses of History*, pp. 15–16, 155–64; Eric Hobsbawm, *On History* (Abacus, 1998), p. 41; Donella Meadows, *Thinking in Systems: A Primer* (Earthscan, 2009); Will Durant and Ariel Durant, *The Lessons of History* (Simon & Schuster, 2010).

12 A conference on Applied History at Stanford University in 2018 was roundly criticised for featuring 30 white men – and no women – as speakers: https://www. nytimes.com/2018/03/17/us/stanford-conference-white-males.html. There is also a strong tendency among applied historians to focus on seeking insights from history for public policy, especially international relations and diplomacy. There is enormous potential for this to be widened to include other realms such as the strategies of social movements.

13 Abeba Birhane, 'Algorithmic Colonization of Africa', *SCRIPT-ed* 17/2 (August 2020), https://script-ed.org/article/algorithmic-colonization-of-africa/; Kehinde Andrews, *The New Age of Empire: How Racism and Colonialism Still Rule the World* (Allen Lane, 2021).

1: Breaking the Fossil Fuel Addiction

1 Michael Taylor, *The Interest: How the British Establishment Resisted the Abolition of Slavery* (Vintage, 2021), p. 59.

2 Adam Hochschild, *Bury the Chains: The British Struggle to Abolish Slavery* (Pan Books, 2005), p. 324.

3 Taylor, *Interest*, pp. 63, 104, 133; 'The Correspondence Between John Gladstone and James Cropper' (West India Association, 1824), pp. 19–20, https:// westindiacommittee.org/historyheritageculture/wp-content/uploads/2021/12/ The-correspondence-between-John-Gladstone-and-James-Cropper.pdf.

4 Andrews, *New Age of Empire*, p. 56.

5 Anonymous, 'An Attempt to Strip Negro Emancipation of Its Difficulties as Well as Its Terrors' (printed for J.M. Richardson et al., 1824); see also Taylor, *Interest*, p. 118.

6 Van Beurden's comments at the 2021 TED conference can be found at: https:// www.ted.com/talks/countdown_summit_decarbonizing_fossil_fuels.

7 Van Beurden's successor, Wael Sawan, has made similar arguments: https://www. bbc.co.uk/news/business-66108553.

8 For a discussion of the complex similarities and differences between slavery and the carbon economy, see Jean-François Mouhot, 'Past Connections and Present Similarities in Slave Ownership and Fossil Fuel Usage', *Climate Change* 105 (2011), https://doi.org/10.1007/s10584-010-9982-7; Eric Beinhocker, 'I Am a Carbon Abolitionist', *Democracy*, 24 June 2019; Chris Hayes, 'The New Abolitionism', *Nation*, 22 April 2014.

9 https://www.statista.com/statistics/264699/worldwide-co2-emissions/.

10 https://ourworldindata.org/renewable-energy.

11 Lenton et al., 'Operationalising positive tipping points', p. 1; https://www.unep. org/news-and-stories/press-release/cut-global-emissions-76-percent-every-year-next-decade-meet-15degc. Some studies provide a higher figure of around

15 per cent for the required annual decline in greenhouse gas emissions: https://www.carbonbrief.org/unep-1-5c-climate-target-slipping-out-of-reach. On the decline of emissions during COVID, see https://www.nature.com/articles/d41586-021-00090-3.

12 https://www.statista.com/chart/23046/carbon-neutrality-in-china/.

13 Vaclav Smil, *Energy and Civilization: A History* (MIT Press, 2018), p. 395; Clay McShane and Joe Tarr, *The Horse in the City: Living Machines in the Nineteenth Century* (Johns Hopkins University Press, 2007), p. 166.

14 According to energy efficiency expert Jan Rosenow, 'After 30 years of public support and multiple pilot projects, CCS has little to show.' Jan Rosenow and Richard Lowes, 'Will blue hydrogen lock us into fossil fuels forever?', *One Earth* 4/11 (2021): 1527–9.

15 This had long been Wilberforce's position. See Taylor, *Interest*, pp. 24–6, 189.

16 David Olusoga, *Black and British: A Forgotten History* (Macmillan, 2016), p. 229. See also Taylor, *Interest*, p. 197.

17 Taylor, *Interest*, p. 203. David Olusoga takes a slightly different view than Taylor, stressing the revolt's origins in the sit-down strike rather than in a planned rebellion. See Olusoga, *Black and British*, p. 228.

18 Hochschild, *Bury the Chains*, p. 341.

19 https://www.youtube.com/watch?v=7CSRN_qO2jM.

20 Hochschild, *Bury the Chains*, p. 344; Taylor, *Interest*, pp. 230, 250–4, 274; Christopher Brown, 'Later, Not Now', *London Review of Books* 43/14 (15 July 2021).

21 Andrews, *New Age of Empire*, pp. 58, 82.

22 Hochschild, *Bury the Chains*, p. 351. Similarly, Tom Zoellner argues that, 'The story of the Jamaican revolution suggests that methods of calculated revolutionary action transcend historical periods', https://www.zocalopublicsquare.org/2020/05/28/jamaican-uprising-samuel-sharpe-rebellion-christmas-uprising-great-jamaican-slave-revolt/ideas/essay/.

23 Toke Aidt and Raphaël Franck, 'Democratization Under the Threat of Revolution: Evidence from the Great Reform Act of 1832', *Econometrica* 83/2 (2015): 507, 514.

24 Eric Hobsbawm and George Rudé, *Captain Swing* (Verso, 2014), pp. 139–41, 281–97.

25 Daron Acemoglu and James A. Robinson, *Economic Origins of Dictatorship and Democracy* (Oxford University Press, 2006), p. 26.

26 Aidt and Franck, 'Democratization Under the Threat of Revolution', p. 542.

27 Taylor, *Interest*, pp. 253, 274; Hochschild, *Bury the Chains*, p. 343.

28 Herbert Haines, 'Radical Flank Effects', in David A. Snow et al. (eds), *Wiley Blackwell Encyclopedia of Social and Political Movements*, vol. 2 (John Wiley & Sons, 2013), pp. 1048–50; Todd Schifeling and Andrew J. Hoffman, 'Bill McKibben's

Influence on US Climate Change Discourse: Shifting Field-Level Debates Through Radical Flank Effects', *Organization and Environment* 32/3 (2019): 216, https://doi.org/10.1177/1086026617744278.

29 See, for instance, Malcolm X with Alex Haley, *The Autobiography of Malcolm X* (Grove Press, 1965), and Angela Davis, *An Autobiography* (Random House, 1974).

30 Herbert Haines, *Black Radicals and the Civil Rights Mainstream, 1954–1970* (University of Tennessee Press, 1988), pp. 159–64.

31 https://open.library.okstate.edu/introphilosophy/chapter/letter-from-the-birmingham-city-jail/.

32 Andreas Malm, *How to Blow Up a Pipeline* (Verso, 2021), pp. 48–9.

33 Quoted in Diane Atkinson, *Rise Up, Women! The Remarkable Lives of the Suffragettes* (Bloomsbury, 2018), p. 362.

34 June Purvis, 'Did Militancy Help or Hinder the Granting of Women's Suffrage in Britain?', *Women's History Review* 28/7 (2019), https://doi.org/10.1080/09612025.2019.1654638.

35 Malm, *How to Blow Up a Pipeline*, pp. 50–9. Radical flank organisations appear across the political spectrum and on multiple issues, including in far-right politics and the pro-choice movement in the United States.

36 Erica Chenoweth and Maria Stephan, *Why Civil Resistance Works: The Strategic Logic of Nonviolent Campaigns* (Columbia University Press, 2011), p. 43; Haines, 'Radical Flank Effects', p. 1048.

37 Erica Chenoweth and Kurt Schock, 'Do Contemporaneous Armed Challenges Affect the Outcomes of Mass Nonviolent Campaigns?', *Mobilization: An International Quarterly* 20 (2015), p. 443, https://doi.org/10.17813/1086-671x-20-4-427; https://web.archive.org/web/20150320024433/http://anc.org.za.

38 Chenoweth and Stephan, *Why Civil Resistance Works*, p. 7; Erica Chenoweth, 'The Success of Non-Violent Resistance', TEDx Boulder, 2013, https://www.youtube.com/watch?v=YJSehRlU34w.

39 The apparent failure of radical flank movements is discussed more explicitly in Chenoweth and Schock, 'Do Contemporaneous Armed Challenges Affect the Outcomes of Mass Nonviolent Campaigns?', pp. 428–30, though note that their analysis focuses primarily on the negative impacts of armed resistance struggles rather than unarmed direct action movements such as Extinction Rebellion or Just Stop Oil.

40 On the widespread influence of Chenoweth and Stephan's book, see https://www.bbc.com/future/article/20190513-it-only-takes-35-of-people-to-change-the-world.

41 In a recent article, Erica Chenoweth herself acknowledged the weakness of this comparison and questioned the relevance of the 3.5 per cent threshold: 'But there are several limitations to applying the 3.5 per cent rule specifically to the climate

movement. First, the rule has been created from looking at historical cases in which people were trying to topple their own governments. These people were not necessarily pursuing policy reform, much less trying to coordinate durable international change', Erica Chenoweth, 'People Power', in Greta Thunberg (ed.), *The Climate Book* (Allen Lane, 2022), p. 366. In contrast to Chenoweth and Stephan's advocacy of peaceful movements, there is also a growing literature arguing that 'unarmed collective violence' (including damaging private property) has positive impacts on social movement outcomes. See, for example, Mohammad Ali Kadivar and Neil Ketchley, 'Sticks, Stones and Molotov Cocktails: Unarmed Collective Violence and Democratization', *Socius* 4 (2018), https://doi.org/10.1177%2F2378023118773614.

42 For a summary of recent studies on the benefits of a radical flank, including the positive impacts of organisations such as Extinction Rebellion and Just Stop Oil, see Brett Simpson, Robb Willer and Matthew Feinberg, 'Radical Flanks of Social Movements Can Increase Support for Moderate Factions', *PNAS Nexus* 1/3 (2022), https://doi.org/10.1093/pnasnexus/pgac110; Ozden and Glover 2022; https://earth.org/grassroots-campaigns-can-influence-climate-policy-extinction-rebellion/.

43 James Ozden and Sam Glover, 'Protest Movements: How Effective Are They?', Social Change Lab (2022), pp. 9–10, https://commonslibrary.org/protest-movements-how-effective-are-they/.

44 https://nltimes.nl/2023/10/10/mp-majority-favor-potential-phase-fossil-fuel-subsidies.

45 Extinction Rebellion's positioning as a radical flank organisation has been subject to some discussion. According to one of its leading figures, Rupert Read, it was 'founded as a radical flank to the existing environmental movement, to pull the whole debate more in the kind of direction it needed to be pulled in'. In April 2023, however, it experimented with a more moderate strategy of mass mobilisation in its The Big One protest in London, which emphasised broad coalition building with trade unions, racial justice campaigners and mainstream environmental groups such as Friends of the Earth, rather than more classic radical flank strategies such as getting large numbers of people arrested for disruptive actions. At the time of writing, it is unclear whether it will continue with this more moderate approach. In the eyes of the mass media, XR is still identified as a disruptive radical flank organisation like Just Stop Oil. See 'Radical Flank or Moderate Flank: Roger Hallam and Rupert Read Dialogue on Movement Strategy', https://www.youtube.com/watch?v=eVhpcpJcNkQ.

46 https://forum.effectivealtruism.org/posts/YDtsGHmDJMsAWB7Wt/disruptive-climate-protests-in-the-uk-didn-t-lead-to-a-loss#Likelihood_of_Engaging_in_Activism; Ozden and Glover, 'Protest Movements'.

47 https://www.tiktok.com/@greenpeaceuk/video/7237112736449088794; https://
www.theguardian.com/sport/2023/jul/06/lewis-hamilton-backs-peaceful-just-stop-
oil-protest-at-british-grand-prix; https://www.ft.com/content/
4a0ab6f3-83fc-4e89-b6a2-c05c85f3791b.

48 Abbie Hoffman, *The Autobiography of Abbie Hoffman* (Four Walls Eight Windows,
2000), p. 64.

49 Chenoweth and Stephan, *Why Civil Resistance Works*, p. 13.

50 https://www.theguardian.com/environment/2022/mar/18/tyre-extinguishers-
deflating-suv-tyres-as-a-form-of-climate-action. The Tyre Extinguishers may have
been inspired by an earlier organisation in Sweden – see Malm, *How to Blow Up a
Pipeline*, pp. 79–80. The figure of 12,000 deflated tyres is based on a personal
communication with activists.

51 Zinn, *On History*, p. 39.

52 https://www.un.org/press/en/2022/sgsm21228.doc.htm; https://media.un.org/en/
asset/k1x/k1xcijxjhp.

53 Jay Griffiths, *Why Rebel* (Penguin, 2021), p. 4.

2: Nurturing Tolerance

1 Felicita Tramontana, 'Five Lessons History Can Teach Us About Migration',
Warwick Knowledge Centre, 14 August 2018, https://warwick.ac.uk/
newsandevents/knowledgecentre/arts/history/migration.

2 Hein de Haas, Stephen Castles and Mark Miller, *The Age of Migration: International
Population Movements in the Modern World* (Guilford, 2019), p. 7; https://www.
un.org/en/development/desa/population/migration/data/estimates2/estimates19.
asp; https://www.unhcr.org/uk/admin/hcspeeches/48873def4/people-move-
challenges-displacement-21st-century-international-rescue-committee.html;
https://publications.iom.int/system/files/pdf/wmr_2020.pdf; https://www.unhcr.
org/uk/about-unhcr/who-we-are/figures-glance.

3 https://reliefweb.int/report/world/climate-migrants-might-reach-one-billion-2050;
https://www.pnas.org/content/117/21/11350; Gaia Vince, *Nomad Century: How to
Survive the Climate Upheaval* (Allen Lane, 2022), pp. xi, xvi.

4 Leo Lucassen and Felicita Tramontana, 'Migration in Historical Perspective',
OpenDemocracy, 11 August 2017, https://www.opendemocracy.net/en/can-
europe-make-it/migration-in-historical-perspective/.

5 Parag Khanna, *Move: How Mass Migration Will Reshape the World – and What It
Means for You* (Weidenfeld & Nicolson, 2021), pp. 29–45.

6 Afroditi-Maria Koulaxi, 'Convivial reflexivity in the changing city – a tale of
hospitality or hostility?', *International Journal of Cultural Studies* 25/2 (2021): 5,
https://doi.org/10.1177/13678779211055490.

7 Theodore Zeldin, *An Intimate History of Humanity* (Minerva, 1995), p. 272.

8 https://www.smithsonianmag.com/blogs/smithsonian-center-folklife-cultural-heritage/2021/04/20/chinese-poetry-angel-island-immigration-station/.

9 http://www.cetel.org/1854_hall.html.

10 Sven Lindqvist, *The Skull Measurer's Mistake – and Other Portraits of Men and Women Who Spoke Out Against Racism* (The New Press, 1997), pp. 72–3. See also the excellent Bill Moyers documentary series, *Becoming American – The Chinese Experience* (2003), https://www.youtube.com/watch?v=1IkDn08i-A4.

11 Andrew Gyory, *Closing the Gate: Race, Politics, and the Chinese Exclusion Act* (University of North Carolina, 1998); Robert Chang, 'The Dark History of the Chinese Exclusion Act', TED-Ed (2021), https://www.youtube.com/watch?v=2K88pWCimZg; Gary Okihiro, *The Columbia Guide to Asian American History* (Columbia University Press, 2001), Chapter 4.

12 John Kuo Wei Tchen and Dylan Yeats, *Yellow Peril! An Archive of Anti-Asian Fear* (Verso, 2014), pp. 7–16; Lindqvist, *Skull Measurer's Mistake*, pp. 114–15; https://www.gutenberg.org/files/173/173-h/173-h.htm.

13 Kevin Scott Wong, *Americans First: Chinese Americans and the Second World War* (Harvard University Press, 2005), p. 70.

14 Lisa Kiang et al., 'Moving Beyond the Model Minority', *Asian American Journal of Psychology* 8/1 (2017): 3. On the complex relations between Asian Americans and African Americans, see Saemyi Park, 'Asian Americans' Perception of Intergroup Commonality with Blacks and Latinos: The Roles of Group Consciousness, Ethnic Identity, and Intergroup Contact', *Social Sciences* 10/11 (2021): 441, https://doi.org/10.3390/socsci10110441.

15 https://www.searac.org/wp-content/uploads/2020/02/SEARAC_NationalSnapshot_PrinterFriendly.pdf; https://www.nbcnews.com/news/asian-america/chinese-migrants-are-coming-us-foot-officials-say-rcna77244.

16 https://www.bbc.co.uk/news/world-us-canada-56218684.

17 Robert S. Chang, 'Whitewashing Precedent: From the Chinese Exclusion Case to Korematsu to the Muslim Travel Ban', *Case Western Reserve Law Review* 68/4 (2018), https://heinonline.org/HOL/LandingPage?handle=hein.journals/cwrlrv68&div=53&id=&page=.

18 https://www.washingtonpost.com/news/fact-checker/wp/2015/07/08/donald-trumps-false-comments-connecting-mexican-immigrants-and-crime/; https://time.com/4386240/donald-trump-immigration-arguments/; https://www.theatlantic.com/entertainment/archive/2019/08/trump-immigrant-invasion-language-origins/595579/.

19 Vogt J. Isaksen, 'The impact of the financial crisis on European attitudes toward immigration', *CMS* 7 (2019).

20 https://www.oxfordeconomics.com/resource/the-fiscal-impact-of-immigration-on-the-uk; Haas, Castles and Miller, *Age of Migration*, p. 38.

21 Marco Tabellini, 'Gifts of the Immigrants, Woes of the Natives: Lessons from the Age of Mass Migration', Harvard Business School Working Paper 19-005 (2019), https://www.hbs.edu/ris/Publication%20Files/19-005_a4261e39-175c-4b3f-969a-8e1ce818a3d8.pdf; Haas, Castles and Miller 2019, 39; Vince, *Nomad Century*, pp. 72–3.

22 Edward Gibbon, *The Decline and Fall of the Roman Empire*, vol. 6 (Methuen, 1898), pp. 28–9.

23 María Rosa Menocal, 'Culture in the Time of Tolerance: Al-Andalus as a Model for Our Own Time', *Yale Law School Occasional Papers* (2000): 11, https://openyls.law.yale.edu/bitstream/handle/20.500.13051/17668/Menocal_paper.pdf.

24 María Rosa Menocal, *The Ornament of the World: How Muslims, Jews and Christians Created a Culture of Tolerance in Medieval Spain* (Back Bay, 2002), pp. 72–4.

25 J.H. Elliott, 'A Question of Coexistence', *New York Review of Books*, 13 August 2009, https://www.nybooks.com/articles/2009/08/13/a-question-of-coexistence/.

26 Brian Catlos, *Kingdoms of Faith: A New History of Islamic Spain* (Hurst, 2018), pp. 145, 157, 167, 202, 320, 428–9; Brian Catlos, *Muslims in Medieval Latin Christendom* (Cambridge University Press, 2014), pp. 469–77, 509, 524; Robert Hillenbrand, '"The Ornament of the World": Medieval Córdoba as a Cultural Centre', in Salma Khadra Jayussi (ed.), *The Legacy of Muslim Spain*, vol. 1 (Brill, 2012); Elliott, 'Question of Coexistence'.

27 Catlos, *Kingdoms of Faith*, p. 202.

28 Menocal, 'Culture in the Time of Tolerance', p. 66.

29 Ibid.

30 R.C.H. Davis, *The Normans and Their Myth* (Thames & Hudson, 1976), pp. 8–9, 71, 75; https://www.bl.uk/collection-items/the-harley-trilingual-psalter.

31 Menocal, 'Culture in the Time of Tolerance', pp. 101–9. For other examples of such fusion in a broader historical context, see Tramontana, 'Five Lessons History Can Teach Us'.

32 See, for example, Kenneth Baxter Wolf, 'Convivencia and "The Ornament of the World"', in Connie Scarborough (ed.), *Revisiting Convivencia in Medieval and Early Modern Iberia* (Juan de la Cuesta, 2014); Dario Fernández-Morera, *The Myth of the Andalusian Paradise* (ISI, 2014); Mark Abate (ed.), *Convivencia and Medieval Spain: Essays in Honour of Thomas F. Glick* (Palgrave Macmillan, 2018); David Nirenberg, *Communities of Violence: Persecution of Minorities in the Middle Ages* (Princeton, 1996), pp. 33, 237, 245–9.

33 Even scholars who focus on violence tend to acknowledge the depth of everyday *Convivencia*. For instance, in David Nirenberg's excellent study of communal

violence in the Christian-ruled Kingdom of Aragon, he points out that 'the relations between Christians and non-Christians in the medieval Crown of Aragon were largely nonviolent', Nirenberg, *Communities of Violence*, p. 38.

34 Brian Catlos, 'Islamic Spain Ended in the 15th Century and We Still Can't Agree if It Was a Paradise or Hell?', History News Network, 6 October 2018, https://historynewsnetwork.org/article/168990.

35 Interview in the PBS television series, *The Ornament of the World* (2019), https://www.youtube.com/watch?v=aoMs783m624.

36 Nirenberg, *Communities of Violence*, pp. 38–9.

37 https://onlinelibrary.wiley.com/doi/abs/10.1111/juaf.12141; https://www.bloomberg.com/news/articles/2015-05-29/a-new-study-tries-to-determine-what-a-tolerant-city-looks-like.

38 Thomas Pettigrew and Linda R. Tropp, 'A Meta-Analytic Test of Intergroup Contact Theory', *Journal of Personality and Social Psychology* 90/5 (2006), https://doi.org/10.1037/0022-3514.90.5.751.

39 Catlos, 'Islamic Spain Ended in the 15th Century'.

40 https://www.un.org/development/desa/en/news/population/2018-revision-of-world-urbanization-prospects.html#.

41 David Birmingham, *Kwame Nkrumah: The Father of African Nationalism* (Ohio University Press, 1998), p. 51; Kofi Takyi Asante, 'Individualistic and Collectivistic Orientations: Examining the Relationship Between Ethnicity and National Attachment in Ghana', *Studies in Ethnicity and Nationalism* 20/1 (April 2020): 4, https://doi.org/10.1111/sena.12313. Nkrumah had been influenced by contact with Black socialists in the USA and Britain, which encouraged him to see politics in terms of class rather than ethnic struggles.

42 Note that Nkrumah also espoused an ideology of Pan-Africanism alongside Ghanaian nationalism: Harcourt Fuller, *Building the Ghanaian Nation-State: Kwame Nkrumah's Symbolic Nationalism* (Palgrave Macmillan, 2014), p. 4; Birmingham, *Kwame Nkrumah*, pp. 30–1, 49.

43 Paul Kwame Asamoah, 'Ethnic Conflict: A Threat to Ghana's Internal Stability – A Case Study of the Nkonya–Alavanyo Conflict in the Volta Region', doctoral dissertation, University of Oslo, 2014, p. 2, https://www02.core.ac.uk/download/pdf/30903716.pdf; Birmingham, *Kwame Nkrumah*, p. 59.

44 Although it is important to note that Ghana also ranks among the lowest in Africa on tolerance of different sexual identities and orientations: https://www.afrobarometer.org/wp-content/uploads/migrated/files/publications/Dispatches/ab_r7_dispatchno362_pap17_tolerance_in_africa_2.pdf.

45 Jeffrey Paller, *Democracy in Ghana: Everyday Politics in Urban Africa* (Cambridge University Press, 2019), pp. 212–13; Konadu Adam, Frederick Mensah-Bonsu and

Dorcas Amedorme, 'Fostering Religious Tolerance and Harmonization in Ghana: A Discussion on Efforts Made by Various Stakeholders', *E-Journal of Humanities, Arts and Social Sciences (EHASS)* 3/5 (May 2022): 185, https://doi.org/10.38159/ehass.2022352.

46 https://www.nas.gov.sg/archivesonline/data/pdfdoc/lky19650809b.pdf.

47 Selina Lim et al., 'Reconfiguring the Singapore Identity Space', *International Journal of Intercultural Relations* 43 (2014), https://doi.org/10.1016/j.ijintrel.2014.08.011.

48 Amanda Wise and Selvaraj Velayutham, 'Conviviality in Everyday Multiculturalism: Some Brief Comparisons Between Singapore and Sydney', *European Journal of Cultural Studies* 17/4 (2014): 411, https://doi.org/10.1177/1367549413510419.

49 Hong Liu and Lingli Huang, 'Paradox of Superdiversity: Contesting Racism and "Chinese Privilege" in Singapore', *Journal of Chinese Overseas* 18/2 (2022), https://doi.org/10.1163/17932548-12341468.

50 Vince, *Nomad Century*, p. 134; Claudia Finotelli and Sebastian Rinken, 'A Pragmatic Bet: The Evolution of Spain's Immigration System', Migration Policy Institute, 18 April 2023, https://www.migrationpolicy.org/article/spain-immigration-system-evolution.

51 Tilmann Heil, 'Are Neighbours Alike? Practices of Conviviality in Catalonia and Casamance', *European Journal of Cultural Studies* 17/4 (2014): 454, 547, 463, 466, https://doi.org/10.1177/1367549413510420.

3: Kicking the Consumer Habit

1 Victor Lebow, 'Price Competition in 1955', *Journal of Retailing* (Spring 1955).

2 Bon Marché was originally a small Left Bank shop founded in 1838 and which Boucicaut took over in 1863. But it wasn't until the opening of the main flagship store in 1872 that Bon Marché became a landmark retail emporium. For an excellent history, see Michael B. Miller, *The Bon Marché: Bourgeois Culture and the Department Store, 1869–1920* (George Allen & Unwin, 1981).

3 Keith Thomas, *The Ends of Life: Roads to Fulfilment in Early Modern England* (Oxford University Press, 2011), p. 142. See also Chapter 6 of my book *The Wonderbox* for a discussion of the historical origins of consumer culture.

4 Stuart Ewen, *PR! A Social History of Spin* (Basic Books, 1996), pp. 3–4.

5 On Nike's iconic 'Just Do It' campaign, see Naomi Klein, *No Logo* (Flamingo, 2001), pp. 365–79.

6 Juliet Schor, 'Towards a New Politics of Consumption', in Juliet Schor and Douglas Holt (eds), *The Consumer Society Reader* (The New Press, 2000), p. 449.

7 Jason Hickel, *Less Is More: How Degrowth Will Save the Planet* (Windmill, 2021), pp. 102, 109.

8 Kenneth Boulding, 'The Economics of the Coming Spaceship Earth', in H. Jarrett (ed.), *Environmental Quality in a Growing Economy* (Resources for the Future/ Johns Hopkins University Press, 1966), pp. 3–14.

9 Kate Raworth, *Doughnut Economics: Seven Ways to Think Like a 21st-Century Economist* (Random House Business Books, 2017), pp. 206–42.

10 David E. Shi, *The Simple Life: Plain Living and High Thinking in American Culture* (Oxford University Press, 1985), p. 39.

11 Duane Elgin, 'Voluntary Simplicity and the New Global Challenge', in Juliet Schor and Douglas Holt (eds), *The Consumer Society Reader* (The New Press, 2000), pp. 397–413.

12 James Wallman, *Stuffocation: Living More with Less* (Penguin Books, 2013), pp. 7–9.

13 https://www.theguardian.com/environment/2021/nov/07/few-willing-to-change-lifestyle-climate-survey.

14 https://yougov.co.uk/topics/society/articles-reports/2022/12/29/how-many-britons-will-attempt-vegan-diet-and-lifes.

15 https://www.statista.com/statistics/298322/chicken-broiler-slaughterings-in-the-united-kingdom-uk-by-breed/; George Monbiot, *Regenesis: Feeding the World without Devouring the Planet* (Allen Lane, 2022), pp. 39–41; https://www.monbiot.com/2015/11/19/pregnant-silence/.

16 Quoted in Nana Supriatna, 'Confronting Consumerism as a New Imperialism', *Journal of Social Studies Education* 6 (2017).

17 https://edoflourishing.blogspot.com/2014/01/recycling-and-reuse.html; Eisuke Ishikawa, *Japan in the Edo Period – An Ecologically Conscious Society* (Kodansha, 2000).

18 Azby Brown, *Just Enough: Lessons in Living Green from Traditional Japan* (Kodansha, 2010); Azby Brown, 'Building a Circular Economy: Lessons from Edo Japan', TEDx (2001), https://www.youtube.com/watch?v=zKkQ2PIjAas; Duncan Baker-Brown, *The Re-Use Atlas: A Designer's Guide Towards the Circular Economy* (RIBA, 2017); Susan Hanley, 'Urban Sanitation in Preindustrial Japan', *Journal of Interdisciplinary History* 18/1 (1987): 1–26.

19 Conrad Totman, *The Green Archipelago: Forestry in Pre-Industrial Japan* (Ohio University Press, 1998), p. 171. Note that I briefly discuss Tokugawa timber and forestry policy in my book *The Good Ancestor: How to Think Long Term in a Short-Term World* (WH Allen, 2020), pp. 104–6.

20 Totman, *Green Archipelago*, pp. 85–9, 115; Conrad Totman, *Early Modern Japan* (University of California Press, 1993), pp. 245–7. On the successes of timber rationing, see also Osamu Saito, 'Forest History and the Great Divergence: China, Japan and the West', Institute of Economic Research, Hitotsubashi University,

2008, https://warwick.ac.uk/fac/soc/economics/seminars/seminars/conferences/
econchange/programme/saito_-_venice.pdf, p. 20. Sumptuary laws linked to social
status also limited the wearing of silk clothes, the use of gold leaf in buildings and
the display of elaborate decorations at weddings, although they often proved
difficult to enforce. The first Tokugawa shogun, Ieyasu, was especially known for
advocating material frugality. See Donald H. Shively, 'Sumptuary Regulation and
Status in Early Tokugawa Japan', *Harvard Journal of Asiatic Studies* 25 (1964),
https://doi.org/10.2307/2718340.

21 Totman, *Green Archipelago*, pp. 114–5, 136, 163; Conrad Totman, 'Land-Use
Patterns and Afforestation in the Edo Period', *Monumenta Nipponica* 39/1 (1984):
4–5, https://doi.org/10.2307/2384477; Junichi Iwamoto, 'The Development of
Japanese Forestry', in Yorshiya Iwai (ed.), *Forestry and Forest Industry in Japan*
(University of British Columbia Press, 2002), p. 5. For further details on the Edo
economy, see also Roman Krznaric, 'Food Coupons and Bald Mountains: What
the History of Resource Scarcity Can Teach Us About Tackling Climate Change',
Human Development Report Office Occasional Paper 2007/63, United Nations
Development Programme (2007).

22 Sustainability designer Isao Kitabayashi first coined the term 'Edonomy'. See
https://zenbird.media/circular-edonomy-japans-original-circular-economy-model/.
'Edonomics' was by no means a perfect system. Rationing rules were often broken
and the country's large urban populations could not have been easily supported
without the overexploitation of fish stocks, especially in the northern frontier region;
Tessa Morris-Suzuki, 'Sustainability and ecological colonialism in Edo period Japan',
Japanese Studies 15/1 (1995), https://doi.org/10.1080/10371399508571520.

23 Eiichiro Ochiai, 'Japan in the Edo Period: Global Implications for a Model of
Sustainability', *Asia Pacific Journal* 5/2 (2007): 2.

24 Ishikawa, 'Japan in the Edo Period', p. 11; Brown, *Just Enough*; Brown, 'Building a
Circular Economy'.

25 The idea of 'choice editing' was pioneered by the UK's Sustainable Consumption
Roundtable in its 2006 report, 'Looking Forward, Looking Back: Lessons in
Choice Editing for Sustainability'.

26 Brown, 'Building a Circular Economy'.

27 https://www.fairphone.com/en/impact/fair-materials.

28 William McDonough and Michael Braungart, *The Upcycle: Beyond Sustainability –
Designing for Abundance* (North Point Press, 2013), p. 11.

29 Jo Williams, 'Circular Cities: Planning for Circular Development in European
Cities', *European Planning Studies* 31/1 (2022), https://doi.org/10.1080/09654313.20
22.2060707; https://www.amsterdam.nl/en/policy/sustainability/circular-economy/.

30 'The Circularity Gap Report 2023', Circle Economy, Amsterdam, 2023, https://www.circularity-gap.world/2023#download.

31 Hickel, *Less Is More*, pp. 158–9.

32 Kate Raworth, 'Towards 1.5°C Lifestyles', in Greta Thunberg (ed.), *The Climate Book* (Penguin, 2022), p. 334.

33 https://www.nature.com/articles/s41586-021-03821-8.

34 Ina Zweiniger-Bargielowska, *Austerity in Britain: Rationing, Controls and Consumption, 1939–1955* (Oxford University Press, 2000), p. 31; John Kenneth Galbraith, *A Life in Our Times* (André Deutsch, 1981), p. 127; Meg Jacobs, 'How About Some Meat?: The Office of Price Administration, Consumption Politics, and State Building from the Bottom Up, 1941–46', *Journal of American History* (December 1997): 911, 921, https://doi.org/10.2307/2953088; Geoffrey Mills and Hugh Rockoff, 'Compliance with Price Controls in the United States and the United Kingdom During World War II', *Journal of American History* 47/1 (1987), https://www.jstor.org/stable/2121945, p. 209.

35 Paul M. O'Leary, 'Wartime Rationing and Governmental Organization', *American Political Science Review* 39/6 (December 1945): 1103, https://doi.org/10.2307/1949657.

36 Thomas Piketty, *A Brief History of Equality* (Belknap Press, 2022), pp. 25–6.

37 Lewis Akenji et al., '1.5 Degree Lifestyles: Towards a Fair Consumption Space for All', Hot or Cool Institute, Berlin, 2021, pp. 94–102; https://ecocore.org/lahti-25-reduction-carbon-footprint/; Fuso F. Nerini et al., 'Personal carbon allowances revisited', *Nature Sustainability* 4 (2012), https://doi.org/10.1038/s41893-021-00756-w; Judith Deutsch, 'Lessons for the Climate Emergency: Rationing, Moratoriums, Ending War', *Bullet*, 27 June 2019.

38 https://takethejump.org/.

4: Taming Social Media

1 Marshall McLuhan, *The Gutenberg Galaxy* (University of Toronto Press, 1962), p. 1.

2 Tom Standage, *Writing on the Wall: Social Media, the First 2,000 Years* (Bloomsbury, 2013), p. 22. Standage's book is an exemplar of applied history and an important source of inspiration for this chapter.

3 Stanley Stowers, *Letter Writing in Greco-Roman Antiquity* (John Knox Press, 1989); Marcus Tullius Cicero, *The Letters of Cicero: The Whole Extant Correspondence in Chronological Order*, ed. Evelyn Shirley Shuckburgh (Legare Street Press, 2022).

4 Standage, *Writing on the Wall*, pp. 21–47; Robert Morstein-Marx, 'Political Graffiti in the Late Roman Republic: "Hidden Transcripts" and "Common Knowledge"', in Cristina Kuhn (ed.), *Politische Kommunikation und öffentliche Meinung in der antiken Welt* (Franz Steiner Verlag, 2012), pp. 191–217.

5 Marshall McLuhan, *Understanding Media* (Abacus, 1973), p. 15.

6 Elizabeth Eisenstein, *The Printing Revolution in Early Modern Europe* (Cambridge University Press, 2005), p. 176. Wooden block printing had emerged far earlier, in ninth-century China. Gutenberg's genius was to combine three technologies: individually cast metal letters, durable oil-based ink and a modified screw press.

7 Friedrich Myconius quoted in A. Skevington Wood, *Captive to the Word – Martin Luther: Doctor of Sacred Scripture* (Paternoster Press, 1969), p. 65.

8 Standage, *Writing on the Wall*, pp. 51–60; Eisenstein, *Printing Revolution*, pp. 171, 187; Mark Edwards, *Printing, Propaganda and Martin Luther* (University of California Press, 1994), pp. 14–40.

9 Eisenstein, *Printing Revolution*, p. 165.

10 Ibid., p. 176; Neil Postman, *Technopoly: The Surrender of Culture to Technology* (Vintage, 1993), p. 15.

11 Natalie Grace, 'Vermin and Devil-Worshippers: Exploring Witch Identities in Popular Print in Early Modern Germany and England', *Midlands Historical Review* 5 (2021): 2–6.

12 Lyndal Roper, *Witch Craze: Terror and Fantasy in Baroque Germany* (Yale University Press, 2006); Abaigéal Warfield, 'Witchcraft Illustrated: The Crime of Witchcraft in Early Modern German News Broadsheets', in Andrew Pettegree (ed.), *Broadsheets: Single-Sheet Publishing in the First Age of Print* (Brill, 2017), p. 459; Keith Thomas, *Religion and the Decline of Magic* (Penguin, 1973), pp. 521–3, 612.

13 https://pursuit.unimelb.edu.au/articles/bewitched-and-beguiled-by-art. See also Charles Zika, *The Appearance of Witchcraft: Print and Visual Culture in Sixteenth-Century Europe* (Routledge, 2007), pp. 2–4; Wolfgang Behringer, 'Witchcraft and the Media', in Marjorie Elizabeth Plummer (ed.), *Ideas and Cultural Margins in Early Modern Germany* (Routledge, 2009), pp. 218–19.

14 Zika, *Appearance of Witchcraft*, pp. 182–3; Behringer, 'Witchcraft and the Media', pp. 220–3; Warfield, 'Witchcraft Illustrated', pp. 461, 464; http://www.geschichte-schiltach.de/themen/aufsaetze/der-teufel-von-schiltach/der-teufel-von-schiltach.html.

15 Grace, 'Vermin and Devil-Worshippers', p. 11; Warfield, 'Witchcraft Illustrated', p. 484; Zika, *Appearance of Witchcraft*, p. 179; Thomas, *Religion and the Decline of Magic*, p. 561.

16 Some scholars point to earlier examples of fake news in the history of printing, such as bloodthirsty tales about the Transylvanian Count Dracula first published in the late fifteenth century: Brian Winston and Matthew Winston, *The Roots of Fake News: Objecting to Objective Journalism* (Routledge, 2021).

17 Behringer, 'Witchcraft and the Media', pp. 219–20; Warfield, 'Witchcraft Illustrated', p. 460; Zoey Strzelecki, 'Printing Witchcraft', *Manchester Historian*, 12 November 2014; Jon Crabb, 'Woodcuts and Witches', *Public Domain Review*, 4 May 2017.

18 Accusations of witchcraft remain common in some countries and continue to result in human rights abuses – for instance against people with albinism in several African nations – prompting the UN Human Rights Commission to pass a special resolution on the issue in July 2021, https://jogh.org/wp-content/uploads/2022/06/jogh-12-03029.pdf.

19 Zika, *Appearance of Witchcraft*, p. 9.

20 Paul Mason, *Why It's Still Kicking Off Everywhere: The New Global Revolutions* (Verso, 2013).

21 S. Schumann et al., 'Social Media Use and Support for Populist Radical Right Parties: Assessing Exposure and Selection Effects in a Two-wave Panel Study', *Information, Communication and Society* 24/7 (2019), https://doi.org/10.1080/13691 18X.2019.1668455; Paolo Gerbaudo, 'Social Media and Populism: An elective affinity', *Media, Culture and Society* 40/5 (2018), https://doi.org/10.1177/0163443718772192.

22 Paul Barrett, Justin Hendrix and J. Grant Sims, 'Fuelling the Fire: How Social Media Intensifies US Political Polarization – And What Can Be Done About It', Stern Center for Business and Human Rights, New York University, 2021.

23 https://scrapsfromtheloft.com/movies/the-social-dilemma-movie-transcript/.

24 Eisenstein, *Printing Revolution*, p. 48.

25 Steve Pincus, '"Coffee Politicians Does Create": Coffeehouses and Restoration Political Culture', *Journal of Modern History* 67/4 (1995): 813, 819, https://www.jstor.org/stable/2124756; https://www.bl.uk/restoration-18th-century-literature/articles/newspapers-gossip-and-coffee-house-culture; https://www.newstatesman.com/culture/2023/01/social-media-culture-coffeehouse-history.

26 Standage, *Writing on the Wall*, pp. 107, 109.

27 Quoted in Pincus, '"Coffee Politicians Does Create"', p. 821; Thomas Brennan, 'Coffeehouses and Cafes', in Alan Charles Kors (ed.), *Encyclopedia of the Enlightenment* (Oxford University Press, 2002).

28 https://www.spectator.co.uk/article/1711-and-all-that-the-untold-story-of-the-spectator/.

29 Jürgen Habermas, *The Structural Transformation of the Public Sphere: An Inquiry into a Category of Bourgeois Society* (Polity Press, 1992), pp. 57–60.

30 Quoted in Pincus, '"Coffee Politicians Does Create"', p. 815. See also Richard Sennett, *The Fall of Public Man* (Faber and Faber, 1986), pp. 80–2.

31 John Barrell, 'Coffee-House Politicians', *Journal of British Studies* 43/2 (2004): 206–10, https://doi.org/10.1086/380950; John Keane, *Tom Paine: A Political Life* (Bloomsbury, 2009), pp. 321, 336.

32 James Curran and Jean Seaton, *Power without Responsibility: Press, Broadcasting and the Internet in Britain* (Routledge, 2018), pp. 10–14; Jürgen Habermas, 'The Public

Sphere: An Encyclopedia Article', *New German Critique* 3 (1974): 54, https://doi.org/10.2307/487737.

33 https://www.theatlantic.com/technology/archive/2018/05/when-did-tv-watching-peak/561464/. For a fuller discussion of the rise and impact of television, see my book *Carpe Diem Regained: The Vanishing Art of Seizing the Day* (Unbound, 2017), pp. 60–7.

34 To get a sense of this utopian vision of the internet and its liberating potential, see John Perry Barlow's 1996 'Declaration of the Independence of Cyberspace', https://www.eff.org/cyberspace-independence. For a fine antidote, read Evgeny Morozov, *The Net Delusion: How Not to Liberate the World* (Allen Lane, 2011), especially Chapter 7.

35 Jürgen Habermas, 'Reflections and Hypotheses on a Further Structural Transformation of the Political Public Sphere', *Theory, Culture & Society* 39/4 (2022): 66, https://doi.org/10.1177/02632764221112341.

36 Advocates of this include Lizzie O'Shea, *Future Histories: What Ada Lovelace, Tom Paine and the Paris Commune Can Teach Us About Digital Technology* (Verso, 2019), p. 168.

37 https://medium.com/@teamwarren/heres-how-we-can-break-up-big-tech-9ad9e0da324c.

38 Azeem Azhar, *Exponential: How Accelerating Technology Is Leaving Us Behind and What to Do About It* (Random House Business, 2021), pp. 120–2.

39 Rishab Nithyanand, Brian Schaffner and Phillipa Gill, 'Online Political Discourse in the Trump Era', *arXiv* (2017), https://doi.org/10.48550/arXiv.1711.05303, pp. 1, 2, 5; https://www.newscientist.com/article/2154743-politics-chat-on-reddit-reads-like-it-was-written-by-6-year-olds/.

40 https://www.metafilter.com/guidelines.mefi.

41 https://www.statista.com/statistics/978010/coffee-shop-numbers-united-kingdom-uk/.

42 The conversation meals we organised at the Oxford Muse foundation are profiled in a BBC radio documentary called *The Art of Conversation* (2005), produced by Eka Morgan: https://www.bbc.co.uk/sounds/play/p03cgdhb.

43 http://news.bbc.co.uk/1/hi/world/middle_east/6948034.stm.

44 https://www.timesofisrael.com/education-ministry-bars-israeli-palestinian-bereavement-group-from-schools/.

45 Theodore Zeldin, *Conversation* (Harvill Press, 1998), p. 14.

46 McLuhan, *Understanding Media*, p. 26.

47 David Dunér and Christer Ahlberger (eds), *Cognitive History: Mind, Space, and Time* (De Gruyter Oldenbourg, 2019).

48 Marshall McLuhan and Quentin Fiore, *The Medium Is the Massage* (Penguin Books, 2008), pp. 44–50; Walter Ong, *Orality and Literacy: The Technologizing of the World* (Routledge, 1982), p. 121.

49 Postman, *Technopoly*, p. 65; Eisenstein, *Printing Revolution*, pp. 105–7.

50 Ong, *Orality and Literacy*, pp. 123–5; Eisenstein, *Printing Revolution*, pp. 71–81.

51 McLuhan, *Understanding Media*, p. 189.

52 McLuhan, *Gutenberg Galaxy*, pp. 22–7, 72, 125, 151, 175. The invention of the mechanical clock also contributed to the development of linear thinking, a subject I discuss in my book *The Good Ancestor*, pp. 40–4.

53 John Naughton, *From Gutenberg to Zuckerberg: What You Really Need to Know About the Internet* (Quercus, 2012), pp. 25–6.

5: Securing Water for All

1 William Ligtvoet et al., *The Geography of Future Water Challenges* (PBL Netherlands Environmental Assessment Agency, 2018), pp. 14, 39.

2 Vandana Shiva, *World Water Wars* (Sound End Press, 2002), p. 1; https://www.wri. org/insights/17-countries-home-one-quarter-worlds-population-face-extremely-high-water-stress; https://www.bbc.co.uk/news/world-42982959; https://www. rd.com/list/water-shortages-cities/.

3 https://www.wri.org/insights/ranking-worlds-most-water-stressed-countries-2040.

4 Ligtvoet et al., *Geography of Future Water Challenges*, p. 10.

5 The Chinese character *zhì* 治 appears in such modern terms as 政 治 (*zhèngzhì*: politics), 治理 (*zhìlǐ* : governance) and 法治 (*fǎzhì*: rule of law). Thanks to sinologist David Kelly for advising on this issue. See also https:// languagelog.ldc.upenn.edu/nll/?p=19251.

6 Steven Solomon, *Water: The Epic Struggle for Wealth, Power, and Civilization* (Harper Perennial, 2011), Chapter 5; Brian Fagan, *Elixir: A Human History of Water* (Bloomsbury, 2011), Chapter 12. Mark Elvin, *The Retreat of the Elephants: An Environmental History of China* (Yale University Press, 2004), pp. 117–19, questions the extent to which Chinese water management was a 'changeless bedrock of despotism', pointing out important regional variations.

7 William Rowe, *Saving the World: Chen Hongmou and Elite Consciousness in Eighteenth-Century China* (Stanford University Press, 2001), pp. 1–10, 24–44, 222–31, 453; Fagan, *Elixir*, pp. 235–8.

8 Mike Davis, *Late Victorian Holocausts: El Niño Famines and the Making of the Third World* (Verso, 2002), p. 81.

9 Ibid., pp. 67–86, 187–98. The sale of human beings and consumption of human flesh during famines in Chinese history is also documented in Elvin, *Retreat of the Elephants*, pp. 193–4, 443–4.

10 Thomas Glick, *Irrigation and Society in Medieval Valencia* (Harvard University Press, 1970), pp. 65–8; Julia Hudson-Richards and Cynthia Gonzales, 'Water as a Collective Responsibility: The Tribunal de las Aguas and the Valencian

Community', *Bulletin for Spanish and Portuguese Historical Studies* 38/1 (2013), https://asphs.net/wp-content/uploads/2020/02/Water-as-a-Collective-Responsibility.pdf.

11 Note that traditional forms of water management are under threat in some regions in Spain: https://www.bbc.com/future/article/20221011-the-moorish-invention-that-tamed-spains-mountains.

12 Elinor Ostrom, *Governing the Commons: The Evolution of Institutions of Collective Action* (Cambridge University Press, 2015 [reprint]), pp. 69–76.

13 https://research.com/scientists-rankings/political-science.

14 https://wiki.p2pfoundation.net/Water_Cooperatives.

15 David Bollier, *Think Like a Commoner: A Short Introduction to the Life of the Commons* (New Society Publishers, 2014), pp. 26–33.

16 Stephen Lansing, *Perfect Order: Recognizing Complexity in Bali* (Princeton University Press, 2006).

17 *Crafting Institutions for Self-Governing Irrigation Systems* video (1992), https://www.canr.msu.edu/resources/video-crafting-institutions-for-self-governing-irrigation-systems.

18 https://www.newyorker.com/magazine/2002/04/08/leasing-the-rain; see also the documentary *Blue Gold: World Water Wars* (2008).

19 On conflicts over water privatisation, see https://www.opendemocracy.net/en/tc-lagos-water-privatisation/; https://ourworld.unu.edu/en/water-privatisation-a-worldwide-failure. Multiple studies reveal that privatisation tends to push up the price of water. See, for example, Naren Prasad, 'Privatisation of Water: A Historical Perspective', *Law, Environment and Development* 3/2 (2007): 231–3, https://lead-journal.org/content/07217.pdf.

20 Ariel Sharon, *Warrior: An Autobiography* (Simon & Schuster, 2001).

21 Ofira Seliktar, 'Turning Water into Fire: The Jordan River as the Hidden Factor in the Six-Day War', *Middle East Review of International Affairs* 9/2 (June 2005); Brahma Chellaney, *Water, Peace, and War: Confronting the Global Water Crisis* (Rowman and Littlefield, 2015).

22 https://www.btselem.org/sites/default/files/publications/202305_parched_eng.pdf, p. 7; https://www.amnesty.org/en/latest/campaigns/2017/11/the-occupation-of-water/; https://reliefweb.int/report/occupied-palestinian-territory/allocation-water-resources-occupied-palestinian-territory; United Nations Development Programme, *Human Development Report 2006: Beyond Scarcity* (New York, 2006), p. 216.

23 Chellaney, *Water, Peace, and War*, Chapter 1.

24 Quoted in Chellaney, *Water, Peace, and War*, p. 7.

25 https://www.wri.org/insights/how-solve-water-related-conflicts.

26 Peter Gleick, Charles Iceland and Ayushi Trivedi, *Ending Conflicts Over Water: Solutions to Water and Security Challenges* (World Resources Institute, 2020), https://pacinst.org/wp-content/uploads/2020/09/Ending-Conflicts-Over-Water-Pacific-Institute-Sept-2020.pdf.

27 United Nations Development Programme, *Human Development Report 2006*, Chapter 6; https://www.independent.co.uk/climate-change/news/syria-drought-climate-change-civil-war-isis-b1947711.html; 'Global Water Wars' (2017), an episode of the National Geographic series, *Parched*, https://www.youtube.com/watch?v=A0yu7nP50rM.

28 https://www.youtube.com/watch?v=B1gPCwErTr4&t=613s.

29 https://hispagua.cedex.es/en/documentacion/noticia/82752.

30 https://ecopeaceme.org/wp-content/uploads/2021/03/A-Green-Blue-Deal-for-the-Middle-East-EcoPeace.pdf; https://www.usip.org/publications/2022/12/water-can-be-rare-win-win-israelis-palestinians-and-region; https://www.jpost.com/middle-east/article-714896.

31 Vincent Ostrom, *The Meaning of American Federalism: Constituting a Self-Governing Society* (ICS Books, 1991); Elinor Ostrom, 'A Polycentric Approach for Coping with Climate Change', World Bank Policy Research Working Paper 5095 (October 2009).

32 https://www.icpdr.org/sites/default/files/nodes/documents/lessons-from-the-danube-a-world-leader-in-transboundary-river-basin-management.pdf.

33 Jeremy Rifkin, *The Age of Resilience: Reimagining Existence on a Rewilding Earth* (Swift, 2022), pp. 201–2.

34 Tarek Majzoub and Fabienne Quilleré Majzoub, 'The Time Has Come for a Universal Water Tribunal', *Pace Environmental Law Review* 36/1 (2018), https://doi.org/10.58948/0738-6206.1822.

35 https://tragua.org/.

36 https://theconversation.com/zero-day-for-california-water-not-yet-but-unprecedented-water-restrictions-send-a-sharp-warning-173479.

37 Petri Juuti, Tapio Katko and Heikki Vuorinen, *Environmental History of Water: Global Views on Community Water Supply and Sanitation* (IWA Publishing, 2007), p. 241; Colin Ward, *Reflected in Water: A Crisis of Social Responsibility* (Cassel, 1997), Chapters 1 and 8.

6: Reviving Faith in Democracy

1 Quoted in Roderick McIntosh, *Ancient Middle Niger: Urbanism and the Self-Organizing Landscape* (Cambridge University Press, 2005), p. 9.

2 https://www.worldhistory.org/Djenne-Djenno/.

3 See Roderick McIntosh's Yale lecture, 'Why Study African Cities?', 5 July 2016, https://www.youtube.com/watch?app=desktop&v=0IJJIVEkk7A. In this lecture he

points out that, 'It's in some ways amazing that earlier colonial period archaeologists didn't go to this very large floodplain … They didn't imagine that these mounds that they saw topping it up, covered in potsherds, weren't cities as well.' Elsewhere he argues that Western society has a 'deeply rooted view of the non-Western city as despotic, depraved, and a place of bondage.' See Roderick McIntosh, 'Western Representations of Urbanism and Invisible African Towns', in Susan Keech McIntosh (ed.), *Beyond Chiefdoms: Pathways to Complexity in Africa* (Cambridge University Press, 1999), p. 56.

4　Damola Adejumo-Ayibiowu, 'Western style "democracy" in Africa is just a way of pushing the neoliberal agenda', OpenDemocracy, 6 November 2019, www. opendemocracy.net/en/oureconomy/ western-style-democracy-in-africa-is-just-a-way-of-pushing-the-neoliberal-agenda/.

5　R. McIntosh, *Ancient Middle Niger*, pp. 5, 10–14, 36–7, 42–3, 187–9. Djenné-Djeno is not the only example of an ancient city that fails to display signs of hierarchical politics. Others include Teotihuacan in Mesoamerica and the Neolithic settlement of Talianki in Ukraine. As David Graeber and David Wengrow argue, 'a surprising number of the world's earliest cities were organised on robustly egalitarian lines, with no need for authoritarian rulers, ambitious warrior politicians, or even bossy administrators', *The Dawn of Everything: A New History of Humanity* (Penguin, 2022), pp. 4, 292, 330–2.

6　Kwasi Wiredu, 'Democracy and Consensus in African Traditional Politics: A Plea for a Non-Party Polity', *Centennial Review* 39/1 (1995): 53, https://www.jstor.org/ stable/23739547. For a classic discussion on the history of African democracy and 'chiefless societies', see Chancellor Williams, *The Destruction of Black Civilization: Great Issues of a Race From 4500 BC to 2000 AD* (Third World Press, 1971), pp. 172–6.

7　Jan Vansina, *How Societies Are Born: Governance in Central West Africa Before 1600* (University of Virginia Press, 2005), pp. 209, 216, 224–37, 248, 255–9; https://www. vaguelyinteresting.co.uk/what-a-palaver/.

8　Ikpechukwuka E. Ibenekwu, 'Igbo Traditional Political System and the Crisis of Governance in Nigeria', *Ikoro Journal of the Institute of African Studies* UNN 9/1–2 (2015); Susan Keech McIntosh, 'Pathways to Complexity: An African Perspective', in Susan Keech McIntosh (ed.), *Beyond Chiefdoms: Pathways to Complexity in Africa* (Cambridge University Press, 1999), p. 9.

9　Elizabeth Isichei, *Igbo Worlds: An Anthology of Oral Histories and Historical Descriptions* (Institute for the Study of Human Issues, 1978), pp. 71–5.

10　David Van Reybrouck, *Against Elections: The Case for Democracy* (Seven Stories Press, 2018), pp. 1–16.

11　https://www.v-dem.net/documents/19/dr_2022_ipyOpLP.pdf, pp. 6, 14.

12 David Graeber, 'There Never Was a West: Or, Democracy Emerges from the Spaces in Between', *Possibilities: Essays on Hierarchy, Rebellion, and Desire* (AK Press, 2007), p. 331.

13 James Madison, *The Federalist Papers, Number 10* (1787).

14 Francis Dupuis-Déri, 'The Political Power of Words: The Birth of Pro-democratic Discourse in the Nineteenth Century in the United States and France', *Political Studies* 52/1 (2004), https://doi.org/10.1111/j.1467-9248.2004.00467.x. See also Bernard Manin, *The Principles of Representative Government* (Cambridge University Press, 1997), pp. 1–7; Van Reybrouck, *Against Elections*, pp. 62–3; Hélène Landemore, *Open Democracy: Reinventing Popular Rule for the Twenty-First Century* (Princeton University Press, 2020), pp. 3–4.

15 Jean-Jacques Rousseau, *The Social Contract* (1762), Book 3 Section 15.

16 Quoted in Philip Kotler, *Democracy in Decline: Rebuilding Its Future* (Sage, 2016), p. 17.

17 Van Reybrouck, *Against Elections*, pp. 62–9; Murray Bookchin, *From Urbanization to Cities: Toward a New Politics of Citizenship* (Cassell, 1995), pp. 74–5; Murray Bookchin, *The Ecology of Freedom* (AK Press, 2005), pp. 204–5; Graeber and Wengrow, *Dawn of Everything*, p. 306. Participation in the *Boule* was not obligatory for those who were selected: poorer male citizens often chose not to take part; https://www.britannica.com/topic/boule-ancient-Greek-council.

18 Aristotle, *The Politics* (Cambridge University Press, 1988), Book 4, Part 9, Book 6, Part 2.

19 Piero Gualtieri, 'Institutional Practices of the Florentine Republic: From the Regime del Popolo to the Electoral Reform 1282–1328', *Revue Française de Science Politique* 64/6 (2014): 1109–21. While it is difficult to precisely trace the impact of Athenian democracy on the Italian city-states, there is evidence that the democratic traditions of the ancient Greeks helped justify and legitimise practices such as sortition in Renaissance Italy; https://jamesk508.medium.com/is-democracy-western-the-case-of-sortition-1f0bbfaa78e8; M. Bookchin, *From Urbanization to Cities*, pp. 100–5.

20 Quoted in Van Reybrouck, *Against Elections*, p. 74. Note that sortition was also used for the selection of public officials in imperial China, and has long been practised by Adivasi communities in the remote forests of eastern India; Alpa Shah, 'What if We Selected Our Leaders by Lottery? Democracy by Sortition, Liberal Elections and Communist Revolutionaries', *Development and Change* 52/4 (2021), https://doi.org/10.1111/dech.12651.

21 Benjamin Barber, *The Death of Communal Liberty: A History of Freedom in a Swiss Mountain Canton* (Princeton University Press, 1974), pp. 49, 172–82, 193; Randolph Head, *Early Modern Democracy in the Grisons: Social Order and Political*

Language in a Swiss Mountain Canton, 1470–1620 (Cambridge University Press, 1995), pp. 74–109.

22 Barber, *Death of Communal Liberty*, pp. 171–2.

23 Barber, *Death of Communal Liberty*, p. 170.

24 Peter Kropotkin, *Mutual Aid: A Factor of Evolution* (Freedom Press, 1987), Chapter 7; M. Bookchin, *From Urbanization to Cities*, pp. 87–116; Peter Marshall, *Demanding the Impossible: A History of Anarchism* (Fontana Press, 1993), pp. 462–3.

25 I am not the first person to use the term 'communal democracy'. See, for example, Daniel J. Elazar, 'Communal Democracy and Liberal Democracy: An Outside Friend's Look at the Swiss Political Tradition', *Publius* 23/2 (1993): 3–18, http://www.jstor.org/stable/3330856. Note also that there are many historical examples of communal democratic practices that I have not discussed, such as the creation of a six-nation decentralised confederation by the Haudenosaunee people (once known as the Iroquois), ruled by a great council of 50 peace chiefs: https://www.onondaganation.org/government/chiefs/. A more recent example can be found in the Zapatista communities in southern Mexico.

26 M. Bookchin, *From Urbanization to Cities*, p. 118.

27 M. Bookchin, *From Urbanization to Cities*, p. 8. Note that Bookchin's *From Urbanization to Cities* has also been published under the title, *Urbanization without Cities*. For detailed analysis of the influence of Bookchin's ideas on Öcalan and the Kurdish liberation struggle, see Damian Gerber and Shannon Brincat, 'When Öcalan Met Bookchin: The Kurdish Freedom Movement and the Political Theory of Democratic Confederalism', *Geopolitics* 26/4 (2018), https://doi.org/10.1080/14650045.2018.1508016; Debbie Bookchin, 'How My Father's Ideas Helped the Kurds Create a New Democracy', *New York Review of Books*, 15 June 2018; https://theanarchistlibrary.org/library/various-authors-bookchin-ocalan-correspondence. Bookchin's communalism, sometimes called 'libertarian municipalism', has similarities with Elinor Ostrom's model of 'polycentric governance' (see Chapter 5).

28 https://www.versobooks.com/blogs/2368-murray-bookchin-and-the-ocalan-connection-the-new-york-times-profiles-the-students-of-pkk-rojava. Note that the letter Bookchin received from Öcalan was written on his behalf by an intermediary.

29 http://new-compass.net/articles/bookchin-%C3%B6calan-and-dialectics-democracy.

30 Öcalan called the political model 'democratic confederalism' or 'stateless democracy'. See Abdullah Öcalan, *Democratic Confederalism* (Transmedia Publishing, 2011); https://www.bakonline.org/wp-content/uploads/2018/12/NWA-Reader-5.pdf.

31 https://www.ft.com/content/50102294-77fd-11e5-a95a-27d368e1ddf7.

32 https://www.resilience.org/stories/2019-07-01/making-rojava-green-again/.

33 https://www.nytimes.com/2015/09/30/opinion/the-kurds-democratic-experiment. html.

34 On critiques of communal democracy, see Landemore, *Open Democracy*, p. 212. On Taiwan, see the 2019 TEDx talk by Audrey Tang, Taiwan's digital minister: https://www.ted.com/talks/audrey_tang_digital_social_innovation_to_empower_democracy.

35 George Monbiot, 'Feeling the urge to take back control from power-mad governments? Here's an idea', *Guardian*, 13 July 2022, https://www.theguardian.com/commentisfree/2022/jul/13/take-back-control-governments.

36 The title of Öcalan's book *The Sociology of Freedom* is a homage to Bookchin's *The Ecology of Freedom*. Öcalan has also been influenced by other historical writers such as Fernand Braudel and Immanuel Wallerstein; Abdullah Öcalan, *The Sociology of Freedom: Manifesto of the Democratic Civilization*, vol. III (PM Press, 2020), pp. 10, 387 n. 7.

37 Landemore, *Open Democracy*, p. 13.

38 Data sources: https://www.oecd.org/gov/open-government/innovative-citizen-participation-new-democratic-institutions-catching-the-deliberative-wave-highlights.pdf, p. 20; https://involve.org.uk/citizens-assembly-tracker; J.-B. Pilet et al., 'The POLITICIZE Dataset: an inventory of Deliberative Mini-Publics (DMPs) in Europe', *European Political Science* 20 (2022), https://doi.org/10.1057/s41304-020-00284-9; Nabila Abbas and Yves Sintomer, 'Three Contemporary Imaginaries of Sortition: Deliberative, Antipolitical, or Radically Democratic?', *Raisons Politiques* 82/2 (2021): 33–54.

39 Reybrouk, *Against Elections*, p. 148.

40 For details of the selection process, see https://www.citizensassembly.ie/recruitment/; also based on direct communication with the chair of the assembly, Dr Aoibhinn Ní Shúilleabháin, 28 July 2023.

41 The talk, based on ideas in my book *The Good Ancestor*, is available here: https://www.youtube.com/watch?v=2pXjLg3dhVg.

42 A Children and Young People's Assembly on Biodiversity Loss also took place in parallel, involving youths aged 7 to 17. Its recommendations were fed into the main adult assembly; https://cyp-biodiversity.ie.

43 https://globalassembly.org/resources/downloads/GlobalAssembly2021-FullReport.pdf.

44 For critical appraisals of the French Citizens' Convention for the Climate, see Graham Smith, 'Placing the Convention: An Outlier Amongst Climate Assemblies?', paper prepared for *Participations* journal Special Issue on Climate

Assemblies, ed. Jean-Michel Fourniau and Hélène Landemore (2022), p. 3; Charles Girard, 'Lessons from the French Citizens' Climate Convention: On the role and legitimacy of citizens' assemblies', *VerfBlog*, 28 July 2021, https://verfassungsblog. de/lessons-from-the-french-citizens-climate-convention/.

45 France's Citizens' Convention for the Climate (2019/20) and Spain's Citizens' Climate Assembly (2022) both proposed to make ecocide a crime, as did the Global Assembly on the Climate and Ecological Crisis (2021).

46 For a discussion of these efforts to institutionalise citizens' assemblies, see Graham Smith, *Can Democracy Safeguard the Future?* (Polity, 2021), pp. 104–12.

47 Proposals for replacing the House of Lords with a chamber based on sortition go back to Anthony Barnett and Peter Carty's pathbreaking book, *The Athenian Option: Radical Reform for the House of Lords* (Imprint Academic, 1998). On citizens' assemblies in Gdansk, see https://www.resilience.org/stories/2017-11-22/ solutions-how-the-poles-are-making-democracy-work-again-in-gdansk/. On the radical potential of citizens' assemblies see Abbas and Sintomer, 'Three Contemporary Imaginaries of Sortition'; and the Yves Sintomer interview at Equality By Lot, 21 June 2019, https://equalitybylot.com/2019/06/21/ interview-with-yves-sintomer-part-2-of-2-with-sortition-the-scale-is-immaterial/.

48 The term 'electoral fundamentalism' comes from the Belgian democratic thinker David Van Reybrouck (*Against Elections*, p. 39).

7: Managing the Genetic Revolution

1 Lawrence Principe, *The Secrets of Alchemy* (University of Chicago Press, 2013), p. 51.

2 Ibid., p. 129. See also Thomas, *Religion and the Decline of Magic*, p. 321, and Carl Jung, *The Psychology of the Transference* (Ark Paperbacks, 1983).

3 Paracelsus, *Of the Nature of Things* (1537). Some scholars believe this tract was written by one of his followers.

4 Annette Burfoot, 'Life Light: Explorations in Alchemy and the Magic of Enlightenment', *Public* 18 (1999): 108, https://public.journals.yorku.ca/index.php/ public/article/view/30303.

5 https://www.focusonreproduction.eu/article/ESHRE-News-COP23_adamson; https://www.hfea.gov.uk/treatments/embryo-testing-and-treatments-for-disease/ pre-implantation-genetic-testing-for-monogenic-disorders-pgt-m-and-pre-implantation-genetic-testing-for-chromosomal-structural-rearrangements-pgt-sr/.

6 On the significance and development of CRISPR (clustered regularly interspaced short palindromic repeats), see Jamie Metzl, *Hacking Darwin: Genetic Engineering and the Future of Humanity* (Sourcebooks, 2019), Chapter 5.

7 https://www.zetafertility.com/profiling.

8 The legal landscape is currently in a state of flux. While embryo screening for sex is legal in the US, in the UK it is currently only legal to choose the baby's sex if you have a serious genetic condition that you risk passing on to your children and which affects only one of the two sexes. Screening for genetic diseases is now permitted in most countries, but it is generally still illegal to edit genetically a human embryo except for research purposes. In 2018, Chinese scientist He Jiankui announced that he had genetically edited the embryos of twin girls to give them immunity to HIV. His actions were widely condemned by the international scientific community and he was sentenced to three years in prison by the Chinese government. There is also debate about the relative ethics of 'germline' editing, which is passed down intergenerationally, in contrast to 'somatic' editing, which is not transmitted to the next generation. Germline editing is categorically prohibited in at least 70 countries. See Françoise Baylis et al., 'Human Germline and Heritable Genome Editing: The Global Policy Landscape', *CRISPR Journal* 3/5 (2020), http://doi.org/10.1089/crispr.2020.0082; Metzl, *Hacking Darwin*, pp. 216–17.

9 According to Alexandra Minna Stern, 'by excluding African American children, the contests reinforced patterns of segregation' and 'promoted the idea that only white babies could achieve perfection'. The contests, she writes, 'were segregated in practice not on paper'; Alexandra Minna Stern, 'Making Better Babies: Public Health and Race Betterment in Indiana, 1920–35', in Osagie Obasogie and Marcy Darnovsky (eds), *Beyond Bioethics: Toward a New Biopolitics* (University of California Press, 2018), pp. 41, 50 n. 51.

10 Quoted in Adam Rutherford, *Control: The Dark History and Troubling Present of Eugenics* (Weidenfeld & Nicolson, 2022), p. 48.

11 Ibid., p. 66; https://scholarworks.iupui.edu/communities/4e5f76bf-5f6c-4328-82c6-d6327848d4d1.

12 https://www.johnlocke.org/two-quotes-from-obamas-new-heroe-teddy-roosevelt/.

13 Philip R. Reilly, 'Eugenics and Involuntary Sterilization: 1907–2015', *Annual Review of Genomics and Human Genetics* 16 (2015), https://doi.org/10.1146/annurev-genom-090314-024930. Forced sterilisation also became common in other countries, such as Sweden from 1906 to 1975, and in India in the 1970s.

14 Edwin Black, 'Eugenics and the Nazis: The California Connection', in Osagie Obasogie and Marcy Darnovsky (eds), *Beyond Bioethics: Toward a New Biopolitics* (University of California Press, 2018), pp. 52–9; Jeremy Rifkin, *The Biotech Century: Harnessing the Gene and Remaking the World* (Tarcher/Putnam, 1999), pp. 26–7; James Whitman, 'Why the Nazis Studied American Race Laws for Inspiration', *Aeon*, December 2016, https://aeon.co/ideas/why-the-nazis-studied-american-race-laws-for-inspiration.

15 Lia Weintraub, 'The Link Between the Rockefeller Foundation and Racial Hygiene in Nazi Germany', dissertation, Tufts University, 2013, http://hdl.handle.net/10427/77753.

16 Rutherford, *Control*, p. 135.

17 Transcript from the documentary film *Human Nature* (2019), https://www.imdb.com/title/tt9612680/.

18 Ibid.

19 https://bioedge.org/enhancement/eugenics/more-protests-over-eugenics-this-time-at-michigan-state/; https://statenews.com/article/2020/06/michigan-state-geu-calls-to-remove-vp-research-administrator-stephen-hsu?ct=content_open&cv=cbox_featured.

20 Tom Shakespeare, 'Inheritance after genetics', undated, https://farmerofthoughts.co.uk/collected_pieces/inheritance-after-genetics/. See also Harriet McBryde Johnson's superb essay 'Unspeakable Conversations', *New York Times*, 16 February 2003, where the author questions the argument of philosopher Peter Singer that disability necessarily makes a person 'worse off' and that their 'suffering' may render their life not worth living.

21 For discussion of some of these problems with what has been called the 'personal service model' of genetic intervention, see Allen Buchanan et al., *From Chance to Choice: Genetics and Justice* (Cambridge University Press, 2000), pp. 13, 51.

22 Rutherford, *Control*, p. 177; https://www.newscientist.com/article/mg24032041-900-exclusive-a-new-test-can-predict-ivf-embryos-risk-of-having-a-low-iq/. There are also philosophers, such as Julian Savulescu, who argue in favour of 'moral enhancement' – that we have an obligation genetically to enhance our species to improve morality. Given the current state of genetic knowledge about how to make us good – which is close to zero, and will probably stay that way – such discussions remain largely theoretical. See Julian Savulescu and Ingmar Persson, 'Moral Enhancement', *Philosophy Now* 91 (2012), https://philosophynow.org/issues/91/Moral_Enhancement. For critiques of Savulescu, see Michael Sandel, *The Case Against Perfection: Ethics in the Age of Genetic Engineering* (Belknap Press, 2009), pp. 47–9; Michael Parker, 'The Best Possible Child', *Journal of Medical Ethics* 33/5 (2007), https://doi.org/10.1136/jme.2006.018176.

23 Nathaniel Comfort, 'Can We Cure Genetic Diseases without Slipping into Eugenics?', in Osagie Obasogie and Marcy Darnovsky (eds), *Beyond Bioethics: Toward a New Biopolitics* (University of California Press, 2018), pp. 184–5.

24 Lee Silver, *Remaking Eden: How Genetic Engineering and Cloning Will Remake the American Family* (Harper Perennial, 2007). See also Yuval Harari, *Homo Deus: A Brief History of Tomorrow* (Vintage, 2016), pp. 403–8.

25 https://www.openaccessgovernment.org/covid-19-vaccines-genetic-modification/
112020/.

26 Amitai Etzioni, *The Common Good* (Polity, 2004), p. 3. See also M. Jaede, 'The
Concept of the Common Good', PSRP Working Paper No. 8 (2017), Global
Justice Academy, University of Edinburgh.

27 It has recently been suggested that he may have suffered from a different but
closely related illness.

28 David Oshinsky, *Polio: An American Story* (Oxford University Press, 2005),
pp. 53–5.

29 Ibid., p. 211.

30 https://www.history.com/news/salk-polio-vaccine-shortages-problems.

31 Jonas Salk, 'Are We Being Good Ancestors?', *World Affairs: The Journal of
International Issues* 1/2 (1992), https://www.jstor.org/stable/45064193.

32 Quoted in James Boyle, 'The Second Enclosure Movement and the Construction
of the Public Domain', *Law and Contemporary Problems* 66/1 (2003): 33, https://
scholarship.law.duke.edu/lcp/vol66/iss1/2/.

33 On the history of enclosures, see Ellen Meiksins Wood, *The Origin of Capitalism: A
Longer View* (Verso, 2002), pp. 108–15; Edward Thompson, *The Making of the
English Working Class* (Pelican, 1968), pp. 237–43; https://www.parliament.uk/
about/living-heritage/transformingsociety/towncountry/landscape/overview/
enclosingland/.

34 Karl Polanyi, *The Great Transformation: The Political and Economic Origins of Our
Time* (Beacon Press, 2001), p. 37.

35 Tom Athanasiou and Marcy Darnovsky, 'The Genome as Commons', in Osagie
Obasogie and Marcy Darnovsky (eds), *Beyond Bioethics: Toward a New Biopolitics*
(University of California Press, 2018), pp. 157–62; Boyle, 'Second Enclosure
Movement', p. 33; Stephen Scharper and Hilary Cunningham, 'The Genetic
Commons: Resisting the Neoliberal Enclosure of Life', *Social Analysis: The
International Journal of Anthropology* 50/3 (2006), https://www.jstor.org/
stable/23182119.

36 There are many other dangers associated with genetic engineering that I am not
addressing in this chapter, but which deserve consideration, such as the use of
genetic technology to create bioweapons, and the prospect that CRISPR editing
could have unintended side effects such as creating cancers.

37 https://www.fiercepharma.com/pharma/situation-untenable-bluebird-will-wind-
down-its-operations-broken-europe; https://investor.bluebirdbio.com/
news-releases/news-release-details/bluebird-bio-licenses-lentiviral-vector-patent-
rights; Fyodor Urnov, 'Imagine CRISPR Cures', TEDx Berkeley talk, 2022, https://
www.youtube.com/watch?v=eql8XUxM6Ss.

38 https://www.reuters.com/business/healthcare-pharmaceuticals/breakthrough-gene-editing-technology-belongs-harvard-mit-us-tribunal-2022-03-01/.

39 Katharina Pistor, *The Code of Capital: How the Law Creates Wealth and Inequality* (Princeton University Press, 2019), pp. 114, 131.

40 https://www.precisionmedicineonline.com/cancer/23andme-gets-50m-payment-gsk-extends-companies-drug-discovery-alliance.

41 Pistor, *Code of Capital*, pp. 112, 127; Osagie Obasogie, 'Your Body, Their Property', in Osagie Obasogie and Marcy Darnovsky (eds), *Beyond Bioethics: Toward a New Biopolitics* (University of California Press, 2018), p. 212.

42 Mariana Mazzucato, *The Entrepreneurial State: Debunking Public vs Private Sector Myths* (Anthem Press, 2013), Chapter 5; Mariana Mazzucato, *The Value of Everything: Making and Taking in the Global Economy* (Allen Lane, 2018), pp. 194–9.

43 https://gh.bmj.com/content/6/12/e007321; Mazzucato, *Entrepreneurial State*, pp. 67–71.

44 https://www.genomicsengland.co.uk/patients-participants/participant-panel; 'A public dialogue on genomic medicine: time for a new social contract?', Ipsos, 25 April 2019, https://www.ipsos.com/en-uk/public-dialogue-genomic-medicine-time-new-social-contract-report.

45 https://www.euractiv.com/section/coronavirus/news/german-government-takes-a-stake-in-vaccine-developer-curevac/.

46 At present these alternative models remain rare in the biotech industry, in part due to the large start-up costs, which typically require funding from outside investors. There are, however, a growing number of B Corps (Benefit Corporations) in the sector; https://www.forbes.com/sites/christophermarquis/2021/04/19/why-are-so-few-life-sciences-companies-certified-b-corps/.

47 Rifkin, *Biotech Century*, p. 9.

48 Simon Singh, *Fermat's Last Theorem* (Harper Perennial, 2011), pp. 48–9; Alberto Manguel, *The Library at Night* (Yale University Press, 2008), pp. 24–6.

8: Bridging the Inequality Gap

1 Piketty, *Brief History of Equality*, p. 2.

2 Michael Wood, *The Story of England* (Penguin, 2011), Chapter 10.

3 R.H. Hilton, 'Kibworth Harcourt: A Merton College Manor in the Thirteenth and Fourteenth Centuries', *Transactions of the Leicestershire Archaeological Society* 24 (1949): 38–40.

4 Wood, *Story of England*, Chapter 13.

5 Walter Scheidel, *The Great Leveler: Violence and the History of Inequality from the Stone Age to the Twenty-First Century* (Princeton University Press, 2017), p. 463.

6 Piketty, *Brief History of Equality*, p. 185.

7 Scheidel, *Great Leveler*, pp. 9, 165, 434–6.

8 Richard Wilkinson and Kate Pickett, *The Spirit Level: Why Equality Is Better for Everyone* (Penguin, 2010), pp. 19–20; Dixson-Declève et al., *Earth for All*, Chapter 4.

9 https://www.brookings.edu/articles/the-black-white-wealth-gap-left-black-households-more-vulnerable/.

10 Timothy Snyder, *On Tyranny: Twenty Lessons from the Twentieth Century* (Bodley Head, 2017), p. 12; Tony Judt, *Ill Fares the Land* (Penguin, 2011), p. 235; Luke Kemp et al., 'Climate Endgame: Exploring Catastrophic Climate Change Scenarios', *PNAS* 119 (2022): 6, https://doi.org/10.1073/pnas.2108146119; Diamond, *Collapse*, pp. 430, 519–20; https://www-cdn.oxfam.org/s3fs-public/file_attachments/bp172-no-accident-resilience-inequality-of-risk-210513-en_1_0.pdf.

11 Aristotle, *Politics*, 1296a16–17.

12 https://www.weforum.org/agenda/2021/12/global-income-inequality-gap-report-rich-poor/.

13 Kerala is the highest-ranked Indian state on the UN's Human Development Index: https://globaldatalab.org/shdi/table/shdi/IND/?levels=1+4&years=2019&extrapolation=0. For Kerala's performance on indicators such as the Gini coefficient, women's empowerment, school enrolment and healthcare spending per capita, see Aviral Pandey and Richa Gautam, 'Regional Inequality in India: A State Level Analysis', MRPA Paper No. 101980 (2020), https://mpra.ub.uni-muenchen.de/101980/. For other data, see https://www.bbc.co.uk/news/world-asia-india-62951951.

14 Jean Dreze and Amartya Sen (eds), *Indian Development: Selected Regional Perspectives* (United Nations University, 1999), pp. 15–18; Barbara H. Chasin and Richard W. Franke, 'The Kerala Difference', with reply by Amartya Sen, *New York Review of Books*, 24 October 1991; https://www.rbi.org.in/Scripts/PublicationsView.aspx?id=20675.

15 Robin Jeffrey, *Politics, Women and Well-Being: How Kerala Became a 'Model'* (Oxford University Press, 2001), pp. 1–2; Manali Desai, *State Formation and Radical Democracy in India* (Routledge, 2007).

16 Rajan Gurukkal and Raghava Varier, *History of Kerala: Prehistoric to the Present* (Orient BlackSwan, 2018), pp. 250–1, 258–9; Eliza Kent, *Converting Women: Gender and Protestant Christianity in Colonial South India* (Oxford University Press, 2004), pp. 204–10; K.D. Binu and Manosh Manoharan, 'Absence in Presence: Dalit Women's Agency, Channar Lahala, and Kerala Renaissance', *Journal of International Women's Studies* 22/10 (2021): 24, https://vc.bridgew.edu/jiws/vol22/iss10/3.

17 Jeffrey, *Politics, Women and Well-Being*, pp. xxvii, 35, 55–6; Robin Jeffrey, 'Legacies of Matriliny: The Place of Women and the "Kerala Model"', *Pacific Affairs* 77/4 (2004): 648–9, 655, http://www.jstor.org/stable/40023536; V.K. Ramachandran, 'On

Kerala's Development Achievements', in Jean Dreze and Amartya Sen (eds), *Indian Development: Selected Regional Perspectives* (United Nations University, 1999), pp. 265–80, 305–8; Desai, *State Formation*, p. 51; Udaya Kumar, 'Subjects of New Lives: Reform, Self-Making and the Discourse of Autobiography in Kerala', in Bharati Ray (ed.), *Different Types of History* (Pearson Education India, 2009), p. 329.

18 Desai, *State Formation*, p. 35; Benny Kuruvilla, 'Kerala's Web of Cooperatives: Advancing the Solidarity Economy', in Lavinia Steinfort and Satoko Kishimoto (eds), *Public Finance for the Future We Want* (Transnational Institute, 2019); Jeffrey, 'Legacies of Matriliny', pp. 663–4; Jos Chathukulam and Joseph Tharamangalam, 'The Kerala Model in the Time of COVID 19: Rethinking State, Society and Democracy', *World Development* 137 (2020), https://doi.org/10.1016/j.worlddev.2020.105207.

19 Ramachandran, 'On Kerala's Development Achievements', pp. 317–18.

20 Jeffrey, *Politics, Women and Well-Being*, pp. 124–5; Gurukkal and Varier, *History of Kerala*, p. 298.

21 https://countercurrents.org/2021/09/what-made-keralas-women-achievers-of-the-last-century/.

22 Jeffrey, *Politics, Women and Well-Being*, pp. 83–9; Ramachandran, 'On Kerala's Development Achievements', pp. 207, 292; Desai, *State Formation*, pp. 85–7; V. Bijukumar, 'Radicalised Civil Society and Protracted Political Actions in Kerala (India): A Socio-Political Narrative', *Asian Ethnicity* 20/4 (2019), https://doi.org/10.1080/14631369.2019.1601005. The tiny republic of San Marino had an elected Communist government before Kerala, but Kerala was the first example with a substantive population.

23 Bill McKibben, *Hope, Human and Wild: True Stories of Living Lightly on Earth* (Milkweed Editions, 2007), p. 145; Ramachandran, 'On Kerala's Development Achievements', pp. 294–300; G.K. Lieten, 'Human Development in Kerala: Structure and Agency in History', *Economic and Political Weekly* 37/16 (2002): 1542, https://www.jstor.org/stable/4412015.

24 https://thewire.in/agriculture/keralas-women-farmers-rise-above-the-flood; https://kudumbashree.org; Kuruvilla, 'Kerala's Web of Cooperatives', pp. 83–5; Glyn Williams et al., 'Performing Participatory Citizenship – Politics and Power in Kerala's Kudumbashree Programme', *Journal of Development Studies* 47/8 (2011), https://doi.org/10.1080/00220388.2010.527949.

25 Jesha Mohammedali Mundodan, Lamiya K.K. and Sheela P. Haveri, 'Prevalence of spousal violence among married women in a rural area in North Kerala', *Journal of Family Medicine and Primary Care* 10/8 (2021), https://doi.org/10.4103/jfmpc.jfmpc_2313_20; https://english.mathrubhumi.com/news/kerala/

domestic-violence-in-kerala-data-shows-calls-to-women-helpline-almost-doubled-in-2021-1.7398704.

26 Jeffrey, *Politics, Women and Well-Being*, p. xxvi.

27 https://twitter.com/TNiskakangas/status/1203729511658995713?ref_src=twsrc%5Etfw.

28 Danny Dorling and Annika Koljonen, *Finntopia: What We Can Learn from the World's Happiest Country* (Agenda, 2020), pp. xvi, 249–55.

29 https://harvardpolitics.com/nordic-racism/.

30 Dorling and Koljonen, *Finntopia*.

31 https://www.youtube.com/watch?v=jQwosjKbhH0&t=37s.

32 Aura Korppi-Tommola, 'Fighting Together for Freedom: Nationalism, Socialism, Feminism, and Women's Suffrage in Finland 1906', *Scandinavian Journal of History* 15/1–2 (1990): 181–3, https://doi.org/10.1080/03468759008579196; Riita Jallinoja, 'The Women's Liberation Movement in Finland: The Social and Political Mobilisation of Women in Finland, 1880–1910', *Scandinavian Journal of History* 5/1–4 (1980): 40–2, https://doi.org/10.1080/03468758008578965.

33 Eric Blanc, 'Finland 1906: The Revolutionary Roots of Women's Suffrage', March 2015, https://johnriddell.com/2015/03/04/finland-1906-the-revolutionary-roots-of-womens-suffrage-an-international-womens-day-tribute/. See also Eric Blanc, *Revolutionary Social Democracy: Working-Class Politics Across the Russian Empire (1882–1917)* (Brill, 2021); Korppi-Tommola, 'Fighting Together', p. 188.

34 Aura Korppi-Tommola, 'A Long Tradition of Equality: Women's Suffrage in Finland', in Blanca Rodriguez Ruiz and Ruth Rubio Marín (eds), *The Struggle for Female Suffrage in Europe* (Brill, 2012), p. 56.

35 https://encyclopedia.1914-1918-online.net/article/finnish_civil_war_1918.

36 Pauli Kettunen, 'Wars, Nation, and the Welfare State in Finland', in Herbert Obinger et al. (eds), *Warfare and Welfare: Military Conflict and Welfare State Development in Western Countries* (Oxford University Press, 2018), pp. 277–8; Anne Ollila, 'Women's Voluntary Associations in Finland during the 1920s and 1930s', *Scandinavian Journal of History* 20/2 (1995), https://doi.org/10.1080/03468759508579297; Maria Lahteenmaki, 'To the Margins and Back? The Role of Women in the Finnish Labour Movement in the Twentieth Century', *Scandinavian Journal of History* 23/3–4 (1998), https://doi.org/10.1080/03468759850115909.

37 Dorling and Koljonen, *Finntopia*, p. 100; Ilkka Taipale (ed.), *100 Social Innovations from Finland* (Finnish Literature Society, 2013), pp. 101–3.

38 Martti Siisiäinen, 'Social Movements, Voluntary Associations and Cycles of Protest in Finland 1905–91', *Scandinavian Political Studies* 15/1 (1992): 23–4; Jaakko Kiander, Pekka Sauramo and Hannu Tanninen, 'The Finnish Incomes Policy as Corporatist Political Exchange: Development of Social Capital and Social Wage',

Palkansaajien Tutkimuslaitos, Labour Institute for Economic Research, Working Paper 256 (2009).

39 Tapio Bergholm, 'Decade of Equality: Employment, Pay and Gender in Finland in the 1970s', *Moving the Social: Journal of Social History and the History of Social Movements* 48 (2012): 85, https://doi.org/10.13154/mts.48.2012.73-88.

40 Dorling and Koljonen, *Finntopia*, pp. 81–91; https://www.thetimes.co.uk/article/ private-schools-row-what-can-we-learn-from-other-countries-jkj9xbc2g; https:// factual.afp.com/en-finlandia-no-esta-prohibida-la-educacion-privada. Note that Finland does have a small number of fee-paying schools, such as international schools.

41 Quoted in Dorling and Koljonen, *Finntopia*, p. 136.

42 https://fra.europa.eu/sites/default/files/fra_uploads/fra-2019-being-black-in-the-eu-summary_en.pdf.

43 OECD data available at https://ec.europa.eu/eurostat/statistics-explained/SEPDF/ cache/36609.pdf. Material footprint data from the Sustainable Development Index, https://www.sustainabledevelopmentindex.org/time-series.

44 Hickel, *Less Is More*, pp. 185–6.

45 https://oxfamilibrary.openrepository.com/bitstream/handle/10546/621341/ bp-inequality-kills-170122-en.pdf, pp. 2, 13.

46 Piketty, *Brief History of Equality*, pp. 2, 155; https://www.nytimes.com/ interactive/2022/04/03/magazine/thomas-piketty-interview.html.

47 Angela Davis, *Freedom Is a Constant Struggle: Ferguson, Palestine and the Foundations of a Movement* (Haymarket Books, 2016).

9: Keeping the Machines Under Control

1 https://www.gatesnotes.com/The-Age-of-AI-Has-Begun.

2 https://liveblog.digitalimages.sky/lc-images-sky/lcimg-89e9134e-cd33-435b-8b03-1c8d42146c14.png.

3 As an experiment I asked ChatGPT to cut an early draft of this chapter by 500 words while retaining content and style. The resulting prose was so lifeless and generic that I swiftly abandoned using an AI editor.

4 Humans have created other large-scale systems that they have found difficult to restrain. For instance, we developed states – gigantic bureaucratic machines to administer huge territories and wage war on their enemies – as well as organised religions, which have directed the lives of countless millions across global networks of communities and institutions. As this chapter reveals, neither of these examples resembles AI as closely as financial capitalism.

5 Kate Crawford, *Atlas of AI: Power, Politics, and the Planetary Costs of Artificial Intelligence* (Yale University Press, 2021), p. 8.

6 Niall Ferguson, *The Ascent of Money: A Financial History of the World* (Penguin, 2009), p. 133.

7 Simon Schama, *The Embarrassment of Riches: An Interpretation of Dutch Culture in the Golden Age* (Fontana Press, 1988), p. 323.

8 Ferguson, *Ascent of Money*, Chapter 3; David Graeber, *Debt: The First 5,000 Years* (Melville House, 2021), pp. 341–2; John Kenneth Galbraith, *The Age of Uncertainty* (BBC, 1997), Chapter 6. Financial crashes had happened before the Mississippi Bubble, such as the Dutch tulip collapse of 1637, but none had been on such a large scale and with such far-reaching consequences.

9 This has been effectively illustrated in analysis of the global financial system by former Bank of England chief economist Andy Haldane: https://www. businessinsider.com/these-two-charts-show-how-the-worlds-banking-system- exploded-in-size-before-the-2008-crash-2015-3.

10 Fernand Braudel, *Civilization and Capitalism*, vol. I (Collins/Fontana, 1981), p. 437.

11 Dominic Leggett, 'Feeding the Beast: Superintelligence, Corporate Capitalism and the End of Humanity', *Proceedings of the 2021 AAAI/ACM Conference on AI, Ethics, and Society* (July 2021), https://doi.org/10.1145/3461702.3462581; George Dyson, *Analogia: The Entangled Destinies of Nature, Human Beings and Machines* (Allen Lane, 2020), p. 251; Max Tegmark, *Life 3.0: Being Human in the Age of Artificial Intelligence* (Penguin, 2017), pp. 86–91.

12 See Daniel Schmachtenberger in conversation with Nate Hagens on the podcast *The Great Simplification*, episode 71, 17 May 2023, https://www.thegreatsimplification. com/episode/71-daniel-schmachtenberger.

13 Tristan Harris and Aza Raskin, 'The A.I. Dilemma', 2023, https://www.youtube. com/watch?v=xoVJKj8lcNQ; https://www.washingtonpost.com/ technology/2023/03/05/ai-voice-scam/.

14 https://www.ansa.it/documents/1680080409454_ert.pdf

15 https://fortune.com/2022/12/08/pentagon-cloud-contract-to-be-shared-by-google- amazon-microsoft-and-oracle-in-9-billion-deal/; https://www.thegamer.com/ microsoft-proxy-statement-investigations-military-contracts/; https://www.nytimes. com/2018/10/26/us/politics/ai-microsoft-pentagon.html; https://www.defenseone. com/technology/2022/06/new-google-division-will-take-aim-pentagon-battle- network-contracts/368691/.

16 https://theconversation.com/why-a-computer-will-never-be-truly-conscious-120644#.

17 https://www.lesswrong.com/posts/zRn6aQyD8uhAN7qCc/sam-altman-planning- for-agi-and-beyond; https://www.telegraph.co.uk/business/2023/05/23/ chatgpt-sam-altman-ai-regulation-risk-fears/. See also the open letter on AI risk signed by dozens of tech CEOs: https://www.safe.ai/statement-on-ai-risk# open-letter.

18 https://www.theatlantic.com/technology/archive/2023/06/ai-regulation-sam-altman-bill-gates/674278/.

19 For a comprehensive definition of capitalism, on which my own is based, see the one given by economist Kate Raworth, which is informed by the work of Nancy Fraser, Marjorie Kelly and Katharina Pistor: https://twitter.com/KateRaworth/status/1632661786426998784. The distinction I make between financial, industrial, colonial and consumer capitalism broadly mirrors that made by sociologist James Fulcher in *Capitalism: A Very Short Introduction* (Oxford University Press, 2004), pp. 1–13. Rather than using the term 'colonial capitalism', he refers to a pre-industrial mode of 'merchant capitalism'.

20 Crawford, *Atlas of AI*, p. 53; https://www.huckmag.com/article/speaking-to-amazon-uk-workers-on-the-picket-lines-in-coventry-2023.

21 Crawford, *Atlas of AI*, p. 68.

22 https://www.smithsonianmag.com/science-nature/history-human-computers-180972202/.

23 https://www.marxists.org/archive/marx/works/1848/communist-manifesto/ch01.htm.

24 This colonialist relationship between centre and periphery is fundamental to what is known as 'dependency theory', which is making an intellectual comeback today after having been popularised in the 1970s by thinkers such as Immanuel Wallerstein and Andre Gunder Frank.

25 Eduardo Galeano, *The Open Veins of Latin America* (Latin America Bureau, 1997), pp. 20–37; https://www.theguardian.com/cities/2016/mar/21/story-of-cities-6-potosi-bolivia-peru-inca-first-city-capitalism.

26 https://www.theguardian.com/world/2023/jan/25/bolivia-lithium-mining-salt-flats.

27 AI is highly resource and energy intensive: by 2040 the tech sector will be responsible for 14 per cent of global greenhouse gas emissions (Crawford, *Atlas of AI*, p. 42). For an excellent analysis of the scramble for mineral resources in the Global South to power the tech industry, see Olivia Lazard, 'The Blind Spots of the Global Energy Transition', TED Countdown New York Session, June 2022, https://www.ted.com/talks/olivia_lazard_the_blind_spots_of_the_green_energy_transition?language=en.

28 Birhane, 'Algorithmic Colonization of Africa'.

29 Michael Kwet, 'Digital Colonialism: US Empire and the New Imperialism in the Global South', *Race & Class* 60/4 (2019), https://doi.org/10.1177/0306396818823172. In 2020, Facebook launched a product similar to Free Basics called Discover, which has many of the same extractive qualities: https://restofworld.org/2021/facebook-connectivity-discover/.

30 Milford Bateman, 'The Problem with Microcredit in Africa', *Africa Is a Country*, 9 October 2019, https://africasacountry.com/2019/09/a-fatal-embrace.

31 https://www.aclu.org/blog/privacy-technology/surveillance-technologies/ amazons-face-recognition-falsely-matched-28; https://www.washingtonpost.com/ technology/2019/12/19/federal-study-confirms-racial-bias-many-facial-recognition-systems-casts-doubt-their-expanding-use/. See also the documentary film *Coded Bias* (2020).

32 Crawford, *Atlas of AI*, p. 128.

33 Shoshana Zuboff, *The Age of Surveillance Capitalism* (Profile, 2019), Chapter 3; https://www.cigionline.org/articles/shoshana-zuboff-undetectable-indecipherable-world-surveillance-capitalism/.

34 https://www.forbes.com/sites/kashmirhill/2012/02/16/how-target-figured-out-a-teen-girl-was-pregnant-before-her-father-did.

35 Crawford, *Atlas of AI*; https://www.youtube.com/watch?v=UCxPMF2htEs; https://www.facebook.com/watch/?v=530638791417727.

36 Quoted in Mark Fisher, *Capitalist Realism: Is There No Alternative?* (Zero Books, 2009), p. 2.

37 https://www.vice.com/en/article/5d3naz/openai-is-now-everything-it-promised-not-to-be-corporate-closed-source-and-for-profit; https://www.wired.com/story/you-yes-you-would-be-a-better-owner-for-twitter-than-elon-musk/; https://www.nytimes.com/2023/03/31/business/tesla-union-musk-twitter.html; https://www.reuters.com/technology/pentagon-awards-9-bln-cloud-contracts-each-google-amazon-oracle-microsoft-2022-12-07/.

38 https://www.yesmagazine.org/economy/2016/07/05/the-italian-place-where-co-ops-drive-the-economy-and-most-people-are-members; https://core.ac.uk/download/pdf/58774993.pdf; Colin Ward, *Welcome, Thinner City* (Bedford Square Press, 1989), pp. 90–5. Emilia-Romagna's cooperative network is more extensive than Spain's celebrated Mondragon cooperative federation, employing around three times as many people.

39 Robert Putnam, *Making Democracy Work: Civic Traditions in Modern Italy* (Princeton University Press, 1993), p. 126.

40 https://historyofeducation.org.uk/puncta-for-professors-the-university-of-bologna-and-its-fining-system/.

41 Putnam, *Making Democracy Work*, pp. 121, 139, 142, 161. For a critical appraisal of Putnam's views on the history of Emilia-Romagna, see Sarah Blanshei, *Politics and Justice in Late Medieval Bologna* (Brill, 2010).

42 Margaret Lund and Matt Hancock, 'Stewards of Enterprise: Lessons in Economic Democracy from Northern Italy', International Centre for Co-operative Management, St Mary's University, Canada, Working Paper 2020/01 (2020): 15–16; Matt Hancock, 'The Cooperative District of Imola: Forging the High Road to Globalization', manuscript, University of Bologna, 2004, p. 21, https://base.

socioeco.org/docs/imola_0.pdf; Stefano Zamagni and Vera Zamagni, *Cooperative Enterprise: Facing the Challenge of Globalization* (Edward Elgar, 2010), pp. 46–8.

43 Matt Hancock, 'The Communist Party in the Land of Cooperation', manuscript, University of Bologna, 2005, https://institute.coop/resources/communist-party-land-cooperation.

44 Lund and Hancock, 'Stewards of Enterprise', pp. 4, 16–17; Vera Zamagni, 'Why We Need Cooperatives to Make the Business World More People-Centred', paper presented at the UN Inter-Agency Task Force on Social and Solidarity Economy International Conference, Geneva, 25–6 June 2019, pp. 7–8; https://www.lowimpact.org/posts/why-is-the-co-operative-movement-so-successful-in-emilia-romagna-with-matt-hancock-no-not-that-one.

45 https://www.technologyreview.com/2020/06/17/1003316/what-the-1930s-can-teach-us-about-dealing-with-big-tech-today/; https://www.americamagazine.org/politics-society/2017/09/07/how-communists-and-catholics-built-commonwealth; Nathan Schneider, 'An Internet of Ownership: Democratic Design for the Online Economy', *Sociological Review* 66/2 (2018), https://doi.org/10.1177/0038026118758533; https://www.electric.coop/electric-cooperative-fact-sheet.

46 https://www.fastcompany.com/90651242/how-the-drivers-cooperative-built-a-worker-owned-alternative-to-uber-and-lyft; https://nextcity.org/urbanist-news/new-yorks-driver-owned-ride-hailing-app-is-putting-its-foot-on-the-accelera.

47 Connor Spelliscy et al., 'Toward Equitable Ownership and Governance in the Digital Public Sphere', Belfer Center for Science and International Affairs, Harvard University, 2023, p. 18.

48 https://platform.coop/blog/is-bologna-on-the-verge-of-becoming-the-italian-co-op-valley/; https://www.ifabfoundation.org.

49 https://www.project-syndicate.org/magazine/break-up-big-tech-companies-by-robert-b-reich-2020-04.

50 https://www.europarl.europa.eu/news/en/press-room/20231206IPR15699/artificial-intelligence-act-deal-on-comprehensive-rules-for-trustworthy-ai.

51 Harris and Raskin, 'A.I. Dilemma'.

52 Coralie Koonce, *Thinking Toward Survival* (iUniverse, 2010), p. 337.

10: Averting Civilisational Breakdown

1 Smil, *Energy and Civilization*, pp. 1–2.

2 Nate Hagens, 'Economics for the Future – Beyond the Superorganism', *Ecological Economics* 169 (2020): 14, https://doi.org/10.1016/j.ecolecon.2019.106520.

3 Hagens, 'Economics for the Future'. See also his video *The Great Simplification* (2022), https://www.youtube.com/watch?v=-xr9rIQxwj4. Hagens's theory has some resonances with Joseph Tainter's research on civilisational collapse emerging from

'diminishing returns to complexity', which can be resolved through enforced 'simplification', as occurred with the Eastern Roman Empire. See Joseph Tainter, 'Problem Solving: Complexity, History, Sustainability', *Population and Environment* 22 (2000), https://doi.org/10.1023/A:1006632214612.

4　Hagens, 'Economics for the Future', p. 13.

5　Jefim Vogel and Jason Hickel, 'Is Green Growth Happening? An Empirical Analysis of Achieved Versus Paris-Compliant CO2-GDP Decoupling in High-Income Countries', *Lancet Planetary Health* 7/9 (2023), https://doi.org/10.1016/S2542-5196(23)00174-2.

6　The evidence that we are on the pathway towards catastrophic ecological breakdown grows every day. See, for instance: Kemp et al., 'Climate Endgame'; Will Steffen et al., 'Trajectories of the Earth System in the Anthropocene', *PNAS* 115/33 (2019): 35–44, https://doi.org/10.1073/pnas.1810141115; Gaya Herrington, 'Update to Limits to Growth: Comparing the World3 model with Empirical Data', *Journal of Industrial Ecology* 25/3 (2020), https://doi.org/10.1111/jiec.13084.

7　Luke Kemp, 'Are we on the road to civilisation collapse?', BBC Future, 19 September 2019, https://www.bbc.com/future/article/20190218-are-we-on-the-road-to-civilisation-collapse.

8　Peter Turchin, *Ultrasociety: How 10,000 Years of War Made Humans the Greatest Cooperators on Earth* (Beresta Books, 2016), p. 28. Among the most effective attempts to create an integrative framework for understanding collapse, and which challenges the 'single theory' approach, is Cumming and Peterson, 'Unifying Research on Social-Ecological Resilience and Collapse'.

9　Arnold Toynbee, *A Study of History*, vol. III (Oxford University Press, 1935), p. 322.

10　Khaldun's writings are infused with the idea of drawing lessons from history, especially warnings from the past. His later historical work known as the *Kitāb al-'Ibar* (an expansion of *The Muqaddimah*) has been variously translated with the title *The Book of Lessons* and *The Book of Warning and Collection of New Things and Historical Information*.

11　Robert Irwin, *Ibn Khaldun: An Intellectual Biography* (Princeton University Press, 2018), pp. x, 3–9, 24–38, 96–100; Albert Hourani, *A History of the Arab Peoples* (Faber and Faber, 1991), pp. 1–4.

12　Ibn Khaldun, *The Muqaddimah: An Introduction to History*, trans. Franz Rosenthal (Princeton University Press, 2015), pp. 45–6, 97–137; Irwin, *Ibn Khaldun*, pp. 19, 45–9, 53–5, 89–90; Sohail Inayatullah, 'Ibn Khaldun: The Strengthening and Weakening of Asabiya', *Periodica Islamica* 6/3 (1996): 3–11.

13　Khaldun, *Muqaddimah*, p. 39.

14 Kemp, 'Are we on the road to civilisation collapse?'. See also Luke Kemp, 'Diminishing Returns on Extraction: How Inequality and Extractive Hierarchy Create Fragility', in Miguel Centeno et al. (eds), *How Worlds Collapse* (Routledge, 2023), pp. 37–60. For further discussion of the way that social cohesion can mediate and lessen the impacts of environmental and other crises that threaten civilisational breakdown, see Daniel Hoyer, 'Navigating Polycrisis: Long-Run Socio-Cultural Factors Shape Response to Changing Climate', *Philosophical Transactions B: Climate Change Adaptation Need a Science of Culture* (March 2023), https://doi.org/10.31235/osf.io/h6kma.

15 Rebecca Solnit, *A Paradise Built in Hell: The Extraordinary Communities that Arise in Disaster* (Penguin, 2010), pp. 2, 14; Diamond, *Collapse*, pp. 430–1; Putnam, *Making Democracy Work*, pp. 121–62.

16 Turchin, *Ultrasociety*, p. i.

17 Peter Turchin, *War and Peace and War: The Rise and Fall of Empires* (Plume, 2007), p. 108.

18 Stefan Gössling and Andreas Hume, 'Millionaire Spending Incompatible with 1.5°C Ambitions', *Cleaner Production Letters* 4 (2023), https://doi.org/10.1016/j.clpl.2022.100027.

19 Ronald Wright, *A Short History of Progress* (Canongate, 2004), pp. 8, 78–9; Cumming and Petersen, 'Unifying Research on Social-Ecological Resilience and Collapse', pp. 702–6.

20 Diamond, *Collapse*, pp. 306–7; Lansing, *Perfect Order*.

21 Robin Wall Kimmerer, 'Mending Our Relationship with the Earth', in Greta Thunberg (ed.), *The Climate Book* (Penguin, 2022), pp. 415–20; https://www.yesmagazine.org/issue/good-health/2015/11/26/the-honorable-harvest-lessons-from-an-indigenous-tradition-of-giving-thanks.

22 Stephen Kellert and Edward O. Wilson, *The Biophilia Hypothesis* (Island Press, 1993); https://www.nature.com/articles/s41598-022-20207-6; Rifkin, *Age of Resilience*, pp. 224, 233, 239.

23 Keith Thomas, *Man and the Natural World: Changing Attitudes in England 1500–1800* (Penguin, 1984), pp. 25, 197; Lynn White Jr, 'The Historical Roots of our Ecological Crisis', *Science* 155/3767 (1967), https://doi.org/10.1126/science.155.3767.1203; Richard Tawney, *Religion and the Rise of Capitalism* (Penguin, 1980).

24 Masashi Soga et al., 'Gardening Is Beneficial for Health: A Meta-Analysis', *Preventative Medicine Reports* 5 (2017), https://doi.org/10.1016/j.pmedr.2016.11.007.

25 Thomas, *Man and the Natural World*, p. 15.

26 Quoted in ibid., p. 221.

27 Martin Hoyles, *Gardeners Delight: Gardening Books from 1560–1960* (Pluto Press, 1994, 2 vols); Laura Rival (ed.), *The Social Lives of Trees: Anthropological Perspectives*

  on Tree Symbolism (Berg, 1998); Simon Schama, *Landscape and Memory* (Fontana, 1996), pp. 159–68.

28 Thomas, *Man and the Natural World*, pp. 102–12.

29 Ibid., pp. 65–6, 130, 141, 247.

30 James George Frazer, *The Illustrated Golden Bough* (Macmillan, 1978), pp. 58–64, 73–7, 144–52.

31 Teri Frances Brewer, 'May Morning in Oxford: History and Social Change in an Urban Tradition', PhD dissertation, University of California, Los Angeles, 1995, pp. 76–7.

32 Thomas, *Man and the Natural World*, p. 166.

33 Rifkin, *Age of Resilience*, p. 240.

34 https://www.bbc.co.uk/news/science-environment-47976184.

35 https://pinyin.info/chinese/crisis.html.

36 Reinhart Koselleck, 'Crisis', *Journal of the History of Ideas* 67/2 (2006), https://www.jstor.org/stable/30141882.

37 Jacobs, 'How About Some Meat?'; O'Leary, 'Wartime Rationing'; https://www.monbiot.com/2021/10/24/miracle-of-reduction/. I further discuss US rationing policy in Krznaric, 'Food Coupons and Bald Mountains', pp. 8–12.

38 Rutger Bregman, 'This Is What Climate Change Means if Your Country Is Below Sea Level', *The Correspondent*, 24 September 2020, https://thecorrespondent.com/685/this-is-what-climate-change-means-if-your-country-is-below-sea-level.

39 Ruth Supko, 'Perspectives on the Cuban National Literacy Campaign', paper delivered to the Latin American Studies Association, Chicago, 24–6 September 1998; Arlo Kempf, 'The Cuban Literacy Campaign at 50: Formal and Tacit Learning in Revolutionary Education', *Critical Education* 5/4 (2014), https://doi.org/10.14288/ce.v5i4.183269; Catherine Murphy, *Maestra* (documentary film, 2012); Illona Otto et al., 'Social Tipping Dynamics for Stabilizing Earth's Climate by 2050', *PNAS* 117/5 (2020): 2361, https://doi.org/10.1073/pnas.1900577117.

40 Note that my first three crisis contexts of war, disaster and revolution have some overlaps with the 'four horsemen of leveling' described by Walter Scheidel, which historically have resulted in major erosions of wealth inequality: mass mobilisation warfare, transformative revolution, state failure and pandemics (see Chapter 8). There is nothing resembling my crisis category of 'disruption' in Scheidel's model, which displays little faith in disruptive social movements for creating radical change. This is a fundamental area of difference.

41 Naomi Klein, *This Changes Everything: Capitalism vs the Climate* (Allen Lane, 2014), p. 14.

42 Mary Elise Sarotte, *The Collapse: The Accidental Opening of the Berlin Wall* (Basic Books, 2015), pp. 85–103.

43 In his 1982 preface to Milton Friedman, *Capitalism and Freedom* (Chicago University Press, 2002), p. xiv.

44 Steven DeCaroli, 'Arendt's Krisis', *Ethics and Education* 15/2 (2020), https://doi.org/ 10.1080/17449642.2020.1732121, pp. 175, 177; Jeff Jurgens, 'Arendt on Crisis', The Hannah Arendt Center (2018), https://medium.com/quote-of-the-week/arendt-on-crisis-e24ab8225289; Hannah Arendt, 'Understanding Politics', *Partisan Review* 20/4 (1953); Hannah Arendt, 'The Crisis in Culture: Its Social and Political Significance', in *Between Past and Future: Eight Exercises in Political Thought* (Penguin, 2006), pp. 194–223.

45 Peter Frankopan, *The Earth Transformed: An Untold Story* (Bloomsbury, 2023), p. 654; Fagan and Durrani, *Climate Chaos*, pp. 59–62, 239.

46 Note that biophilia and *asabiya* are consistent with the model of Doughnut Economics developed by economist Kate Raworth and discussed in my previous book *The Good Ancestor*. Biophilia provides the basis for the ecological ceiling of the doughnut model, while *asabiya* underpins the social foundation.

Conclusion: Five Reasons for Radical Hope

1 Zinn, *On History*, p. 44.

2 Ibid., p. 45. Etymologically, the origin of the word 'radical' derives from the Latin *radic*, meaning 'root'. Hence why I talk about *radical* hope, which is based on the values you are rooted in.

3 https://halifax.citynews.ca/2023/04/07/hanging-in-david-suzuki-shares-insights-as-he-retires-from-the-nature-of-things/.

4 Many existing university courses on applied history are relatively narrow in scope, focusing on learning from the history of international affairs and diplomacy, such as a course offered at Harvard University: https://www.hks.harvard.edu/courses/ reasoning-past-applied-history-and-decision-making.

5 https://remolino.qc.ca/2023/10/11/une-chaise-des-generations-pour-lassemblee-nationale/.

List of Illustrations

Page 163: Associated Press / Alamy Stock Photo

Page 182: Image courtesy of Benny Kuruvilla

Page 185: Wikimedia Commons / Ministry for Foreign Affairs of Finland

Page 188: Associated Press / Alamy Stock Photo

Page 196: BTEU/RKMLGE / Alamy Stock Photo

Page 204: Malcolm Haines / Alamy Stock Photo

Page 214: Wikimedia Commons / Kupferstichkabinett

Page 227: Gado Images / Alamy Stock Photo

Page 236: Photo courtesy of Oxford University Morris

Bibliography

Abate, Mark (ed.), *Convivencia and Medieval Spain: Essays in Honour of Thomas F. Glick* (Palgrave Macmillan, 2018)

Abbas, Nabila and Sintomer, Yves, 'Three Contemporary Imaginaries of Sortition: Deliberative, Antipolitical, or Radically Democratic?', *Raisons Politiques* 82/2 (2021)

Acemoglu, Daron and Robinson, James A., *Economic Origins of Dictatorship and Democracy* (Oxford University Press, 2006)

Adam, Konadu, Mensah-Bonsu, Frederick and Amedorme, Dorcas, 'Fostering Religious Tolerance and Harmonization in Ghana: A Discussion on Efforts Made by Various Stakeholders', *E-Journal of Humanities, Arts and Social Sciences (EHASS)* 3/5 (May 2022), https://doi.org/10.38159/ehass.2022352

Aidt, Toke and Franck, Raphaël, 'Democratization Under the Threat of Revolution: Evidence from the Great Reform Act of 1832', *Econometrica* 83/2 (2015)

Akenji, Lewis et al., '1.5 Degree Lifestyles: Towards a Fair Consumption Space for All', Hot or Cool Institute, Berlin (2021)

Andrews, Kehinde, *The New Age of Empire: How Racism and Colonialism Still Rule the World* (Allen Lane, 2021)

Arendt, Hannah, 'The Crisis in Culture: Its Social and Political Significance', in *Between Past and Future: Eight Exercises in Political Thought* (Penguin, 2006)

Arendt, Hannah, 'Understanding Politics', *Partisan Review* 20/4 (1953)

Aristotle, *The Politics* (Cambridge University Press, 1988)

Asamoah, Paul Kwame, 'Ethnic Conflict: A Threat to Ghana's Internal Stability – A Case Study of the Nkonya–Alavanyo Conflict in the Volta Region', doctoral dissertation, University of Oslo, 2014, https://www02.core.ac.uk/download/pdf/30903716.pdf

Asante, Kofi Takyi, 'Individualistic and Collectivistic Orientations: Examining the Relationship Between Ethnicity and National Attachment in Ghana', *Studies in Ethnicity and Nationalism* 20/1 (April 2020), https://doi.org/10.1111/sena.12313

Athanasiou, Tom and Darnovsky, Marcy, 'The Genome as Commons', in Osagie Obasogie and Marcy Darnovsky (eds), *Beyond Bioethics: Toward a New Biopolitics* (University of California Press, 2018), pp. 153–62

Atkinson, Diane, *Rise Up, Women! The Remarkable Lives of the Suffragettes* (Bloomsbury, 2018)

Azhar, Azeem, *Exponential: How Accelerating Technology Is Leaving Us Behind and What to Do About It* (Random House Business, 2021)

Baker-Brown, Duncan, *The Re-Use Atlas: A Designer's Guide Towards the Circular Economy* (RIBA, 2017)

Barber, Benjamin, *The Death of Communal Liberty: A History of Freedom in a Swiss Mountain Canton* (Princeton University Press, 1974)

Bardi, Hugo, *The Seneca Effect: Why Growth is Slow but Collapse is Rapid* (Springer, 2017)

Barnett, Anthony and Carty, Peter, *The Athenian Option: Radical Reform for the House of Lords* (Imprint Academic, 1998)

Barrell, John, 'Coffee-House Politicians', *Journal of British Studies* 43/2 (2004), https://doi.org/10.1086/380950

Barrett, Paul, Hendrix, Justin and Sims, J. Grant, 'Fuelling the Fire: How Social Media Intensifies US Political Polarization – And What Can Be Done About It', Stern Center for Business and Human Rights, New York University, 2021

Bateman, Milford, 'The Problem with Microcredit in Africa', *Africa Is a Country*, 9 October 2019, https://africasacountry.com/2019/09/a-fatal-embrace

Baylis, Françoise et al., 'Human Germline and Heritable Genome Editing: The Global Policy Landscape', *CRISPR Journal* 3/5 (2020), http://doi.org/10.1089/crispr.2020.0082

Behringer, Wolfgang, 'Witchcraft and the Media', in Marjorie Elizabeth Plummer (ed.), *Ideas and Cultural Margins in Early Modern Germany* (Routledge, 2009)

Beinhocker, Eric, 'I Am a Carbon Abolitionist', *Democracy*, 24 June 2019

Bergholm, Tapio, 'Decade of Equality: Employment, Pay and Gender in Finland in the 1970s', *Moving the Social: Journal of Social History and the History of Social Movements* 48 (2012), https://doi.org/10.13154/mts.48.2012.73-88

Bijukumar, V., 'Radicalised Civil Society and Protracted Political Actions in Kerala (India): A Socio-Political Narrative', *Asian Ethnicity* 20/4 (2019), https://doi.org/10.1080/14631369.2019.1601005

Binu, K.D. and Manoharan, Manosh, 'Absence in Presence: Dalit Women's Agency, Channar Lahala, and Kerala Renaissance', *Journal of International Women's Studies* 22/10 (2021), https://vc.bridgew.edu/jiws/vol22/iss10/3

Birhane, Abeba, 'Algorithmic Colonization of Africa', *SCRIPT-ed* 17/2 (August 2020), https://script-ed.org/article/algorithmic-colonization-of-africa/

Birmingham, David, *Kwame Nkrumah: The Father of African Nationalism* (Ohio University Press, 1998)

Black, Edwin, 'Eugenics and the Nazis: The California Connection', in Osagie Obasogie and Marcy Darnovsky (eds), *Beyond Bioethics: Toward a New Biopolitics* (University of California Press, 2018), pp. 52–9

Blanc, Eric, 'Finland 1906: The Revolutionary Roots of Women's Suffrage' (March 2015), https://johnriddell.com/2015/03/04/finland-1906-the-revolutionary-roots-of-womens-suffrage-an-international-womens-day-tribute/

Blanc, Eric, *Revolutionary Social Democracy: Working-Class Politics Across the Russian Empire (1882–1917)* (Brill, 2021)

Blanshei, Sarah, *Politics and Justice in Late Medieval Bologna* (Brill, 2010)

Bollier, David, *Think Like a Commoner: A Short Introduction to the Life of the Commons* (New Society Publishers, 2014)

Bookchin, Debbie, 'How My Father's Ideas Helped the Kurds Create a New Democracy', *New York Review of Books*, 15 June 2018

Bookchin, Murray, *The Ecology of Freedom* (AK Press, 2005)

Bookchin, Murray, *From Urbanization to Cities: Toward a New Politics of Citizenship* (Cassell, 1995)

Boulding, Kenneth, 'The Economics of the Coming Spaceship Earth', in H. Jarrett (ed.), *Environmental Quality in a Growing Economy* (Resources for the Future/Johns Hopkins University Press, 1966)

Boyle, James, 'The Second Enclosure Movement and the Construction of the Public Domain', *Law and Contemporary Problems* 66/1 (2003), https://scholarship.law.duke.edu/lcp/vol66/iss1/2/

Braudel, Fernand, *Civilization and Capitalism*, vol. 1 (Collins/Fontana, 1981)

Brennan, Thomas, 'Coffeehouses and Cafes', in Alan Charles Kors (ed.), *Encyclopedia of the Enlightenment* (Oxford University Press, 2002)

Brewer, Teri Frances, 'May Morning in Oxford: History and Social Change in an Urban Tradition', PhD dissertation, University of California, Los Angeles, 1995

Brown, Azby, *Just Enough: Lessons in Living Green from Traditional Japan* (Kodansha, 2010)

Buchanan, Allen et al., *From Chance to Choice: Genetics and Justice* (Cambridge University Press, 2000)

Burfoot, Annette, 'Life Light: Explorations in Alchemy and the Magic of Enlightenment', *Public* 18 (1999), https://public.journals.yorku.ca/index.php/public/article/view/30303

Butzer, Karl, 'Collapse, Environment, and Society', *PNAS* (2012), https://doi.org/10.1073/pnas.1114845109

Catlos, Brian, 'Islamic Spain Ended in the 15th Century and We Still Can't Agree if It Was a Paradise or Hell?', History News Network, 6 October 2018, https://historynewsnetwork.org/article/168990

Catlos, Brian, *Kingdoms of Faith: A New History of Islamic Spain* (Hurst, 2018)

Catlos, Brian, *Muslims in Medieval Latin Christendom* (Cambridge University Press, 2014)

Chasin, Barbara H. and Franke, Richard W., 'The Kerala Difference', with reply by Amartya Sen, *New York Review of Books*, 24 October 1991

Chathukulam, Jos and Tharamangalam, Joseph, 'The Kerala Model in the Time of COVID 19: Rethinking State, Society and Democracy', *World Development* 137 (2020), https://doi.org/10.1016/j.worlddev.2020.105207

Chellaney, Brahma, *Water, Peace, and War: Confronting the Global Water Crisis* (Rowman and Littlefield, 2015)

Chenoweth, Erica, 'People Power', in Greta Thunberg (ed.), *The Climate Book* (Allen Lane, 2022)

Chenoweth, Erica and Schock, Kurt, 'Do Contemporaneous Armed Challenges Affect the Outcomes of Mass Nonviolent Campaigns?', *Mobilization: An International Quarterly* 20 (2015), https://doi.org/10.17813/1086-671x-20-4-427

Chenoweth, Erica and Stephan, Maria, *Why Civil Resistance Works: The Strategic Logic of Nonviolent Campaigns* (Columbia University Press, 2011)

Cicero, Marcus Tullius, *The Letters of Cicero: The Whole Extant Correspondence in Chronological Order*, ed. Evelyn Shirley Shuckburgh (Legare Street Press, 2022)

Comfort, Nathaniel, 'Can We Cure Genetic Diseases without Slipping into Eugenics?', in Osagie Obasogie and Marcy Darnovsky (eds), *Beyond Bioethics: Toward a New Biopolitics* (University of California Press, 2018), pp. 184–5

Cox, Pamela, 'The Future Uses of History', *History Workshop Journal* 75/1 (2013), https://doi.org/10.1093/hwj/dbs007

Crabb, Jon, 'Woodcuts and Witches', *Public Domain Review*, 4 May 2017

Crawford, Kate, *Atlas of AI: Power, Politics, and the Planetary Costs of Artificial Intelligence* (Yale University Press, 2021)

Cumming, Graeme and Peterson, Gary, 'Unifying Research on Social-Ecological Resilience and Collapse', *Trends in Ecology and Evolution* 32/9 (2017)

Curran, James and Seaton, Jean, *Power without Responsibility: Press, Broadcasting and the Internet in Britain* (Routledge, 2018)

Davis, Angela, *Freedom Is a Constant Struggle: Ferguson, Palestine and the Foundations of a Movement* (Haymarket Books, 2016)

Davis, Mike, *Late Victorian Holocausts: El Niño Famines and the Making of the Third World* (Verso, 2002)

Davis, R.C.H., *The Normans and Their Myth* (Thames & Hudson, 1976)

DeCaroli, Steven, 'Arendt's Krisis', *Ethics and Education* 15/2 (2020), https://doi.org/10.1080/17449642.2020.1732121

Desai, Manali, *State Formation and Radical Democracy in India* (Routledge, 2007)

Deutsch, Judith, 'Lessons for the Climate Emergency: Rationing, Moratoriums, Ending War', *Bullet*, 27 June 2019

Diamond, Jared, *Collapse: How Societies Choose or Fail to Survive* (Penguin, 2011)

Dixson-Declève, Sandrine et al., *Earth for All: A Survival Guide for Humanity* (New Society Publishers, 2022)

Bibliography

Dorling, Danny and Koljonen, Annika, *Finntopia: What We Can Learn from the World's Happiest Country* (Agenda, 2020)

Dreze, Jean and Sen, Amartya (eds), *Indian Development: Selected Regional Perspectives* (United Nations University, 1999)

Dunér, David and Ahlberger, Christer (eds), *Cognitive History: Mind, Space, and Time* (De Gruyter Oldenbourg, 2019)

Dupuis-Derí, Francis, 'The Political Power of Words: The Birth of Pro-democratic Discourse in the Nineteenth Century in the United States and France', *Political Studies* 52/1 (2004), https://doi.org/10.1111/j.1467-9248.2004.00467.x

Durant, Will and Durant, Ariel, *The Lessons of History* (Simon & Schuster, 2010)

Dyson, George, *Analogia: The Entangled Destinies of Nature, Human Beings and Machines* (Allen Lane, 2020)

Edwards, Mark, *Printing, Propaganda and Martin Luther* (University of California Press, 1994)

Eisenstein, Elizabeth, *The Printing Revolution in Early Modern Europe* (Cambridge University Press, 2005)

Elazar, Daniel J., 'Communal Democracy and Liberal Democracy: An Outside Friend's Look at the Swiss Political Tradition', *Publius* 23/2 (1993), http://www.jstor.org/stable/3330856

Elgin, Duane, 'Voluntary Simplicity and the New Global Challenge', in Juliet Schor and Douglas Holt (eds), *The Consumer Society Reader* (The New Press, 2000)

Elvin, Mark, *The Retreat of the Elephants: An Environmental History of China* (Yale University Press, 2004)

Etzioni, Amitai, *The Common Good* (Polity, 2004)

Ewen, Stuart, *PR! A Social History of Spin* (Basic Books, 1996)

Fagan, Brian, *Elixir: A Human History of Water* (Bloomsbury, 2011)

Fagan, Brian and Durrani, Nadia, *Climate Chaos: Lessons on Survival from Our Ancestors* (Public Affairs, 2021)

Ferguson, Niall, *The Ascent of Money: A Financial History of the World* (Penguin, 2009)

Fernández-Morera, Dario, *The Myth of the Andalusian Paradise* (ISI, 2014)

Finotelli, Claudia and Rinken, Sebastian, 'A Pragmatic Bet: The Evolution of Spain's Immigration System', Migration Policy Institute, 18 April 2023, https://www.migrationpolicy.org/article/spain-immigration-system-evolution

Fisher, Mark, *Capitalist Realism: Is There No Alternative?* (Zero Books, 2009)

Frankopan, Peter, *The Earth Transformed: An Untold Story* (Bloomsbury, 2023)

Frazer, James George, *The Illustrated Golden Bough* (Macmillan, 1978)

Friedman, Milton, *Capitalism and Freedom* (Chicago University Press, 2002)

Fulcher, James, *Capitalism: A Very Short Introduction* (Oxford University Press, 2004)

Fuller, Harcourt, *Building the Ghanaian Nation-State: Kwame Nkrumah's Symbolic Nationalism* (Palgrave Macmillan, 2014)

Galbraith, John Kenneth, *The Age of Uncertainty* (BBC, 1997)

Galbraith, John Kenneth, *A Life in Our Times* (André Deutsch, 1981)

Galeano, Eduardo, *The Open Veins of Latin America* (Latin America Bureau, 1997)

Gerbaudo, Paolo, 'Social Media and Populism: An elective affinity?', *Media, Culture and Society* 40/5 (2018), https://doi.org/10.1177/0163443718772192

Gerber, Damian and Brincat, Shannon, 'When Öcalan Met Bookchin: The Kurdish Freedom Movement and the Political Theory of Democratic Confederalism', *Geopolitics* 26/4 (2018), https://doi.org/10.1080/14650045.2018.1508016

Gibbon, Edward, *The Decline and Fall of the Roman Empire*, vol. 6 (Methuen, 1898)

Girard, Charles, 'Lessons from the French Citizens' Climate Convention: On the role and legitimacy of citizens' assemblies', *VerfBlog*, 28 July 2021, https://verfassungsblog. de/lessons-from-the-french-citizens-climate-convention/

Gleick, Peter, Iceland, Charles and Trivedi, Ayushi, *Ending Conflicts Over Water: Solutions to Water and Security Challenges* (World Resources Institute, 2020), https://pacinst.org/ wp-content/uploads/2020/09/Ending-Conflicts-Over-Water-Pacific-Institute-Sept-2020.pdf

Glick, Thomas, *Irrigation and Society in Medieval Valencia* (Harvard University Press, 1970)

Gössling, Stefan and Hume, Andreas, 'Millionaire Spending Incompatible with 1.5°C Ambitions', *Cleaner Production Letters* 4 (2023), https://doi.org/10.1016/j.clpl.2022. 100027

Grace, Natalie, 'Vermin and Devil-Worshippers: Exploring Witch Identities in Popular Print in Early Modern Germany and England', *Midlands Historical Review* 5 (2021)

Graeber, David, *Debt: The First 5,000 Years* (Melville House, 2021)

Graeber, David, 'There Never Was a West: Or, Democracy Emerges from the Spaces in Between', *Possibilities: Essays on Hierarchy, Rebellion, and Desire* (AK Press, 2007)

Graeber, David and Wengrow, David, *The Dawn of Everything: A New History of Humanity* (Penguin, 2022)

Griffiths, Jay, *Why Rebel* (Penguin, 2021)

Gualtieri, Piero, 'Institutional Practices of the Florentine Republic: From the Regime del Popolo to the Electoral Reform 1282–1328', *Revue Française de Science Politique* 64/6 (2014)

Gurukkal, Rajan and Varier, Raghava, *History of Kerala: Prehistoric to the Present* (Orient BlackSwan, 2018)

Gyory, Andrew, *Closing the Gate: Race, Politics, and the Chinese Exclusion Act* (University of North Carolina, 1998)

Haas, Hein de, Castles, Stephen and Miller, Mark, *The Age of Migration: International Population Movements in the Modern World* (Guilford, 2019)

Habermas, Jürgen, 'The Public Sphere: An Encyclopedia Article', *New German Critique* 3 (1974), https://doi.org/10.2307/487737

Bibliography

Habermas, Jürgen, 'Reflections and Hypotheses on a Further Structural Transformation of the Political Public Sphere', *Theory, Culture & Society* 39/4 (2022), https://doi.org/10.1177/02632764221112341

Habermas, Jürgen, *The Structural Transformation of the Public Sphere: An Inquiry into a Category of Bourgeois Society* (Polity Press, 1992)

Hagens, Nate, 'Economics for the Future – Beyond the Superorganism', *Ecological Economics* 169 (2020), https://doi.org/10.1016/j.ecolecon.2019.106520

Haines, Herbert, *Black Radicals and the Civil Rights Mainstream, 1954–1970* (University of Tennessee Press, 1988)

Haines, Herbert, 'Radical Flank Effects', in David A. Snow et al. (eds), *Wiley Blackwell Encyclopedia of Social and Political Movements*, vol. 2 (John Wiley & Sons, 2013)

Hancock, Matt, 'The Communist Party in the Land of Cooperation', manuscript, University of Bologna, 2005, https://institute.coop/resources/communist-party-land-cooperation

Hancock, Matt, 'The Cooperative District of Imola: Forging the High Road to Globalization', manuscript, University of Bologna, 2004, https://base.socioeco.org/docs/imola_0.pdf

Hanley, Susan, 'Urban Sanitation in Preindustrial Japan', *Journal of Interdisciplinary History* 18/1 (1987)

Harari, Yuval, *Homo Deus: A Brief History of Tomorrow* (Vintage, 2016)

Head, Randolph, *Early Modern Democracy in the Grisons: Social Order and Political Language in a Swiss Mountain Canton, 1470–1620* (Cambridge University Press, 1995)

Heil, Tilmann, 'Are Neighbours Alike? Practices of Conviviality in Catalonia and Casamance', *European Journal of Cultural Studies* 17/4 (2014), https://doi.org/10.1177/1367549413510420

Herrington, Gaya, 'Update to Limits to Growth: Comparing the World3 model with Empirical Data', *Journal of Industrial Ecology* 25/3 (2020), https://doi.org/10.1111/jiec.13084

Hickel, Jason, *Less Is More: How Degrowth Will Save the Planet* (Windmill, 2021)

Hillenbrand, Robert, '"The Ornament of the World": Medieval Córdoba as a Cultural Centre', in Salma Khadra Jayussi (ed.), *The Legacy of Muslim Spain*, vol. 1 (Brill, 2012)

Hilton, R.H., 'Kibworth Harcourt: A Merton College Manor in the Thirteenth and Fourteenth Centuries', *Transactions of the Leicestershire Archaeological Society* 24 (1949)

Hobbes, Thomas, *The English Works of Thomas Hobbes of Malmesbury – Volume 8, Thucydides, The History of the Grecian War* (London, 1843)

Hobsbawm, Eric, *On History* (Abacus, 1998)

Hobsbawm, Eric and Rudé, George, *Captain Swing* (Verso, 2014)

Hochschild, Adam, *Bury the Chains: The British Struggle to Abolish Slavery* (Pan Books, 2005)

Hoffman, Abbie, *The Autobiography of Abbie Hoffman* (Four Walls Eight Windows, 2000)

Hourani, Albert, *A History of the Arab Peoples* (Faber and Faber, 1991)

Hoyer, Daniel et al., 'Navigating Polycrisis: Long-Run Socio-Cultural Factors Shape Response to Changing Climate', *Philosophical Transactions B: Climate Change Adaptation Need a Science of Culture* (March 2023), https://doi.org/10.31235/osf.io/h6kma

Hoyles, Martin, *Gardeners Delight: Gardening Books from 1560–1960* (Pluto Press, 1994, 2 vols)

Hudson-Richards, Julia and Gonzales, Cynthia, 'Water as a Collective Responsibility: The Tribunal de las Aguas and the Valencian Community', *Bulletin for Spanish and Portuguese Historical Studies* 38/1 (2013), https://asphs.net/wp-content/uploads/2020/02/Water-as-a-Collective-Responsibility.pdf

Ibenekwu, Ikpechukwuka E., 'Igbo Traditional Political System and the Crisis of Governance in Nigeria', *Ikoro Journal of the Institute of African Studies UNN* 9/1–2 (2015)

Inayatullah, Sohail, 'Ibn Khaldun: The Strengthening and Weakening of Asabiya', *Periodica Islamica* 6/3 (1996), pp. 3–11

Irwin, Robert, *Ibn Khaldun: An Intellectual Biography* (Princeton University Press, 2018)

Isaksen, Vogt J., 'The impact of the financial crisis on European attitudes toward immigration', *CMS* 7 (2019)

Ishikawa, Eisuke, *Japan in the Edo Period – An Ecologically Conscious Society* (Kodansha, 2000)

Isichei, Elizabeth, *Igbo Worlds: An Anthology of Oral Histories and Historical Descriptions* (Institute for the Study of Human Issues, 1978)

Iwamoto, Junichi, 'The Development of Japanese Forestry', in Yorshiya Iwai (ed.), *Forestry and Forest Industry in Japan* (University of British Columbia Press, 2002)

Jacobs, Meg, 'How About Some Meat?: The Office of Price Administration, Consumption Politics, and State Building from the Bottom Up, 1941–46', *Journal of American History* (December 1997), https://doi.org/10.2307/2953088

Jaede, M., 'The Concept of the Common Good', PSRP Working Paper No. 8 (2017), Global Justice Academy, University of Edinburgh

Jallinoja, Riita, 'The Women's Liberation Movement in Finland: The Social and Political Mobilisation of Women in Finland, 1880–1910', *Scandinavian Journal of History* 5/1–4 (1980), https://doi.org/10.1080/03468758008578965

Jeffrey, Robin, 'Legacies of Matriliny: The Place of Women and the "Kerala Model"', *Pacific Affairs* 77/4 (2004), http://www.jstor.org/stable/40023536

Jeffrey, Robin, *Politics, Women and Well-Being: How Kerala Became a 'Model'* (Oxford University Press, 2001)

Judt, Tony, *Ill Fares the Land* (Penguin, 2011)

Jung, Carl, *The Psychology of the Transference* (Ark Paperbacks, 1983)

Jurgens, Jeff, 'Arendt on Crisis', The Hannah Arendt Center (2018), https://medium.com/quote-of-the-week/arendt-on-crisis-e24ab8225289

Juuti, Petri, Katko, Tapio and Vuorinen, Heikki, *Environmental History of Water: Global Views on Community Water Supply and Sanitation* (IWA Publishing, 2007)

Kaal, Harm and van Lottum, Jelle, 'Applied History: Past, Present, and Future', *Journal of Applied History* 3/1–2 (December 2021), https://doi.org/10.1163/25895893-bja10018

Kadivar, Mohammad Ali and Ketchley, Neil, 'Sticks, Stones and Molotov Cocktails: Unarmed Collective Violence and Democratization', *Socius* 4 (2018), https://doi.org/10.1177%2F2378023118773614

Keane, John, *Tom Paine: A Political Life* (Bloomsbury, 2009)

Kellert, Stephen and Wilson, Edward O., *The Biophilia Hypothesis* (Island Press, 1993)

Kemp, Luke, 'Are we on the road to civilisation collapse?', BBC Future, 19 September 2019, https://www.bbc.com/future/article/20190218-are-we-on-the-road-to-civilisation-collapse

Kemp, Luke, 'Diminishing Returns on Extraction: How Inequality and Extractive Hierarchy Create Fragility', in Miguel Centeno et al. (eds), *How Worlds Collapse* (Routledge, 2023)

Kemp, Luke et al., 'Climate Endgame: Exploring Catastrophic Climate Change Scenarios', *PNAS* 119 (2022), https://doi.org/10.1073/pnas.2108146119

Kempf, Arlo, 'The Cuban Literacy Campaign at 50: Formal and Tacit Learning in Revolutionary Education', *Critical Education* 5/4 (2014), https://doi.org/10.14288/ce.v5i4.183269

Kennedy, Robert, *Thirteen Days: A Memoir of the Cuban Missile Crisis* (Signet, 1969)

Kent, Eliza, *Converting Women: Gender and Protestant Christianity in Colonial South India* (Oxford University Press, 2004)

Kettunen, Pauli, 'Wars, Nation, and the Welfare State in Finland', in Herbert Obinger et al. (eds), *Warfare and Welfare: Military Conflict and Welfare State Development in Western Countries* (Oxford University Press, 2018)

Khaldun, Ibn, *The Muqaddimah: An Introduction to History*, trans. Franz Rosenthal (Princeton University Press, 2015)

Khanna, Parag, *Move: How Mass Migration Will Reshape the World – and What It Means for You* (Weidenfeld & Nicolson, 2021)

Kiander, Jaakko, Sauramo, Pekka and Tanninen, Hannu, 'The Finnish Incomes Policy as Corporatist Political Exchange: Development of Social Capital and Social Wage', Palkansaajien Tutkimuslaitos, Labour Institute for Economic Research, Working Paper 256 (2009)

Kiang, Lisa et al., 'Moving Beyond the Model Minority', *Asian American Journal of Psychology* 8/1 (2017)

Kimmerer, Robin Wall, 'Mending Our Relationship with the Earth', in Greta Thunberg (ed.), *The Climate Book* (Penguin, 2022)

Klein, Naomi, *This Changes Everything: Capitalism vs the Climate* (Allen Lane, 2014)

Klein, Naomi, *No Logo* (Flamingo, 2001)

Koonce, Coralie, *Thinking Toward Survival* (iUniverse, 2010)

Korppi-Tommola, Aura, 'Fighting Together for Freedom: Nationalism, Socialism, Feminism, and Women's Suffrage in Finland 1906', *Scandinavian Journal of History* 15/1–2 (1990), https://doi.org/10.1080/03468759008579196

Korppi-Tommola, Aura, 'A Long Tradition of Equality: Women's Suffrage in Finland', in Blanca Rodriguez Ruiz and Ruth Rubio Marín (eds), *The Struggle for Female Suffrage in Europe* (Brill, 2012)

Koselleck, Reinhart, 'Crisis', *Journal of the History of Ideas* 67/2 (2006), https://www.jstor.org/stable/30141882

Kotler, Philip, *Democracy in Decline: Rebuilding Its Future* (Sage, 2016)

Koulaxi, Afroditi-Maria, 'Convivial reflexivity in the changing city – a tale of hospitality or hostility?', *International Journal of Cultural Studies* 25/2 (2021), https://doi.org/10.1177/13678779211055490

Kropotkin, Peter, *Mutual Aid: A Factor of Evolution* (Freedom Press, 1987)

Krznaric, Roman, *Carpe Diem Regained: The Vanishing Art of Seizing the Day* (Unbound, 2017)

Krznaric, Roman, 'Food Coupons and Bald Mountains: What the History of Resource Scarcity Can Teach Us About Tackling Climate Change', Human Development Report Office Occasional Paper 2007/63, United Nations Development Programme (2007)

Krznaric, Roman, *The Good Ancestor: How to Think Long Term in a Short-Term World* (WH Allen, 2020)

Krznaric, Roman, 'How Change Happens: Interdisciplinary Perspectives for Human Development', Oxfam GB, 2007

Krznaric, Roman, *The Wonderbox: Curious Histories of How to Live* (Profile, 2011)

Kumar, Udaya, 'Subjects of New Lives: Reform, Self-Making and the Discourse of Autobiography in Kerala', in Bharati Ray (ed.), *Different Types of History* (Pearson Education India, 2009)

Kuruvilla, Benny, 'Kerala's Web of Cooperatives: Advancing the Solidarity Economy', in Lavinia Steinfort and Satoko Kishimoto (eds), *Public Finance for the Future We Want* (Transnational Institute, 2019)

Kwet, Michael, 'Digital Colonialism: US Empire and the New Imperialism in the Global South', *Race & Class* 60/4 (2019), https://doi.org/10.1177/0306396818823172

Lahteenmaki, Maria, 'To the Margins and Back? The Role of Women in the Finnish Labour Movement in the Twentieth Century', *Scandinavian Journal of History* 23/3–4 (1998), https://doi.org/10.1080/03468759850115909

Landemore, Hélène, *Open Democracy: Reinventing Popular Rule for the Twenty-First Century* (Princeton University Press, 2020)

Lansing, Stephen, *Perfect Order: Recognizing Complexity in Bali* (Princeton University Press, 2006)

Lebow, Victor, 'Price Competition in 1955', *Journal of Retailing* (Spring 1955)

Leggett, Dominic, 'Feeding the Beast: Superintelligence, Corporate Capitalism and the End of Humanity', *Proceedings of the 2021 AAAI/ACM Conference on AI, Ethics, and Society* (July 2021), https://doi.org/10.1145/3461702.3462581

Lenton, Tim et al., 'Operationalising positive tipping points towards global sustainability', *Global Sustainability* 5 (2022), https://doi.org/10.1017/sus.2021.30

Lieten, G.K., 'Human Development in Kerala: Structure and Agency in History', *Economic and Political Weekly* 37/16 (2002), https://www.jstor.org/stable/4412015

Ligtvoet, Willem et al., *The Geography of Future Water Challenges* (PBL Netherlands Environmental Assessment Agency, 2018)

Lim, Selina et al., 'Reconfiguring the Singapore Identity Space', *International Journal of Intercultural Relations* 43 (2014), https://doi.org/10.1016/j.ijintrel.2014.08.011

Lindqvist, Sven, *The Skull Measurer's Mistake – and Other Portraits of Men and Women Who Spoke Out Against Racism* (The New Press, 1997)

Liu, Hong and Lingli Huang, 'Paradox of Superdiversity: Contesting Racism and "Chinese Privilege" in Singapore', *Journal of Chinese Overseas* 18/2 (2022), https://doi.org/10.1163/17932548-12341468

Lund, Margaret and Hancock, Matt, 'Stewards of Enterprise: Lessons in Economic Democracy from Northern Italy', International Centre for Co-operative Management, St Mary's University, Canada, Working Paper 2020/01 (2020)

MacMillan, Margaret, *The Uses and Abuses of History* (Profile, 2010)

Madison, James, *The Federalist Papers, Number 10* (1787)

Majzoub, Tarek and Quilleré Majzoub, Fabienne, 'The Time Has Come for a Universal Water Tribunal', *Pace Environmental Law Review* 36/1 (2018), https://doi.org/10.58948/0738-6206.1822

Malm, Andreas, *How to Blow Up a Pipeline* (Verso, 2021)

Manguel, Alberto, *The Library at Night* (Yale University Press, 2008)

Manin, Bernard, *The Principles of Representative Government* (Cambridge University Press, 1997)

Marshall, Peter, *Demanding the Impossible: A History of Anarchism* (Fontana Press, 1993)

Mason, Paul, *Why It's Still Kicking Off Everywhere: The New Global Revolutions* (Verso, 2013)

Mazzucato, Mariana, *The Entrepreneurial State: Debunking Public vs Private Sector Myths* (Anthem Press, 2013)

Mazzucato, Mariana, *The Value of Everything: Making and Taking in the Global Economy* (Allen Lane, 2018)

McDonough, William and Braungart, Michael, *The Upcycle: Beyond Sustainability – Designing for Abundance* (North Point Press, 2013)

McIntosh, Roderick, *Ancient Middle Niger: Urbanism and the Self-Organizing Landscape* (Cambridge University Press, 2005)

McIntosh, Roderick, 'Western Representations of Urbanism and Invisible African Towns', in Susan Keech McIntosh (ed.), *Beyond Chiefdoms: Pathways to Complexity in Africa* (Cambridge University Press, 1999)

McIntosh, Susan Keech, 'Pathways to Complexity: An African Perspective', in Susan Keech McIntosh (ed.), *Beyond Chiefdoms: Pathways to Complexity in Africa* (Cambridge University Press, 1999)

McKibben, Bill, *Hope, Human and Wild: True Stories of Living Lightly on Earth* (Milkweed Editions, 2007)

McLuhan, Marshall, *The Gutenberg Galaxy* (University of Toronto Press, 1962)

McLuhan, Marshall, *Understanding Media* (Abacus, 1973)

McLuhan, Marshall and Fiore, Quentin, *The Medium Is the Massage* (Penguin Books, 2008)

McShane, Clay and Tarr, Joe, *The Horse in the City: Living Machines in the Nineteenth Century* (Johns Hopkins University Press, 2007)

Meadows, Donella, *Thinking in Systems: A Primer* (Earthscan, 2009)

Menocal, María Rosa, 'Culture in the Time of Tolerance: Al-Andalus as a Model for Our Own Time', *Yale Law School Occasional Papers* (2000), https://openyls.law.yale.edu/bitstream/handle/20.500.13051/17668/Menocal_paper.pdf

Menocal, María Rosa, *The Ornament of the World: How Muslims, Jews and Christians Created a Culture of Tolerance in Medieval Spain* (Back Bay, 2002)

Metzl, Jamie, *Hacking Darwin: Genetic Engineering and the Future of Humanity* (Sourcebooks, 2019)

Miller, Michael B., *The Bon Marché: Bourgeois Culture and the Department Store, 1869–1920* (George Allen & Unwin, 1981)

Mills, Geoffrey and Rockoff, Hugh, 'Compliance with Price Controls in the United States and the United Kingdom During World War II', *Journal of American History* 47/1 (1987), https://www.jstor.org/stable/2121945

Monbiot, George, *Regenesis: Feeding the World without Devouring the Planet* (Allen Lane, 2022)

Morozov, Evgeny, *The Net Delusion: How Not to Liberate the World* (Allen Lane, 2011)

Morris-Suzuki, Tessa, 'Sustainability and ecological colonialism in Edo period Japan', *Japanese Studies* 15/1 (1995), https://doi.org/10.1080/10371399508571520

Morstein-Marx, Robert, 'Political Graffiti in the Late Roman Republic: "Hidden Transcripts" and "Common Knowledge"', in Cristina Kuhn (ed.), *Politische Kommunikation und öffentliche Meinung in der antiken Welt* (Franz Steiner Verlag, 2012)

Mouhot, Jean-François, 'Past Connections and Present Similarities in Slave Ownership and Fossil Fuel Usage', *Climate Change* 105 (2011), https://doi.org/10.1007/s10584-010-9982-7

Mundodan, Jesha Mohammedali, K.K., Lamiya and Haveri, Sheela P., 'Prevalence of spousal violence among married women in a rural area in North Kerala', *Journal of Family Medicine and Primary Care* 10/8 (2021), https://doi.org/10.4103/jfmpc.jfmpc_2313_20

Naughton, John, *From Gutenberg to Zuckerberg: What You Really Need to Know About the Internet* (Quercus, 2012)

Needham, Charles, 'Finding the Ethical Standard of Medical Science in the Age of Sciences', *Journal of Evaluation in Clinical Practice* 5/1 (1999), https://doi.org/10.1046/j.1365-2753.1999.00166.x

Nerini, Fuso F. et al., 'Personal carbon allowances revisited', *Nature Sustainability* 4 (2012), https://doi.org/10.1038/s41893-021-00756-w

Neustadt, Richard and May, Ernest, *Thinking in Time: The Uses of History for Decision Makers* (The Free Press, 1986)

Nirenberg, David, *Communities of Violence: Persecution of Minorities in the Middle Ages* (Princeton, 1996)

Nithyanand, Rishab, Schaffner, Brian and Gill, Phillipa, 'Online Political Discourse in the Trump Era', *arXiv* (2017), https://doi.org/10.48550/arXiv.1711.05303

Obasogie, Osagie, 'Your Body, Their Property', in Osagie Obasogie and Marcy Darnovsky (eds), *Beyond Bioethics: Toward a New Biopolitics* (University of California Press, 2018)

Obasogie, Osagie and Darnovsky, Marcy (eds), *Beyond Bioethics: Toward a New Biopolitics* (University of California Press, 2018)

Öcalan, Abdullah, *Democratic Confederalism* (Transmedia Publishing, 2011)

Öcalan, Abdullah, *The Sociology of Freedom: Manifesto of the Democratic Civilization*, vol. III (PM Press, 2020)

Ochiai, Eiichiro, 'Japan in the Edo Period: Global Implications for a Model of Sustainability', *Asia Pacific Journal* 5/2 (2007)

Okihiro, Gary, *The Columbia Guide to Asian American History* (Columbia University Press, 2001)

O'Leary, Paul M., 'Wartime Rationing and Governmental Organization', *American Political Science Review* 39/6 (December 1945), https://doi.org/10.2307/1949657

Ollila, Anne, 'Women's Voluntary Associations in Finland during the 1920s and 1930s', *Scandinavian Journal of History* 20/2 (1995), https://doi.org/10.1080/03468759508579297

Olusoga, David, *Black and British: A Forgotten History* (Macmillan, 2016)

Ong, Walter, *Orality and Literacy: The Technologizing of the World* (Routledge, 1982)

Ord, Toby, *The Precipice: Existential Risk and the Future of Humanity* (Bloomsbury, 2020)

O'Shea, Lizzie, *Future Histories: What Ada Lovelace, Tom Paine and the Paris Commune Can Teach Us About Digital Technology* (Verso, 2019)

Oshinsky, David, *Polio: An American Story* (Oxford University Press, 2005)

Ostrom, Elinor, 'A Polycentric Approach for Coping with Climate Change', World Bank Policy Research Working Paper 5095 (October 2009)

Ostrom, Elinor, *Governing the Commons: The Evolution of Institutions of Collective Action* (Cambridge University Press, 2015)

Ostrom, Vincent, *The Meaning of American Federalism: Constituting a Self-Governing Society* (ICS Books, 1991)

Otto, Illona et al., 'Social Tipping Dynamics for Stabilizing Earth's Climate by 2050', *PNAS* 117/5 (2020), https://doi.org/10.1073/pnas.1900577117

Ozden, James and Glover, Sam, 'Protest Movements: How Effective Are They?', Social Change Lab (2022), https://commonslibrary.org/protest-movements-how-effective-are-they/

Paller, Jeffrey, *Democracy in Ghana: Everyday Politics in Urban Africa* (Cambridge University Press, 2019)

Pandey, Aviral and Gautam, Richa, 'Regional Inequality in India: A State Level Analysis', MRPA Paper No. 101980 (2020), https://mpra.ub.uni-muenchen.de/101980/

Paracelsus, *Of the Nature of Things* (1537)

Park, Saemyi, 'Asian Americans' Perception of Intergroup Commonality with Blacks and Latinos: The Roles of Group Consciousness, Ethnic Identity, and Intergroup Contact', *Social Sciences* 10/11 (2021), https://doi.org/10.3390/socsci10110441

Parker, Michael, 'The Best Possible Child', *Journal of Medical Ethics* 33/5 (2007), https://doi.org/10.1136/jme.2006.018176

Pettigrew, Thomas and Tropp, Linda R., 'A Meta-Analytic Test of Intergroup Contact Theory', *Journal of Personality and Social Psychology* 90/5 (2006), https://doi.org/10.1037/0022-3514.90.5.751

Piketty, Thomas, *A Brief History of Equality* (Belknap Press, 2022)

Pilet, J.-B. et al., 'The POLITICIZE Dataset: an inventory of Deliberative Mini-Publics (DMPs) in Europe', *European Political Science* 20 (2022), https://doi.org/10.1057/s41304-020-00284-9

Pincus, Steve, '"Coffee Politicians Does Create": Coffeehouses and Restoration Political Culture', *Journal of Modern History* 67/4 (1995), https://www.jstor.org/stable/2124756

Pistor, Katharina, *The Code of Capital: How the Law Creates Wealth and Inequality* (Princeton University Press, 2019)

Plokhy, Serhii, *Nuclear Folly: A New History of the Cuban Missile Crisis* (Penguin, 2021)

Polanyi, Karl, *The Great Transformation: The Political and Economic Origins of Our Time* (Beacon Press, 2001)

Postman, Neil, *Technopoly: The Surrender of Culture to Technology* (Vintage, 1993)

Prasad, Naren, 'Privatisation of Water: A Historical Perspective', *Law, Environment and Development* 3/2 (2007), https://lead-journal.org/content/07217.pdf

Principe, Lawrence, *The Secrets of Alchemy* (University of Chicago Press, 2013)

Purvis, June, 'Did Militancy Help or Hinder the Granting of Women's suffrage in Britain?', *Women's History Review* 28/7 (2019), https://doi.org/10.1080/09612025.2019.1654638

Putnam, Robert, *Making Democracy Work: Civic Traditions in Modern Italy* (Princeton University Press, 1993)

Ramachandran, V.K., 'On Kerala's Development Achievements', in Jean Dreze and Amartya Sen (eds), *Indian Development: Selected Regional Perspectives* (United Nations University, 1999)

Raworth, Kate, *Doughnut Economics: Seven Ways to Think Like a 21st-Century Economist* (Random House Business Books, 2017)

Raworth, Kate, 'Towards 1.5°C Lifestyles', in Greta Thunberg (ed.), *The Climate Book* (Penguin, 2022)

Reilly, Philip R., 'Eugenics and Involuntary Sterilization: 1907–2015', *Annual Review of Genomics and Human Genetics* 16 (2015), https://doi.org/10.1146/annurev-genom-090314-024930

Rifkin, Jeremy, *The Age of Resilience: Reimagining Existence on a Rewilding Earth* (Swift, 2022)

Rifkin, Jeremy, *The Biotech Century: Harnessing the Gene and Remaking the World* (Tarcher/Putnam, 1999)

Rival, Laura (ed.), *The Social Lives of Trees: Anthropological Perspectives on Tree Symbolism* (Berg, 1998)

Roper, Lyndal, *Witch Craze: Terror and Fantasy in Baroque Germany* (Yale University Press, 2006)

Rosenow, Jan and Lowes, Richard, 'Will blue hydrogen lock us into fossil fuels forever?', *One Earth* 4/11 (2021)

Rousseau, Jean-Jacques, *The Social Contract* (1762)

Rowe, William, *Saving the World: Chen Hongmou and Elite Consciousness in Eighteenth-Century China* (Stanford University Press, 2001)

Rutherford, Adam, *Control: The Dark History and Troubling Present of Eugenics* (Weidenfeld & Nicolson, 2022)

Saito, Osamu, 'Forest History and the Great Divergence: China, Japan and the West', Institute of Economic Research, Hitotsubashi University, 2008, https://warwick.ac.uk/fac/soc/economics/seminars/seminars/conferences/econchange/programme/saito_-_venice.pdf

Salk, Jonas, 'Are We Being Good Ancestors?', *World Affairs: The Journal of International Issues* 1/2 (1992), https://www.jstor.org/stable/45064193

Sandel, Michael, *The Case Against Perfection: Ethics in the Age of Genetic Engineering* (Belknap Press, 2009)

Sarotte, Mary Elise, *The Collapse: The Accidental Opening of the Berlin Wall* (Basic Books, 2015)

Savulescu, Julian and Persson, Ingmar, 'Moral Enhancement', *Philosophy Now* 91 (2012), https://philosophynow.org/issues/91/Moral_Enhancement

Schama, Simon, *The Embarrassment of Riches: An Interpretation of Dutch Culture in the Golden Age* (Fontana Press, 1988)

Schama, Simon, *Landscape and Memory* (Fontana, 1996)

Scharper, Stephen and Cunningham, Hilary, 'The Genetic Commons: Resisting the Neoliberal Enclosure of Life', *Social Analysis: The International Journal of Anthropology* 50/3 (2006), https://www.jstor.org/stable/23182119

Scheidel, Walter, *The Great Leveler: Violence and the History of Inequality from the Stone Age to the Twenty-First Century* (Princeton University Press, 2017)

Schifeling, Todd and Hoffman, Andrew J., 'Bill McKibben's Influence on US Climate Change Discourse: Shifting Field-Level Debates Through Radical Flank Effects', *Organization and Environment* 32/3 (2019), https://doi.org/10.1177/1086026617744278

Schneider, Nathan, 'An Internet of Ownership: Democratic Design for the Online Economy', *Sociological Review* 66/2 (2018), https://doi.org/10.1177/0038026118758533

Schor, Juliet, 'Towards a New Politics of Consumption', in Juliet Schor and Douglas Holt (eds), *The Consumer Society Reader* (The New Press, 2000)

Schumann, S. et al., 'Social Media Use and Support for Populist Radical Right Parties: Assessing Exposure and Selection Effects in a Two-wave Panel Study', *Information, Communication and Society* 24/7 (2019), https://doi.org/10.1080/1369118X.2019.1668455

Seliktar, Ofira, 'Turning Water into Fire: The Jordan River as the Hidden Factor in the Six-Day War', *Middle East Review of International Affairs* 9/2 (June 2005)

Sennett, Richard, *The Fall of Public Man* (Faber and Faber, 1986)

Shah, Alpa, 'What if We Selected Our Leaders by Lottery? Democracy by Sortition, Liberal Elections and Communist Revolutionaries', *Development and Change* 52/4 (2021), https://doi.org/10.1111/dech.12651

Sharon, Ariel, *Warrior: An Autobiography* (Simon & Schuster, 2001)

Shi, David E., *The Simple Life: Plain Living and High Thinking in American Culture* (Oxford University Press, 1985)

Shiva, Vandana, *World Water Wars* (Sound End Press, 2002)

Shively, Donald H., 'Sumptuary Regulation and Status in Early Tokugawa Japan', *Harvard Journal of Asiatic Studies* 25 (1964), https://doi.org/10.2307/2718340

Siisiäinen, Martti, 'Social Movements, Voluntary Associations and Cycles of Protest in Finland 1905–91', *Scandinavian Political Studies* 15/1 (1992)

Silver, Lee, *Remaking Eden: How Genetic Engineering and Cloning Will Remake the American Family* (Harper Perennial, 2007)

Simpson, Brett, Willer, Robb and Feinberg, Matthew, 'Radical Flanks of Social Movements Can Increase Support for Moderate Factions', *PNAS Nexus* 1/3 (2022), https://doi.org/10.1093/pnasnexus/pgac110

Singh, Simon, *Fermat's Last Theorem* (Harper Perennial, 2011)

Skevington Wood, A., *Captive to the Word – Martin Luther: Doctor of Sacred Scripture* (Paternoster Press, 1969)

Smil, Vaclav, *Energy and Civilization: A History* (MIT Press, 2018)

Smith, Graham, 'Placing the Convention: An Outlier Amongst Climate Assemblies?', paper prepared for *Participations* journal Special Issue on Climate Assemblies, ed. Jean-Michel Fourniau and Hélène Landemore (2022)

Smith, Graham, *Can Democracy Safeguard the Future?* (Polity, 2021)

Snyder, Timothy, *On Tyranny: Twenty Lessons from the Twentieth Century* (Bodley Head, 2017)

Soga, Masashi et al., 'Gardening Is Beneficial for Health: A Meta-Analysis', *Preventative Medicine Reports* 5 (2017), https://doi.org/10.1016/j.pmedr.2016.11.007

Solnit, Rebecca, *A Paradise Built in Hell: The Extraordinary Communities that Arise in Disaster* (Penguin, 2010)

Solomon, Steven, *Water: The Epic Struggle for Wealth, Power, and Civilization* (Harper Perennial, 2011)

Spelliscy, Connor et al., 'Toward Equitable Ownership and Governance in the Digital Public Sphere', Belfer Center for Science and International Affairs, Harvard University, 2023

Standage, Tom, *Writing on the Wall: Social Media, the First 2,000 Years* (Bloomsbury, 2013)

Steffen, Will et al., 'Trajectories of the Earth System in the Anthropocene', *PNAS* 115/33 (2019), https://doi.org/10.1073/pnas.1810141115

Stern, Alexandra Minna, 'Making Better Babies: Public Health and Race Betterment in Indiana, 1920–35', in Osagie Obasogie and Marcy Darnovsky (eds), *Beyond Bioethics: Toward a New Biopolitics* (University of California Press, 2018)

Stowers, Stanley, *Letter Writing in Greco-Roman Antiquity* (John Knox Press, 1989)

Strzelecki, Zoey, 'Printing Witchcraft', *Manchester Historian*, 12 November 2014

Supko, Ruth, 'Perspectives on the Cuban National Literacy Campaign', paper delivered to the Latin American Studies Association, Chicago, 24–6 September 1998

Supriatna, Nana, 'Confronting Consumerism as a New Imperialism', *Journal of Social Studies Education* 6 (2017)

Tainter, Joseph, 'Problem Solving: Complexity, History, Sustainability', *Population and Environment* 22 (2000), https://doi.org/10.1023/A:1006632214612

Tainter, Joseph, *The Collapse of Complex Societies* (Cambridge University Press, 1988)

Taipale, Ilkka (ed.), *100 Social Innovations from Finland* (Finnish Literature Society, 2013)

Tawney, Richard, *Religion and the Rise of Capitalism* (Penguin, 1980)

Taylor, Michael, *The Interest: How the British Establishment Resisted the Abolition of Slavery* (Vintage, 2021)

Tchen, John Kuo Wei and Yeats, Dylan, *Yellow Peril! An Archive of Anti-Asian Fear* (Verso, 2014)

Tegmark, Max, *Life 3.0: Being Human in the Age of Artificial Intelligence* (Penguin, 2017)

Thomas, Keith, *The Ends of Life: Roads to Fulfilment in Early Modern England* (Oxford University Press, 2011)

Thomas, Keith, *Man and the Natural World: Changing Attitudes in England 1500–1800* (Penguin, 1984)

Thomas, Keith, *Religion and the Decline of Magic* (Penguin, 1973)

Thompson, Edward, *The Making of the English Working Class* (Pelican, 1968)

Tosh, John, 'In Defence of Applied History', *History and Policy* (February 2006)

Tosh, John, *Why History Matters* (Palgrave, 2008)

Totman, Conrad, 'Land-Use Patterns and Afforestation in the Edo Period', *Monumenta Nipponica* 39/1 (1984), https://doi.org/10.2307/2384477

Totman, Conrad, *Early Modern Japan* (University of California Press, 1993)

Totman, Conrad, *The Green Archipelago: Forestry in Pre-Industrial Japan* (Ohio University Press, 1998)

Toynbee, Arnold, *A Study of History*, vol. III (Oxford University Press, 1935)

Tramontana, Felicita, 'Five Lessons History Can Teach Us About Migration', Warwick Knowledge Centre, 14 August 2018, https://warwick.ac.uk/newsandevents/knowledgecentre/arts/history/migration

Turchin, Peter, *Ultrasociety: How 10,000 Years of War Made Humans the Greatest Cooperators on Earth* (Beresta Books, 2016)

Turchin, Peter, *War and Peace and War: The Rise and Fall of Empires* (Plume, 2007)

United Nations Development Programme, *Human Development Report 2006: Beyond Scarcity* (New York, 2006)

Van Reybrouck, David, *Against Elections: The Case for Democracy* (Seven Stories Press, 2018)

Vansina, Jan, *How Societies Are Born: Governance in Central West Africa Before 1600* (University of Virginia Press, 2005)

Vince, Gaia, *Nomad Century: How to Survive the Climate Upheaval* (Allen Lane, 2022)

Vogel, Jefim and Hickel, Jason, 'Is Green Growth Happening? An Empirical Analysis of Achieved Versus Paris-Compliant CO2-GDP Decoupling in High-Income Countries', *Lancet Planetary Health* 7/9 (2023), https://doi.org/10.1016/S2542-5196(23)00174-2

Wahlström, Mattias et al., 'Surveys of Participants in Fridays For Future Climate Protests on 20–28 September, 2019, in 19 Cities around the World', OSF (18 August 2021), https://doi.org/10.17605/OSF.IO/ASRUW

Wallman, James, *Stuffocation: Living More with Less* (Penguin Books, 2013)

Ward, Colin, *Reflected in Water: A Crisis of Social Responsibility* (Cassel, 1997)

Ward, Colin, *Welcome, Thinner City* (Bedford Square Press, 1989)

Warfield, Abaigéal, 'Witchcraft Illustrated: The Crime of Witchcraft in Early Modern German News Broadsheets', in Andrew Pettegree (ed.), *Broadsheets: Single-Sheet Publishing in the First Age of Print* (Brill, 2017)

Weintraub, Lia, 'The Link Between the Rockefeller Foundation and Racial Hygiene in Nazi Germany', dissertation, Tufts University, 2013, http://hdl.handle.net/10427/77753

White, Lynn Jr, 'The Historical Roots of our Ecological Crisis', *Science* 155/3767 (1967), https://doi.org/10.1126/science.155.3767.1203

Wilkinson, Richard and Pickett, Kate, *The Spirit Level: Why Equality Is Better for Everyone* (Penguin, 2010)

Williams, Chancellor, *The Destruction of Black Civilization: Great Issues of a Race From 4500 BC to 2000 AD* (Third World Press, 1971)

Williams, Glyn et al., 'Performing Participatory Citizenship – Politics and Power in Kerala's Kudumbashree Programme', *Journal of Development Studies* 47/8 (2011), https://doi.org/10.1080/00220388.2010.527949

Williams, Jo, 'Circular Cities: Planning for Circular Development\ in European Cities', *European Planning Studies* 31/1 (2022), https://doi.org/10.1080/09654313.2022.2060707

Winston, Brian and Winston, Matthew, *The Roots of Fake News: Objecting to Objective Journalism* (Routledge, 2021)

Wiredu, Kwasi, 'Democracy and Consensus in African Traditional Politics: A Plea for a Non-Party Polity', *Centennial Review* 39/1 (1995), https://www.jstor.org/stable/23739547

Wise, Amanda and Velayutham, Selvaraj, 'Conviviality in Everyday Multiculturalism: Some Brief Comparisons Between Singapore and Sydney', *European Journal of Cultural Studies* 17/4 (2014), https://doi.org/10.1177/1367549413510419

Wolf, Kenneth Baxter, 'Convivencia and "The Ornament of the World"', in Connie Scarborough (ed.), *Revisiting Convivencia in Medieval and Early Modern Iberia* (Juan de la Cuesta, 2014)

Wong, Kevin Scott, *Americans First: Chinese Americans and the Second World War* (Harvard University Press, 2005)

Wood, Ellen Meiksins, *The Origin of Capitalism: A Longer View* (Verso, 2002)

Wood, Michael, *The Story of England* (Penguin, 2011)

Wright, Ronald, *A Short History of Progress* (Canongate, 2004)

Zamagni, Stefano and Zamagni, Vera, *Cooperative Enterprise: Facing the Challenge of Globalization* (Edward Elgar, 2010)

Zamagni, Vera, 'Why We Need Cooperatives to Make the Business World More People-Centred', paper presented at the UN Inter-Agency Task Force on Social and Solidarity Economy International Conference, Geneva, 25–6 June, 2019

Zeldin, Theodore, *Conversation* (Harvill Press, 1998)

Zeldin, Theodore, *An Intimate History of Humanity* (Minerva, 1995)

Zika, Charles, *The Appearance of Witchcraft: Print and Visual Culture in Sixteenth-Century Europe* (Routledge, 2007)

Zinn, Howard, *On History* (Seven Stories Press, 2011)

Zinn, Howard, *A People's History of the United States* (Harper Perennial, 1995)

Zuboff, Shoshana, *The Age of Surveillance Capitalism* (Profile, 2019)

Zweiniger-Bargielowska, Ina, *Austerity in Britain: Rationing, Controls and Consumption, 1939–1955* (Oxford University Press, 2000)

Index

Page references in *italics* indicate images.

Index

Index

Index

Index